Sovereign Borrowers

**Guidelines on
Legal Negotiations
with Commercial Lenders**

Sovereign Borrowers

Guidelines on Legal Negotiations with Commercial Lenders

Edited by

**Lars Kalderén
Qamar S. Siddiqi**

in cooperation with

**Francis Chronnell
Patricia Watson**

Dag Hammarskjöld Foundation
Butterworths 🔲

The Dag Hammarskjöld Foundation was established in 1962 in memory of the Secretary-General of the United Nations. The opinions expressed in its publications are those of the authors and do not necessarily reflect the views of the Foundation.

The address of the Dag Hammarskjöld Foundation is Övre Slottsgatan 2, S-752 20 Uppsala, Sweden.

General editors: Sven Hamrell and Olle Nordberg

The seminar on 'Third World Borrowing in International Capital Markets: Constitutional and Legal Issues' was financed jointly by grants from the Commonwealth Secretariat through the Commonwealth Fund for Technical Cooperation and the Swedish International Development Authority (SIDA).

©Dag Hammarskjöld Foundation 1984
ISBN 91-85214-12-4
Printed in Sweden by Motala Grafiska AB, Motala

Contents

Economic Risks in Sovereign Lending   17
By Göran Ohlin
An economist's view of the current international debt crisis and factors involved in defaults, some limitations of loan documentation and the prospects for the future of sovereign lending.

Negotiating Strategies and the Role of the Lawyer   26
By Lars Kalderén
Loan negotiations from the perspective of the public debt manager, including the effective utilisation of negotiating resources, the impact of market conditions, the formulation of negotiating strategy, the principal aspects of a sovereign borrowing operation, the contributions of in-house and outside lawyers at various stages of the transaction and the benefits of cooperation between sovereign borrowers.

Some Critical Issues in Negotiations and Legal Drafting   44
By Qamar S. Siddiqi
A drawing together of matters of particular importance to the borrower within the context of the borrower's overall negotiating strategy, summarising and emphasising points from other chapters.

The Eurocurrency Loan: Role and Content of the Contract   73
By K. Venkatachari
A general overview of a Eurocurrency loan agreement and a detailed explanation of its provisions.

**Selected Aspects of International Loan Documentation
and Rescheduling**   123
By Philip Wood
A consideration of significant topics in international loan transactions and debt rescheduling, including choice of law, choice of forum, syndication, the substitute basis, illegality and increased costs clauses, financial terms of reschedulings, rescheduling of official debt (Paris Club) and commercial bank reschedulings.

Sovereign Immunity   144
By William Tudor John
A historical and current review of the immunity of sovereign states from jurisdiction and enforcement of judgments in the United States of America and the United Kingdom.

Introductory Note

In November 1981, the Dag Hammarskjöld Foundation and the Commonwealth Secretariat, in cooperation with the Swedish National Debt Office, organised a seminar on 'Third World Borrowing in International Capital Markets: Constitutional and Legal Issues' at the Dag Hammarskjöld Centre in Uppsala. This seminar formed a link in the series of technical seminars organised by the Foundation in such areas as law and development, the automatic mobilisation of resources for development and the law of treaties.

It should be pointed out, however, that the legal seminars constitute only a part of the Foundation's activities, since the purpose of the Foundation is to further not only the legal but also the social, economic and cultural progress of the countries of the Third World by promoting a continuous dialogue on such issues among representatives of both governmental and non-governmental sectors of society. Since its establishment in 1962 in memory of the late Secretary-General of the United Nations, the Foundation has organised over 70 seminars and conferences on a wide variety of subjects in such areas as health, education, rural development, science and technology, information and communication. Around half of these have been held in Uppsala and the rest mainly in Asia, Africa and Latin America.

The background to the seminar, which forms the basis for this book, and to the cooperation between the Commonwealth Secretariat and the Dag Hammarskjöld Foundation, is the following. Like many other countries, especially in the Third World, Sweden was in the late seventies forced to enter the international capital markets as a sovereign borrower. This for Sweden was a new and unexpected development, leading to a considerable expansion of the international activities of the Swedish

National Debt Office and to a rapid accumulation of experience of the processes of international loan negotiations. The relevance of this Swedish experience to the new sovereign borrowers in the Third World was recognised at an early stage by the Commonwealth Secretariat. This relevance was enhanced by Sweden's well-known active involvement in Third World development issues and by its readiness to share its experience with Third World countries. It was therefore not by chance that Qamar Siddiqi of the Commonwealth Secretariat, being responsible for its Capital Markets Programme, turned to Sweden and in particular to the Director General of the Swedish National Debt Office, Lars Kalderén, for advice. Lars Kalderén, who before becoming a loan negotiator and debt manager had had a long career in the field of development cooperation and administration, was well suited to this role. He also declared himself ready to serve as one of the directors of the seminar on Third World Borrowing in International Capital Markets, when the idea of a joint undertaking in this field was suggested by the Secretary-General of the Commonwealth, Shridath S. Ramphal.

The objective of the seminar was to focus on the legal elements in the overall process of international loan negotiations and to deal in particular with those clauses in a loan agreement which are most relevant to the borrower and in which improvements can be sought in its favour.

About 20 participants gathered in Uppsala for the seminar, the majority being highly placed legal officials from the Commonwealth and many of them being from smaller countries with only limited access to the kind of expertise needed in these matters.

Mr Neville Nicholls, Vice-President of the Caribbean Development Bank, served as co-director of the seminar with Lars Kalderén while the papers for the seminar were commissioned by Lars Kalderén and Qamar Siddiqi from some of the most distinguished specialists in this highly esoteric legal field, namely K. Venkatachari, Philip Wood, William Tudor John, Paul I. Harris, Richard G.A. Youard, Nicholas Wilson and J. Speed Carroll.

From the Swedish National Debt Office, Lars Kalderén, Lars Andrén and Bengt Kärde contributed papers based on their experience of Swedish loan negotiations.

The seminar was from the beginning planned in such a way that the material prepared for it would also constitute the basis for a reference work on the constitutional and legal issues involved in sovereign borrowing. In order to produce such a publication, it was necessary not only to expand some of the papers but also to add new material. Thus, Qamar Siddiqi undertook the task of outlining in an early chapter of the book some of the critical issues in negotiations and legal drafting, summarising and emphasising points made in the other chapters, while Professor Göran Ohlin contributed an overview of the current international debt crisis and its effects on the future of sovereign lending. A valuable and practical addition to the seminar material was Francis Chronnell's and Patricia Watson's 'Selected Specimen Clauses for Syndicated Loans'.

This book is primarily intended to provide guidelines for those who are involved in loan negotiations in ministries of justice and finance and in central banks and other government authorities, but it is also addressed to the legal scholar. It is composed in such a way that the first three chapters give an overview of the whole *problématique* from the point of view of the international economist, the debt manager and the international civil servant. These chapters are followed by a detailed examination of a Eurocurrency loan agreement and by a series of interpretations of the crucial clauses in loan agreements, contributed by the legal specialists. This collection of specialist interpretations is a significant feature of the book and is probably a unique contribution to the subject. The book is rounded off by a case study, describing from the borrower's angle the negotiation of an actual syndicated Eurodollar loan facility. To guide the reader in the use of the material presented, the main points advanced in each chapter are indicated in the analytical table of contents.

In concluding, we wish to thank the contributors to the book for responding to the invitation to address the seminar, for re-examining their manuscripts in the light of the seminar discussions and for preparing them for publication. We are most grateful to the Secretary-General of the Commonwealth, Shridath S. Ramphal, for his never-failing interest in the project and for writing the preface to this book. We owe a special debt of gratitude to Francis Chronnell and Patricia Watson, who, in addition to their own contribution, agreed to examine the new material prepared after the seminar. Last, but not least, we wish to thank Lars Kalderén and Qamar Siddiqi, for their efforts on behalf of this project and the publication of this book.

As is evident from the few references made in this book to other works, the literature on constitutional and legal issues involved in international loan negotiations is very limited. It is therefore hoped that this book will prove to be a practical tool for the negotiator and legal draftsman and a valuable addition to the literature on this subject, and that it will be used both in the Third World and in the industrialised countries.

Sven Hamrell   *Olle Nordberg*
Executive Director   Associate Director
Dag Hammarskjöld Foundation   Dag Hammarskjöld Foundation

Preface

BY SHRIDATH S. RAMPHAL

Borrowing by Third World countries in the international capital markets, which is the subject of these Guidelines, is a matter about which the international community has now become concerned. The explosion of Third World debt over the past decade and developments in the world economy which create a predicament for many debtor nations are major aspects of the disturbed condition of the world economy and the precarious state of the whole international financial system.

In the aftermath of the oil price increases in 1973–74, market borrowing inevitably became an important part of the financial strategies of an increasing number of Third World countries. For many of them, this kind of financing represented such wholly unfamiliar territory that special measures were required to assist them to make more effective use of capital markets.

A Capital Markets Programme was instituted by the Commonwealth Secretariat in the mid-seventies at the instance of Finance Ministers. One of its main objectives is to improve our member countries' capabilities to utilise commercial finance and to deal with commercial banks. When the borrowing was taking place it was recognised to be a perfectly natural and desirable development. Today it is tempting, but facile, to ascribe the cause of the debt crisis to poor debt management; present debt servicing difficulties have wider causes and are linked, both in origin and effect, with systemic deficiencies that afflict the world economy as a whole.

In the early seventies, increased commercial borrowing enabled a number of Third World countries to sustain their development efforts and maintain capital goods imports in spite of vastly increased oil bills. It therefore also helped to maintain economic activity and lessen unemployment in the North, which supplied most of the goods imported by the

Third World countries. Today, the picture is a less happy one. A switch from negative to positive real interest rates, adverse movement in Third World countries' terms of trade and increasing difficulties in securing export outlets combined to give rise to acute difficulties in servicing the large volume of accumulated debt. A sustained world economic recovery would certainly help to solve some of these problems. But the pace of recovery has remained unsatisfactory globally and as world trade continues to be depressed Third World exports are being further restrained. With interest rates remaining high, this could further impair debt servicing capacities and heighten the risks facing the international banking system.

Quick and concerted action by some of the major actors in the international financial system has been able to avert a serious breakdown in the system; but the approach has been one of crisis management and therefore piecemeal. The dangers to the financial system have not receded to a significant extent. There remain serious risks for the entire system as well as for individual countries. Those experiencing serious debt service difficulties cannot overcome or even contain them without a more determined, comprehensive and long-term approach to global economic management. Accordingly, there have been many calls for a review of the whole international financial system.

In the Commonwealth we have recently carried out a comprehensive study, by a distinguished group of experts, of the international financial and trading system. It concluded that the time is ripe for a process of reform and renewal to ensure sustained growth in both industrialised and Third World countries. The issues involved were subsequently considered at the political level in the Commonwealth by Finance Ministers and by Heads of Government. The latter agreed that the situation called for a comprehensive review of the relevant issues and decided to establish a Commonwealth Consultative Group to promote consensus on the issues. At the same time, Heads of Government saw a specific need for an examination of all aspects of the Third World debt problem and requested the Secretariat to make such an examination with the help of a group of experts. We are now proceeding with these tasks and are giving them the high priority in our work that they deserve.

But while international efforts, both within and outside the Commonwealth, must continue with the utmost urgency, there also remains a need for individual countries to improve their own capabilities to obtain the necessary finance for their development and deal more effectively with the suppliers of finance, both official and commercial. In order to assist borrowing countries in these tasks, the Dag Hammarskjöld Foundation and the Commonwealth Secretariat joined hands and convened a seminar for sovereign borrowers in November 1981 on the technical and legal aspects of Third World borrowing. The dramatic events of the recent past have, if anything, enhanced the significance of these issues. The recent debt rescheduling packages, while they bring some—and possibly temporary—relief to the hard-pressed countries and to the banks, offer small comfort for many other borrowers and would-be borrowers. The way in which most of these rescheduling arrangements have been devised, as part of a major financial package to ensure that the countries concerned do not lose the ability to raise loans, has meant that the banking system has had to increase its lending exposure to these countries just when many banks were seeking to cut back on their international lending. This in turn has affected the banks' willingness to lend to countries that are not yet in great difficulties and, where they do lend, they seek greater protection against default.

In fact, the crisis psychology of the bankers has made the situation much worse both for themselves and the borrowers than it might have been otherwise. As lenders endeavour to strengthen the protection of their interests they tend to cast their legal net far and wide to include every conceivable financial threat. The result is, at best, over-complicated loan documentation which will unduly protract, at the borrower's expense, the negotiating process. To give an indication of what is or can be involved, a loan document recently circulated in London included a clause, dealing solely with default interest, which ran to four pages. At worst, however, the lender's concern with protection may result in loan documentation which hampers the borrower's ability to conduct normal business and perhaps restricts its ability to borrow in the future.

One of the elements of advice given to sovereign borrowers in this volume is that they should bargain hard in the negotiating arena, but do so judiciously. And it is with these protective clauses that the borrower is advised to be most concerned. Yet, while protection is a central issue for lawyers on both sides of the negotiating table, there is a sense in which it is beyond the reach of the law. For ultimately there is little that lenders can do in terms of applying legal sanctions on a sovereign borrower to enforce repayment in the event that a default is declared. Conversely, however, there does exist a sufficiently powerful economic sanction to render any legal action somewhat superfluous, namely the withholding of further loans. So powerful is this sanction that to date there are hardly any instances of a country repudiating its debt. On the contrary, all parties, including governments, have gone to remarkable lengths in recent years to ensure that debt servicing payments are maintained. When there is no possibility of doing so, borrowers have taken the option of rescheduling rather than that of defaulting on their obligations.

It has to be recognised that the whole system of international lending operates on the basis of an assumption that debts will be serviced promptly if there is any economic possibility of doing so. In the final analysis the relationship between the borrower and the lender goes far beyond the legal relationship represented by the loan agreement; it is defined not by what one party can force upon the other but by a mutuality of interest in wider considerations. Both are members of the world's financial system, and they both have an interest in the preservation of a regime of order. But mutuality of interest goes even beyond the functioning of the world's financial system.

In saying this I do not intend to minimise the legal aspects. Borrowers must continue to try to ameliorate the provisions of the documentation prepared by the lender in order to retain maximum flexibility in their commercial affairs, and these Guidelines should help to strengthen the power of their lawyers to do so. My plea to them, and equally to lawyers on the lender's side, is to bring to their task an awareness of their wider responsibilities and interests. Much is at stake!

Borrowers have a particular responsibility for helping each other in their dealings with international lenders. Although over 90 Third World countries have utilised international capital markets since 1976, only a few have regularly engaged in market negotiations. Most of the others have had insufficient negotiating experience to develop appropriate negotiating skills. This puts them at a great disadvantage relative to the lending banks, which have accumulated a wide range of negotiating experience through dealing with many borrowers of varying types. Countries new to the capital markets can benefit from a sharing of experience both with each other and with more seasoned borrowers.

A large measure of the present inequality in negotiating strength results from the greater ease of communication between lending institutions. They have the advantage of close geographical proximity, and information about events, however confidential, rapidly passes through the various sophisticated official and unofficial channels to become common knowledge among lenders.

In spite of this, however, bankers have come to feel, especially since the Mexican crisis, that their systems of collecting and disseminating information have been inadequate. Accordingly, they have established an Institute for International Finance which will monitor developments in debtor countries and assess their creditworthiness.

Sovereign borrowers should take note of the example of the lending institutions and accelerate their own efforts to exchange ideas and information and provide mutual assistance. This need is particularly great in relation to the legal aspects of a loan agreement. A borrower has relatively easy access to details of the commercial terms of other borrowers' loans, and it can use this information to form a judgement as to the terms it is prepared to offer on its own borrowing. But when it comes to the legal clauses the borrower is out on a limb. Without knowing the full legal environment in which international banks operate, the borrower's representatives have few means of assessing how far to go in seeking to ameliorate the legal conditions.

This book, like the seminar from which it originates, attempts to redress the balance between the relative positions of lenders and borrowers—particularly the weaker Third World borrowers—by familiarising borrowers with the strategies and procedures of a loan negotiation. At the same time, it represents a concrete example of how the knowledge and experience of one very practised borrower (in this case the Kingdom of Sweden) can be shared for the benefit of others.

We are truly indebted to our friends in Sweden for their support and active involvement over the years in our Commonwealth Capital Markets Programme, which assists Third World Commonwealth countries in their operations in the international capital markets and seeks to foster cooperation among borrowers.

This book, which is the product of the joint efforts of the Secretariat, the Dag Hammarskjöld Foundation and the Swedish National Debt Office, is itself a notable achievement and one which we hope will be of value to the government officials and legal practitioners who have to grapple with the legal and technical intricacies of loan negotiations. It is in the interest of all nations, and of the world economy, that they are efficient and effective in these transactions.

Economic Risks
in Sovereign Lending

BY GÖRAN OHLIN

Most of the other contributions in this volume were prepared before the dramatic events of 1982 and 1983 when some of the largest borrowers in the Third World found themselves unable to service their debts to international banks. These events also made it clear that outright default might have such serious implications, not just for the debtors or the creditors but for the world economy at large, that large-scale rescue operations were mounted by governments in creditor countries—directly as well as through intermediaries such as the Bank for International Settlements (BIS) and the International Monetary Fund (IMF)—when it seemed absolutely necessary.

Nonetheless, in early 1984 a state of emergency still prevails in the lending of international banks to the Third World. Although lenders have been persuaded not to press for repayment but to accept some stretching of their loans, there is considerable reluctance to extend new credit, and the future of international trade and finance is clouded.

These economic aspects of the international financial situation may be thought to have little bearing on this volume, which has the primary aim of discussing the legal aspects of sovereign borrowing in international capital markets. But in the first place it does not seem likely that the present crisis will mean the end of sovereign borrowing. No matter how this crisis is resolved, it is overwhelmingly probable that the countries already in the market will stay there, and that in due time others will enter. Secondly, the present debt problems demonstrate the nature of the risks that hover over international lending. It is my view that what a loan contract should do, in addition to providing for debt service in normal circumstances, is to set out procedures for dealing with situations that arise when things do not turn out as both parties expected and especially when the borrower fails to repay. The question arises whether present contracts are well suited to the needs of modern sovereign lending.

Risk and uncertainty

The financial terms of a loan agreement may be fairly simple. The principal terms that have to be specified are the rate of interest and the repayment schedule. These terms may in the future turn out to look different from the way they did at the time of agreement, because the underlying conditions have changed. If the rate of interest falls unexpectedly the borrower might be able to take new loans and repay the more expensive ones prematurely. It may then wish to get rid of a loan which it once regarded as favourable. If the rate of interest rises, the lender would like to have its money back in order to make a more favourable placement, but the contract will not permit it to ask for accelerated repayment on that ground. It will then be disappointed with the transaction.

Generally speaking, the primary risk in lending falls on the lender, and so it is no surprise that creditors will insist on contracts which minimise the risk of not being repaid. With regard to interest payments, the volatility and uncertainty of interest rates in the last decade have reinforced the trend towards loans at variable rates of interest, which now clearly dominate even among commercial loans to Third World countries. These loans, of course, require rules concerning the choice of future interest which are acceptable to both lender and borrower.

The monetary turmoil of the last decade has also meant that the choice of the currency in which a loan is denominated may bring great windfalls to one of the parties and unexpected losses to the other. Many loans are made with multicurrency clauses, and there have also been a number of loans denominated in 'baskets' of currencies, like the SDR or the ECU, which to some extent even out the fluctuations although they cannot remove considerable elements of exchange risk.

Many other innovations have contributed to making the financial terms of international credit increasingly complex. This is necessarily reflected in loan agreements and means that there can be no separation between the financial and the legal aspects of the contract. Economic advisers may have their view of a probable future, but the legal advisers must remember that the international economic environment might turn out very differently and therefore seek to ensure that such unexpected turns of events do not become excessively costly because of some neglected fine print.

Legal traditions in this field are for many reasons likely to give less than complete guidance since they have emerged from lending mainly to private sector companies rather than to governments. The experience of sovereign lending in the pre-war period is of limited relevance in the present international monetary system.

On the other hand, a loan agreement will contain a great number of clauses covering situations that might arise when the obligations are not met. It is natural to think first of all of the possibility that the borrower, for one reason or another, fails to service the debt at a specified time, but it could also happen that the lender fails to provide the funds as promised (although this seldom happens in practice). Once the loan has been paid out, however, the standard assumption is that the borrower is liable to pay, whatever unfavourable turn events might take. It assumes those risks—up to the point where its fortunes turn so bad that it cannot discharge its obligations—i.e. it makes more economic or political sense to renege—at which point the risk is passed to the lender. At that point, national law may provide for seizure of the borrower's assets, if any, to satisfy the creditors, unless some way can be found of reorganising the debtor's operations so as to restore the capacity to service the debt. In the case of international lending, especially lending to sovereign governments, such recourse to the courts in the lending country may be quite ineffectual. The courts may seize some assets of the debtor which fall within their jurisdiction, and they may confiscate ships and aircraft within their reach, but such measures may be counterproductive if they interfere with other principles of maintaining a free flow of commerce and trade.

In sovereign borrowing a default situation is not likely to take the form of a court proceeding, but of a rescheduling or refinancing exercise. Nonetheless, the fine print in the detailed and complex agreements which are characteristic of Anglo-Saxon loan contracts may assume considerable significance at times of distress when they become operative and form the basis for the documentation of subsequent rescheduling arrangements.

The allocation of risk

The essential uncertainty of the future cannot be reduced by any legal arrangements. What a contract can try to do is to shift the risk from one party to the other—and to lay down a procedure to deal with the situation if things do not turn out as expected. The lender wants a contract which minimises its own risk and commits the borrower to repay. If it refuses to do so, claiming inability to pay, a number of questions assume importance whether or not they are dealt with in the contract.

1. Is the failure to meet repayments due to mismanagement and mistakes on the part of the borrower, or is it due to circumstances beyond its control? Although loan contracts usually do not make any reference to this matter, it will be of importance to a creditor's decision whether to press for repayment, even if it can only mean a settlement at a considerable discount, or to consent to a stretching of the term of the debt, or perhaps even to make a new loan, or the complete or partial annulment of an old one (which amounts to much the same thing), in order to restore the borrower's capacity to operate, to service past debts and to generate new financial cooperation in the future. Especially from the borrower's point of view, this question also has a moral and political dimension: payment difficulties due to circumstances beyond its control obviously raise a stronger claim for support and lenience than those occasioned by mindless extravagance. Nonetheless, when there is nothing to take, the lender will have to forgo its money for the time being, regardless of the cause of non-payment.

2. Is the borrower really unable to pay? If it is, there is no point in declaring it in default and invoking paragraphs to 'accelerate' payment of its outstanding debt. Nor is anything to be gained from cross-default. But how could one tell whether the debtor is not the possessor of incomes or assets which the creditors could claim? Corporate assets are, at least in principle, exhaustible to the last penny, but in the case of sovereign lending the situation may be clouded by controversial assessments of a political nature. Gone are the days of gunboat diplomacy when, for instance, an Anglo-French Debt Commission could establish itself in Constantinople just before World War I and claim the proceeds of the salt tax. But where the limit of a country's debt servicing capacity should be drawn in an acute balance of payments crisis, when imports of food, fuel and spare parts have to be restrained, is obviously an extremely delicate matter. The survival of the government may be at stake, perhaps also that of the country or the state. Small wonder that negotiations with the IMF and the banks tend to become heated, for that is where in present conditions very important decisions are made as to whether a sovereign borrower has reached the pain threshold beyond which no-

thing is to be gained from extracting yet another pound of flesh.

3. Is the borrower continuing to pay other creditors? A sure indication that the borrower is able to pay is of course that it continues to pay other creditors, and it is easy to understand that this would incense an unpaid lender. The logic of the situation is quite compelling: in such circumstances the lender must protect itself by whatever device it can write into the contract. A borrower is obviously well advised to treat all creditors alike unless there are very special grounds to expect understanding from the one that is neglected. The 'negative pledge' not to give priority to other creditors' claims by means of unequal security arrangements makes very good sense in this context.

Loan contracts do not seem to make any distinction between the different reasons for a failure to service a loan on time. On the other hand they give extensive attention to procedures in the 'event of default'. However, in the present system of sovereign lending, default clauses are not formulated so as to be invoked automatically even when governments flatly declare that they are not going to pay. Instead, other solutions are found by bankers and borrowers. Sometimes lenders roll over or stretch their commitments. At other times, the starkly political nature of the default raises the non-performance of a term to a level where central banks, treasuries, and the IMF or the BIS step in. Contracts can hardly provide for these events, but a lot of time and effort are spent on submissions to, and immunities from, courts which are never likely to be seised with the case and would not be empowered to do much about it anyway.

The lender to a sovereign borrower is obviously taking a risk of a very different kind from that which a loan in the same currency to a private entity in the same country would entail. But the clauses of the contracts seem in many respects fairly similar despite this difference in risk. The protection they provide to the lender by trying to shift risk to the borrower may turn out to be illusory.

There are of course good reasons for this. The procedures resorted to in the case of a sovereign debt crisis have not been institutionalised. While many debtor countries ask for a clearly defined international lender of last resort, creditor countries resist the idea on various grounds, fearing *inter alia* that it would weaken the resolve of debtors to meet their obligations. The key word tends to be 'discipline'.*

---

* The same arguments were once made against attributing the role of lender of last resort on a national scale to central banks.

There is no denying that the lender shares with the borrower the risk that circumstances beyond the control of the latter will put them both in a situation where the orginal terms have to be reconsidered. If in the future the practices resorted to in rescheduling become more firmly institutionalised one could well imagine that loan agreements might also include references to the procedure to be followed, which would contribute to the recognition of such practices.

It may be objected that, although renegotiation is more probable than acceleration, lenders cannot tie their hands by accepting an obligation to renegotiate (which would effectively amount to a commitment to make concessions) in the future, since the lenders would wish to conduct any such renegotiation in the light of all the surrounding circumstances at that time and to take account of the actions and attitudes of the borrower between the time of entering into the loan agreement and the occurrence of the relevant default (see Youard, p. 179). On the other hand the very uncertainties of how a default may arise and what the circumstances will be at the time make it desirable to specify some of the factors which will come into play at that time, including the possible role of international agencies.

Balance of payment risk

The principal risk of sovereign lending is not that the borrowing government will become destitute or even that it is unwilling to honour its debts but that the lack of foreign exchange makes it reluctant or unable to do so.

This problem is often seen in much the same terms as the management of a company or a household. The wise government does not borrow more than warranted by the ability of the investment to provide future repayment capacity in terms of foreign exchange—and the wise lender does not contribute to extravagance beyond this limit either.

Many countries have a long tradition of overborrowing, which is closely related to political instability and excessive domestic borrowing in the central bank as well. This has often produced rates of inflation of staggering magnitude. If there is then a reluctance to devalue the currency rapidly enough, exports will suffer no matter what development efforts are being undertaken domestically, and the ensuing balance of payments deficit will result in a propensity to seek new foreign loans, especially if the planning horizon of the government is short.

This syndrome is due to fundamental aspects of the situation: a great potential for investment and growth, a strong political call for rapid progress, and an indifference to future consequences which seem remote and are subject to a heavy time discount.

Debt crises have been a regular feature of international lending ever since it began. In the post-war period, some Third World countries refrained from borrowing at all, or borrowed only on IDA terms which were almost equivalent to a grant, but many of those which could borrow both in public and private markets did so and got into trouble repeatedly.

There was a major stepping-up of international lending to governments in the mid-1970s, when the recycling of the oil surpluses began. It was really only at that time that the number of new borrowers in the Euromarkets expanded greatly, and the volume of borrowing from commercial sources began to rise much faster than the borrowing from public sources or the volume of aid.

For a while things seemed to go all right, in spite of the stagnation besetting the industrialised world after the oil crisis of 1974. But the second oil price increase in 1979—which had less to do with OPEC power than with the instability of oil markets and the panic unleashed by the Iranian revolution and the fall of the Shah—combined with a new and decisive effort to eradicate inflation in the US to throw the world economy into reverse gear.

A sudden combination of abruptly falling commodity prices, very high interest rates, and stiffer protectionist treatment of the exports of manufactured goods from some of the biggest debtors in the Third World rapidly made for a situation that became untenable in 1982. Broadly speaking, it is a good rule of thumb that foreign debt situations are manageable as long as export earnings grow at a rate that is higher than the rate of interest on the debt, which had been true until then. But in the new situation, the rate of interest rose to unprecedented levels at the same time as export earnings fell. In such conditions not even the best managed countries could fail to get into trouble if they had run up any debts worth mentioning.

The important determinants of this drastic deterioration in the debt-servicing capacity of Third World debtors were by and large beyond their control. They were not under the control of the private banks either, and it might seem to be very understandable that the problem should escalate to government level fairly quickly.

But if there is to be any learning from experience, the numerous debt renegotiations of the recent past might at least provide many useful clues to the kind of institutionalised procedure previously discussed, and specifically to the assessment and analysis of balance of payments difficulties when they obstruct that repayment. The IMF plays a large role in the life of sovereign borrowers at such times, and it is somewhat anomalous that there should be little mention of the IMF in loan contracts and no clauses dealing with its role in default situations.

The future of sovereign lending

At present, in early 1984, spontaneous bank lending to non-oil producing Third World countries has virtually come to a halt. As mentioned at the outset, there is a state of emergency. Old loans are perforce rolled over, and fresh ones are provided only under pressure from the IMF.

In this climate, disparate views of the future are thriving. Some find it self-evident that major debtors in the Third World will never be able to repay their debts, and that some settlement will be necessary in which these debts are so stretched out over time that they will be less burdensome in real terms. Others emphasise the great need for future investments in the Third World and see a complementary situation developing between the investment in infrastructure in the poorer parts of the world and the symptoms of saturation in the industrialised countries and their excess capacity to produce capital goods which Third World countries need; hence there would be good arguments in favour of continued massive lending.

Any assessment of prospects for a resumption of significant lending depends primarily on whether economic growth in the industrial countries will be resumed or not. It cannot be denied that there is a very great cloud of uncertainty hovering over that issue. Those who at present restrain their economies in order to suppress inflation and the expectation of inflation believe that they are restoring the foundations of non-inflationary growth. Others are preoccupied by the many reasons why one should not expect the same kind of growth in the industrial world as in the 1950s and 60s.

Much of the indignation in Third World countries about their dependency on the North is simply due to the helplessness which they feel in the face of fluctuations in their fortunes over which they have insufficient control. In the case of the debt problem it is not the whole story, but at the present time it is fair to say that most of it is due to developments in the creditor countries.

Inevitably, this raises a set of complex questions for sovereign lending by banks in industrialised countries: it involves them in the policies of their own governments and not just in those of the countries that borrow from them. And, in the end, it is apparent that the search for stability and lesser risks in lending is inseparable from efforts to produce a firmer structure of inter-governmental cooperation in monetary affairs.

The present recovery in the United States is inducing euphoria in some quarters, but it is far too early to say whether it will be long enough and strong enough to make any substantial difference to the deep distress of the world economy.

Negotiating Strategies and the Role of the Lawyer

BY LARS KALDERÉN

Introduction

These Guidelines are written mainly by and for lawyers concerned with international loan negotiations for sovereign borrowers. The present chapter, however, attempts to place the legal negotiations and the work of the lawyers in the somewhat broader context that a public debt manager has to deal with, and to suggest how debt managers could make more effective use of their negotiating resources, including legal expertise.

In negotiating the terms of international commercial loans the debt manager has to contend with a given environment, both domestic and international. With regard to the former, the individual transaction must be viewed against the central borrowing strategy of the government and as part of the financing plan for a particular period such as a year. Thus a sovereign borrower and its debt managers will have a number of basic concerns in formulating and executing an overall strategy for the loan negotiation, e.g. to achieve a diversification of the currency or maturity composition of liabilities, to have the loan widely distributed among sources of finance, and/or to leave the lenders with a favourable attitude towards future lending to the borrower concerned.

The first requirement of the debt manager, after identifying these concerns for the particular loan under consideration, must be to relate them to the given international environment. For example, while lending in the Euromarkets in the second half of the 1970s appeared to carry little risk and therefore hardly required the extensive documentation that bankers and their lawyers insisted upon, the situation has since grown increasingly more difficult—after the Iranian crisis and the debt service problems of many countries in Latin America and elsewhere—so that loan agreements with sovereign borrowers have tended to grow and become more complex in order to meet the preoccupations of the lenders and to provide them with as much legal protection as possible. At the same time, the debt crisis and rescheduling negotiations have underlined the fact that extensive and detailed provisions in loan documentation do not in practice add a great deal of substance in terms of real safeguards. However, the debt manager must accept the world as it is and prepare his negotiating stance accordingly.

Secondly, the debt manager has to be concerned with certain well-defined aspects of international borrowing and with the deployment of a skilled negotiating team, including lawyers. He should therefore be in a position to identify what legal advice is required, and at what stages, both during a loan negotiation and thereafter. In order to obtain such advice, the debt manager should support efforts to build up and improve the capacity of lawyers inside the government to contribute to the negotiating process together with outside consultants.

Finally, experience has shown that sovereign borrowers and their legal advisers could greatly enhance their capabilities through a process of cooperation and exchange of information with their counterparts in other countries.

All these issues are taken up separately in the following pages.

Some general considerations of negotiating strategy

Loan negotiation is the process of reaching agreement on the terms that will govern the relationship between the lender, or lenders, and the borrower during the life of a loan. Partly it entails solving problems of common interest, but to a large extent it serves to resolve problems of opposing interests. It may be a truism to say that negotiating strategies must be based on each party's definition of its own interest; but experience shows that borrowers cannot be too careful in analysing their needs and formulating the goals that they wish to reach through the negotiating process. Moreover, borrowers would do well to try to understand the lender's genuine problems and worries, and to appreciate its negotiating targets. 'Getting into the shoes' of the lending bank or banks should improve the ability of the borrower to get as favourable a deal as the lenders are prepared to agree to at any particular time. An analysis of the lender's side of the market and the situation of individual banks or groups of banks should thus take place at an early stage of a borrower's formulation of strategy. Similarly, greater understanding on the part of negotiating banks of the borrower's position and problems would smooth the negotiation and could well result in fewer and less irksome provisions in the loan documentation. Lenders and borrowers should then find it easier—at least in principle—to share in a common striving for simplicity in substance and in language. Various suggestions are given below on how such greater understanding of the *modus operandi* of major banks—including their legal environment—could be achieved by borrowers.

As for the borrower's own strategy in a more limited sense, it is obvious that business targets must and will be its primary concern. A sovereign borrower is naturally anxious to minimise the cost of servicing the loan out of taxpayers' money and the foreign exchange earnings of the national economy. But the borrower's representatives will also try to avoid legal constraints on the government's future freedom of action, both those that are clearly enforceable and those more dubious ones put in by the bankers' lawyers 'just in case'. Recognising which is which in the first draft presented to the borrower is, of course, much facilitated by an understanding of the other party's position. Ideally, there should be no provisions in the latter category at all; but that seems rarely to be the case.

Borrowers often complain that the draft agreements put before them by the lenders are much too restrictive in substance, i.e. that they do not reflect their real creditworthiness. In particular, small borrowers from Third World countries, which are normally presented with the most numerous and elaborate clauses, may also be told that the proposal is non-negotiable. However, in most cases borrowers will have a certain flexibility at their own level. They will therefore be wise to concentrate their bargaining efforts on items which are of most concern to them and where they have some indication that lenders may be able to show some flexibility. This theme is further developed throughout these Guidelines.

Generally speaking, borrowers should strive to get acceptance of clauses and language that the lender has agreed to in similar contexts. Borrowers are also recommended to try to trim away from the draft agreement clauses and language that they find irrelevant, either because they have no bearing on that borrower's particular situation or because they repeat or follow automatically from something already said elsewhere in the draft, or for other reasons. Unnecessary verbiage is costly in terms of printing charges, handling and storing of bulky documents, etc.; and it is very costly in terms of lawyers' time, which is eventually paid for out of the borrower's pocket. All parties concerned—the lender, the borrower, and especially the lawyers, who ought to know better—should be able to unite in fighting down tendencies to 'pad' loan documentation with 'unnecessary' clauses and language.

The possibility of 'trade-offs'

Central to the idea of negotiation is the concept of trade-offs; that you can gain a point (of importance to you) by sacrificing another (less important) point.* This is possible if the points are of inverse importance to the party across the table. Is it applicable to the negotiation of loan agreements? It is certainly applicable within the area of business terms: for example, a borrower may be willing to pay a higher price in order to extend maturity by another year, while the lender may set a higher value on an improved return on its assets than on the prospect of early repayment. The principle should apply for non-financial terms as well. Thus it can be argued that the 'quality' of the loan agreement could affect, at least marginally, the success of the loan and thereby the cost to the borrower. In each case the lenders and their lawyers will presumably have established the minimum of legal safeguards without which the lenders would not provide funds, no matter how attractive the financial terms might be; at the other end of the scale there would be a set of legal terms that could be called 'the lender's ideal', beyond which they would see no advantage in further safeguarding the loan. Should the lenders and their lawyers seek to achieve the latter position, it will almost inevitably lie on its sovereignty or restrictions on its freedom beyond what the borrower is prepared to accept in the form of limitations on its sovereignty or restrictions on its freedom of action and the borrower will need to push back the lenders' position through negotiation. The borrower might then have to accept that legal terms judged too risky by lenders could somewhat reduce the number of banks that are finally willing to participate in a loan syndicate on the basis of the draft agreement. This could conceivably restrict the size of the loan under negotiation or alternatively, by increasing the final takedown of the len-

---

* This term is sometimes used differently: for example, as used by lawyers negotiating a loan it appears to denote more of a simple 'horse-trading', i.e. an offsetting of each side's unresolved points against those of the other side, at the final stages of the negotiations, in order to achieve a termination of the discussions in time for the set signing date.

ders that do participate, reduce their willingness or ability to lend to the same borrower in the future.

Improved legal terms for a borrower could also lead to less advantageous business terms being offered on future occasions. In this sense, a real conflict could exist between financial and legal terms, although it would be extremely difficult to measure. However, there is not enough evidence of such conflicts being a serious problem to justify borrowers observing excessive self-restraint in seeking improvements in the legal terms for fear they would have to pay a heavy price for it. In any case, what are acceptable terms for the lenders at any particular time will differ a good deal from market to market, and will also differ over time in the same market.

Principal aspects of international borrowing

In order to bring out more clearly the character of legal work and the role of the lawyer, it may be useful to consider first what are the principal aspects of a sovereign borrowing operation.

A sovereign entity or government agency borrowing in the international markets is concerned with at least four aspects of such a transaction, each one of which will require thorough and exacting work employing the best expertise that the borrower can find.

One aspect concerns the business terms of the loan, i.e. amount, maturity, rate of interest, amortisation, prepayment, etc., as well as the choice of bank or banks to lead-manage the loan and handle its syndication, if any, and the compensation to be paid for their services.* It is also necessary to choose an agent bank through which the borrower will maintain contact with the bank syndicate throughout the life of the loan. The financial terms are obviously of the greatest importance for the success of the loan, as well as for the degree of satisfaction that the borrower will derive from the transaction, and they therefore tend to dominate the loan negotiations as well as to receive most of the attention and publicity. To achieve the best possible terms that the market can offer at any one time—and to choose the best time—is every borrower's ambi-

---

* Here and throughout this chapter, the procedures described are those of syndicated bank loans, unless otherwise stated.

tion. For this purpose, the borrower will need to employ some of its best financial experts and negotiators and will need a good information system to follow economic trends, market developments, etc.

Another aspect of the borrower's work concerns the preparation of an information memorandum which will usually be required about the borrowing country and its economy, particularly its economic policies and future financing needs. The memorandum will also describe such things as the financial system, the country's position in international trade, its financial position, its means of repaying the loan and the purpose for which the loan will be used, etc. Much of this information will already be available—*inter alia* in reports drawn up by international organisations such as the IMF and the World Bank—but the production of some of it will require additional work and it must all be put together in a form that will present the borrower fully and fairly to the market. Sometimes such a memorandum has to be followed up by periodic reports to government agencies supervising the lending banks in their home countries, or must be supplemented by oral presentations to lenders. A public sector borrower therefore has to depend on good macro-economists to provide the required background material in connection with its international borrowing operations.

Thirdly, the debt manager in charge of raising a loan is well advised to involve his treasury staff in the preparation for and conduct of the negotiations. Theirs are the skills which will be relied upon once the loan contract has been signed. They will deal with the drawdown of the loan and thereafter be responsible for servicing it, mainly through the payment of interest and fees, and eventually through amortisations. They will also have to maintain close contact with the agent bank. Their help will be needed in structuring the loan in such a way—for example with regard to interest payment dates—that the government's cash management is improved and administrative problems minimised.

Finally, the fourth principal aspect of a sovereign borrowing operation is the legal work itself. This primarily involves negotiating the documentation to be signed, although it also relates to the whole life of the transaction after signing. The loan documentation will contain all the details about the terms and conditions of the loan, including the method of its drawdown, service and repayment, as well as sections to cover jurisdiction, covenants (such as the negative pledge), the functions of the agent bank, etc. Various other documents, for example legal opinions, the transfer guarantee of the central bank and the information memorandum also constitute parts of the loan documentation.

In-house and outside lawyers on the negotiating team

The many aspects involved in commercial borrowing in the international markets require a competent negotiating team which it is not always easy to assemble. Several kinds of specialised staff are required, as we have already seen: macro-economists to keep track of currency developments and long-term trends in the markets, and to review and present the national economy for the benefit of foreign lenders; financial analysts to appraise loan offers; lawyers to handle contract discussions and signing ceremonies; and loan officers to coordinate negotiations and represent the team *vis-à-vis* both the lenders and the domestic authorities, the press, etc. Unless a government has been a heavy borrower from multilateral organisations and of export credits, it is unlikely to have much of this competence available when it starts borrowing in the commercial markets, and what it might have is usually not in one place but spread among a number of agencies such as the treasury or other ministries, the central bank, commercial and development banks, etc.

Internationally trained and experienced lawyers in particular, if available, are not often found in the same organisation as economic and financial experts. Local lawyers seldom have the right training and experience, but if they have they should of course be drawn upon as a matter of priority. The existing national resource base in this area should therefore be examined with a view to identifying individuals and entities that could be helpful. Normally it is necessary to establish a core of a few in-house government lawyers familiar with international loan contracts and to organise their work so that their expertise is continuously used; this probably requires that they should also have other regular tasks within the government. For governments of most small countries this means that —unless they become heavy borrowers—it might not be feasible to keep a full complement of lawyers at the treasury or the central bank but rather in a body that could supply legal services to a broad range of agencies, such as a Solicitor General's office. In that position the lawyers could obtain wide experience from working on several types of financial transaction—in addition to syndicated credits—such as export credits, aid project loans, equity investment in joint ventures, borrowings with state guarantees, etc. However, it should be understood that the lawyers must be able to give top priority to contract negotiations when these are being held or prepared for.

Organising the lawyers as a team within the government also facilitates their recruitment and the upgrading of their skills through further training, at home and abroad. If possible such training should include a few months of practice within an international law firm or the legal department of a major bank. Attending seminars and workshops that are organised from time to time is another useful way for lawyers to keep abreast of the latest developments in the legal profession and to make and maintain contacts with fellow lawyers and international experts in related areas.

Most legal departments within governments, however carefully constructed to achieve a balanced workload over time, now and again find themselves working beyond capacity, i.e. badly in need of temporary reinforcements. Outside consultants are the obvious answer, and it pays, therefore, to keep such individuals more or less on tap. Thus they should be regularly supplied with information in general terms as to what is going on and what may come up—assuming there is no conflict of interest from their serving other clients—and one should not hesitate to use them, for second opinions for example, in the intervals between calling on them to take over a more substantial part of the workload. Such people may also be in a better position than government lawyers (who normally have to operate on a tight budget) to keep abreast of the latest developments in their profession by maintaining contacts in major international banking centres. While it would be preferable to develop such expertise in local law firms wherever possible, most borrowers that go to the markets in London and New York usually rely upon a reputable law firm there for a number of legal and advisory tasks. The newcomer confronted with the job of making the best choice can get advice on firms and individuals from fellow borrowers. A number of commercial and investment banks are also active in assisting borrowers in this as well as other respects.

International organisations, finally, are getting into the act of arranging contacts with good specialised lawyers and even rendering some advice from their own experience. They usually have highly qualified staff with a background in international as well as national law. These organisations include the International Monetary Fund, the World Bank and appropriate agencies of the United Nations as well as the Commonwealth Secretariat and the regional development banks.

The role of the lawyers

It would go beyond the scope of this chapter to try to describe all the contributions that lawyers, whether in-house or outside consultants, can make to financial transactions. In general terms their chief asset—in addition to specific knowledge and experience of the legal field—is their ability to think problems through in a disciplined and orderly manner and to explain or question the consequences and implications of matters which are not fully explained or catered for in the documentation. They are able to keep a sharp look-out for fine detail in the transaction, and through the use of precise language they can improve on the accuracy of the documentation. They are known to make a special effort to 'foresee the unforeseen' and to counsel caution and prudence to the debt manager, who may be under pressure to take quick decisions to get the loan concluded so as to move on to the next operation. In the service of a sovereign borrower, lawyers should be responsible for ensuring conformity between the various financial obligations into which the state enters, as well as for maintaining an historic overview of the evolution of the legal position of the state. It is thus their task to explain to foreign lenders and their lawyers the status of the borrower, i.e. its position within the government structure, its power to speak and act on behalf of the state, and its other rights and obligations.

Once a loan or other financial transaction has been proposed to a sovereign or other governmental borrower, the lawyers will initially have to advise on the proper constitutional requirements for the approval of the transaction, the giving of any licences or consents and the procedure for signature of the relevant documentation. Additionally (but usually at a later stage), they will of course review the text of the documentation to ensure that consistency in substance as well as in the language used is maintained between the various parts of the transaction and for the purpose of detailed negotiations as described later in this chapter.

Considering the unique qualities that lawyers can contribute to international financial negotiations and the important role they must play at all stages, it is highly desirable to bring them in at a very early stage in a government's preparations for a particular loan operation—and to keep them involved throughout as full members of the team. The need for legal advice and the work that lawyers can usefully undertake could be considered in relation to the following: (i) preparatory work; (ii) the pre-negotiation stage; (iii) scope of documentation; (iv) negotiations; and (v) the signing and administration of the loan.

Preparatory work

Legal advice is important for the government's choice of agencies to undertake foreign borrowing. Most governments, in fact, use a number of public borrowers, one of which is the state itself while the others might be state-owned companies or banks, export credit institutions, etc. Some of these public sector borrowers can raise capital on the strength of their own balance sheet while others need a state guarantee to be welcomed by foreign lenders.* Issuing and administering such guarantees for numerous public sector borrowers can be quite a complicated matter, particularly so for the lawyers who have to oversee and coordinate the legal side of these transactions. While the additional work involved is unlikely to be the deciding factor, it must be weighed against other considerations such as the benefits of spreading the country's foreign debt burden somewhat wider over the public sector (thus perhaps achieving a wider use of markets). In any event, legal and financial experts should work closely together in defining a proper strategy in this respect, and in assisting the various public agencies chosen as borrowers to implement it. There is a need for a unified approach to the loan documentation by all public sector borrowers (which should be a factor working against the tendency of each lending bank to promote its own legal style). A coordinated approach will also be useful with regard to obtaining the necessary resolutions and authorities to enable the state to engage in international financing—perhaps changes in the enabling legislation will be required or additional legal instruments will have to be provided, some of which may involve a time-consuming legislative process which should be started sooner rather than later.

The pre-negotiation stage

Beyond the stage of general preparations of the type referred to above, when an actual borrowing is contemplated, the lawyers should make themselves available to assist the macro-economists in putting together

---

* Many lenders, however, would expect a government to assume *de facto* responsibility for the servicing of debt contracted by public sector borrowers, whether or not it has been formally guaranteed by the state.

the information memorandum, i.e. the document, referred to above, which is designed to provide prospective lenders with relevant information about the borrower.

Although concern had been expressed in some quarters as to the status of information memoranda once they started to be used in syndicated bank loans, attention was focused on this question by court proceedings brought in 1976 against a bank which was sued by other banks to which it had sold participations in loans made by it.* The proceedings alleged, *inter alia,* that the first bank had given misleading information by concealing the true financial position of the borrower and misrepresenting the arrangements for securing repayment. The proceedings were settled out of court but the implications of their having been brought were recognised as being applicable not only to banks selling loan participations but also to lead banks engaged in putting together syndicates for international loans. The result has been for lenders to make it clear that the contents of the information memorandum are the responsibility of the borrower, except possibly for the section which would often be included summarising the terms of the loan and/or describing the syndication arrangements (for which the lead bank would usually take responsibility). The Colocotronis proceedings also resulted in lead banks insisting that syndicate members form their own view of the creditworthiness and general financial position of the borrower, and syndicate members are usually required to confirm that they have not for this purpose relied on information given or representations made by the lead bank. It follows that syndicate members are left to rely on the information memorandum and look to the borrower for its accuracy and completeness. Lead banks sometimes have a rather ambiguous attitude to the document: while they may admit that few of their fellow bankers actually read it, they insist in most cases that it must be available (possibly only to enable lead banks formally to disclaim responsibility for the description of the borrower). Considering the risk that the contents of the memorandum will be held against the borrower in one way or the other, it is useful to let legal experts review carefully the wording of specific representations (as well as any disclaimers). However, lawyers in contrast to economists usually provide little of substance for inclusion in the memorandum, except, perhaps, on the description of the borrower's constitutional and legal status.

---

* The so-called 'Colocotronis' case.

Once a decision has been made that a particular loan operation should be undertaken, the bank or group of banks to lead the loan should be chosen with the advice of the government's lawyers guiding the choice of bank for the role of handling the documentation for the loan, in the light of its approach to legal matters. After it is clear which bank will be responsible for the documentation, the government's lawyers should try to obtain copies of that bank's 'standard' loan agreement for the type of transaction being discussed, or its most recent one, in order to study it carefully while the financial negotiators haggle over the business terms of the loan. It is also useful to collect other pertinent documentation, such as the loan agreements used by other borrowers. The more the borrower's lawyers can find out about the lenders' position and their negotiating targets, based on current market preoccupations and practices, the better prepared they will be to devise a workable strategy for the legal part of the negotiations. To conduct the negotiations to a successful conclusion lawyers must thus be reasonably sensitive to the mood of the lenders. Definition of the borrower's own targets is made easier if the lawyers try to draft their own version of important clauses in the loan agreement so as to be prepared for some give-and-take with the lenders' lawyers.

Scope of documentation

The loan agreement and ancillary documents deal with two main areas of the lender/borrower relationship: the mechanics of the loan transaction, and the safeguards which protect the interests of the lenders. The latter are often supplemented by a number of clauses regarding the cooperation of lenders among themselves and their relationship with the borrower, directly and also indirectly through the agent bank. This is an area that has taken on an increasing significance in recent years, particularly after the Iranian crisis and the many reschedulings of public and private debt.

The lenders and the borrower should have little problem in agreeing on clauses setting out the mechanics of the transaction, once the financial and other business terms have been agreed, although in the sometimes very sophisticated loan agreements of today documenting the business side may occasionally give rise to a considerable amount of work for the lawyers. It is obviously in the interests of all parties to have clear provisions on the amount of the loan, when and how it will be drawn down, its repayment schedule, the methods of calculating and paying interest, how notices will be delivered, etc. The more that any potential problems in this area are identified beforehand and solutions prescribed, the better it is for a smooth working relationship between the lenders and the borrower.

The second area, i.e. the clauses protecting the interests of the lenders, is the one of most concern to the lawyers, regardless of the side for which they are working. Usually, almost all the clauses appear to favour the lenders. However, one must bear in mind that, once the loan has been disbursed, the risk of loss is entirely on the lenders and it is reasonable that they should try to reduce that risk as much as possible. Among the main instruments for achieving this are the possibility of accelerating the repayment of the loan in the event of default; representations and warranties on the part of the borrower which form part of the conditions precedent for drawdown of the loan; positive and negative covenants; provisions that changes in the laws of the countries of the lenders or that of the borrower must not reduce the lenders' margin; and provisions concerning jurisdiction, law and immunity. Clauses setting out the rights of the lenders and obligations of the borrower in these matters take up the bulk of the loan agreement and constitute the main battleground for the lawyers, once the financial terms of the transaction have been settled.

One may properly ask why it is deemed necessary by the lenders in a typical Eurocredit to specify in such detail so many legal rules to govern a lender/borrower relationship. Are such rules not already established in generally accepted national and international legislation? The answer is 'yes'—and 'no'. It is 'yes' in the case of certain continental European legal systems, and therefore loans governed by such systems, e.g. the laws of Germany and Switzerland, are much less burdened by extensive documentation. In the case of loans governed by English or United States law (usually that of the State of New York), on the other hand, there is much less of a codified law and so-called 'case law' applies instead.* Regardless of national legislation there is no internationally binding law for a transaction that often involves many participants, with different motives and interests, from a number of countries, each with its own legal system. The loan documentation then provides the only body of rules accepted by the parties to the loan—and therefore 'all the law has to be in there'.

Having cleared out of the way those parts of the loan contract concerned with the documentation of the agreement reached on business

---

*In fact, there is no area of English law specially applicable to bank lending for commercial purposes and the general law of contract applies.

terms, the lawyers will concentrate on the clauses regarded as particularly 'legal', such as representations and warranties, and positive and negative covenants.

Negotiations

Much has been said elsewhere about strategy and tactics in international negotiations and the reader is referred to such sources for a general discussion.[1] As pointed out elsewhere in these Guidelines, the lawyers usually come to grips with the substance and language of the loan agreement only after the business terms have been settled. This naturally creates the expectation that differences on legal matters will speedily be overcome and the transaction concluded. However, the borrower should guard against falling in with such expectations and should make sure that there is sufficient scope for a real negotiation.

While it may be tempting for the borrower's lawyers to question almost every point in the draft agreement put forward by the lenders, to feel free to request changes in any clause that concerns them and to press their views until they are absolutely sure that the lenders will yield no more, this tactic has its obvious dangers, since the lawyers will normally be under pressure from the heads of both negotiating teams to conclude their work in order for the transaction to be completed while the financial terms agreed remain in line with prevailing market conditions. Of course the lawyers should try to make certain that they are given adequate time to complete their part of the negotiations and should resist attempts to set too early a signing date for the agreement, but it is nevertheless wise for the borrower to concentrate its negotiating efforts on points which really matter.

What are the chances of really improving the loan agreement through negotiation on legal matters? On the one hand, the lead manager will have won the borrower's mandate in competition with other banks and will therefore be anxious to accommodate the borrower's wishes as far as is possible; but if the loan is to be sold to other banks, the lead manager must always bear in mind that the loan has to be marketed on the strength of its terms, including the loan agreement. Incidentally, it is an interesting (and sometimes for the borrower, an alarming) transformation that the lead manager undergoes, from being the ardent suitor of the borrower to being the borrower's sales agent in the market, to being further (as agent bank) the chief representative of the lenders in any rescheduling. The problem of choosing the agent bank—not least in view of this possible evolution of its relationship to the borrower—is treated in greater detail in the following chapter.

Even if the borrower has a strong interest in changing certain clauses, and can justify that wish to the lender, the latter may appear to be equally anxious to safeguard the contents and language of those clauses. The borrower must then try to find out if the lender's wish expresses its real fears and preoccupations, or if the clause has merely been put into the draft by the lawyers 'just in case'. Borrowers should be particularly wary of what the lender is likely to call 'boilerplate' clauses, which may or may not be applicable in the case of a particular transaction—the borrower should not without adequate explanation accept any clause in the draft agreement which does not seem to have a good reason for being there. By skilfully using a wide knowledge of precedents, i.e. terms achieved by other borrowers, it is often possible for the borrower to improve on both substance and language. Simple language can be an advantage for the administration of the loan: unforeseen circumstances often appear and require adjustments in the *de facto* relationship between lender and borrower. Flexibility in the loan agreement is then valuable, in order to lessen the need for formal changes through renegotiation. Here the usefulness of the borrower employing experienced international financial lawyers in the country whose law governs the agreement must again be stressed. If it is the first time that the borrower appears in a particular market, such lawyers will be invaluable in assisting its in-house lawyers to evaluate the draft loan agreement.

The signing and administration of the loan

The signing of a syndicated Eurocredit can be a very simple affair, with only a few banks present, or it can be a highly elaborate event involving a great number of banks as well as several representatives of the borrower. Whatever the format, this is an occasion when the lawyers—of both sides—usually play an important role in ensuring that the ceremony goes smoothly and in producing all the documents to be signed.

During the drawdown and loan administration period, the lawyers may be called upon to draw up or review certain certificates in connection with the drawings. During the term of the loan, assignments may be requested (i.e. a transfer of a portion of the loan from one of the original banks in the syndicate to another bank) that will require legal work. From time to time, the legal file on the loan will receive additions through such assignments and other actions, and the lawyers' office will thus serve as a storehouse of legal documentation and information on the loan. In the same manner, the agent bank's file will serve the same purpose for the banks in the syndicate.

Cooperation between borrowers

It is clear from the complexity of modern loan negotiations that few debt managers, particularly in countries which have only recently entered the international credit markets, are likely to have all the negotiating resources, skills and knowledge that they ideally require. In fact, the difficulty increases as borrowers become relatively more sophisticated and in their attempts to minimise the cost of their debt find that they are faced with a variety of sources and markets, each with its own special features. In general terms, it makes sense for a borrower to tap many rather than few of the sources open to it, in order to diversify its liabilities and keep its creditworthiness in individual markets high. However, borrowers following this policy will complicate life for their debt managers. Their lawyers also will have to have some knowledge of several national laws and be able to master many kinds of legal practices including new loan techniques. As mentioned earlier, most debt managers have to rely, therefore, on the services of outside international lawyers as well as other professional advisers, including merchant banks. These services are expensive and the debt managers need to develop in-house expertise, both to be able to handle legal business on their own and to make the best possible use of outside experts.

One way in which debt managers can help to increase the capabilities of the negotiating team, including the lawyers, is to arrange for a systematic exchange of views and information with debt managers in other countries. Short of completing a transaction, the best way to learn about new markets and loan instruments is to ask somebody who has had first-hand experience—preferably the debt manager of a borrower that has a roughly similar credit standing. While there are limits to which debt managers would be willing to provide sensitive information, some would be prepared, for example, to make available copies of loan agreements and other related documents. The more time one has to study and discuss such documentation before negotiations the better. More seasoned borrowers in a particular market can also advise on such questions as a realistic timetable for the negotiations. It is also useful to get an idea of the amount of legal work that can be expected in connection with the transaction, both before and after the signing of the agreement.

This may all sound eminently reasonable, almost self-evident, but cooperation among sovereign borrowers is in fact rather recent and uncertain. For most countries, borrowing in the international markets has become important only during the last few years, and initially they often had reason to believe that it would only be for a short period while their economies adjusted to the oil price shocks. The ranks of sovereign borrowers swelled during the second half of the 1970s from a handful to over one hundred, the majority, however, being infrequent customers in the markets and looking for modest volumes.

In the present world economic situation, borrowers realise that it will take longer than they thought to get back into equilibrium on their balance of payments, let alone to repay their outstanding loans. Meanwhile, debts keep rising, as do debt service payments, as a result of high interest levels. International borrowing—at least to roll over old debt —will therefore be a requirement of most governments for many years to come. In this situation, borrowers' lack of experience and of adequate resources to match those of the lenders are becoming important and call for action. The superiority of major lending banks has been further enhanced by their rapid accumulation of negotiating experience all over the world in recent years; the electronic revolution in information and communications; and the intimate cooperation of banks within syndicates and in dealing with debt crises. The international banking industry, with its supporting law firms, is also concentrated in a few major centres, notably New York, London, Frankfurt and Tokyo, with head offices within walking distance of each other. It is further strengthening its joint efforts by the establishment of an information-gathering Institute of International Finance in Washington, D.C. In contrast, borrowers are often far away from these centres and may be ill-equipped to receive and transmit relevant information with speed and accuracy. They have low travel budgets, in contrast to the banks, and are likely to suffer from a severe lack of trained and experienced staff to match the highly qualified personnel of the international banks. This disequilibrium obviously makes for inequality at the bargaining table, something which can at least partly be corrected by borrowers helping each other through an exchange of information on markets, borrowing techniques and legal practices based on their own experience. The Nordic countries have operated an informal system of consultation at regular meetings of government foreign debt managers held semi-annually over the past five years, and have found it quite useful. A good deal of informal consultation goes on a bilaterally between meetings. Similar practices occur in other regions of the world. In addition to a network of government-to-government contacts, consultations take place with regional development banks, which are well equipped to take on a leading role to assist their members' international borrowing because of their own experience in this area. Borrowers may also help each other by arranging for lawyers from a fellow but less experienced government to spend some time with its own legal experts. For countries that are friendly neighbours or otherwise have good relations—preferably sharing a common language and having similar legal traditions—this could yield substantial, mutual benefits.

Note

1. See, for example, Lipton C.J., *Government Negotiating Techniques and Strategies,* United Nations, 1973 (doc. ESA/RT/AC. 7/11), and Soliven, Guillermo V., *Loan Negotiating Strategies for Developing Country Borrowers,* Central Bank of the Philippines Staff Paper No. 2, 1982.

Some Critical Issues in Negotiations and Legal Drafting

By QAMAR S. SIDDIQI

Apart from the general policy and strategy questions considered in the earlier chapters, these Guidelines are largely concerned with specific issues which are likely to arise during negotiations for a Eurocurrency loan, particularly where the borrower is a sovereign entity or a governmental agency of some kind. These issues are examined mainly in the context of syndicated or other bank loans, but some consideration is also given to bond loans, i.e. loans involving the issue of securities such as bonds, notes, loan stock or debentures (although these types of loan, depending as they do on the marketing of a known name, are in practice inevitably little used by Third World borrowers); and project financing where, typically, the lenders look to the project itself to generate the funds for servicing the loan (whether or not coupled with completion guarantees and 'take or pay' contracts designed to procure a sufficient flow of funds to the project to ensure repayment of borrowings) and may not even have direct recourse to the borrower for repayment of the whole of the loan.

The aim of this chapter is to draw together and emphasise those points which are particularly important to the borrower. Such points may be referred to in more detail in the specialist contributions appearing elsewhere in these Guidelines; appropriate references are given to the relevant chapters.

This chapter also attempts to put various points in the context of the borrower's overall negotiating strategy and point out their relative importance, which may not be readily appreciated when there is so much other relevant material to be considered in the chapters dealing with particular topics.

Borrower's lawyers and their approach to legal negotiations

It was stressed in the previous chapter that the lawyers of the borrower should be involved at an early stage with the preparatory work for any loan negotiations (see Kalderén, pp. 34–36 and 37). In many cases the borrower will have its own 'in-house' lawyers available to it and these will be essential for dealing with questions concerning the status and powers of the borrower, the authorisations required by the borrower and other internal legal matters. These in-house lawyers will typically have detailed knowledge of the borrower and can advise as to the practical effect on the borrower of many provisions of the documentation. No less important, however, at any rate where the in-house lawyers are not experienced in handling international loan transactions, are specialist outside lawyers, qualified to advise on the law chosen as the governing law of the loan documentation and familiar with the considerations of the relevant market. The two kinds of lawyer should form a complementary team, with the outside lawyers critically reviewing the documents from the borrower's point of view in the light of documentation generally accepted in the relevant market and bringing to bear their experience of many similar lending transactions. The in-house lawyers of the borrower, in consultation wherever appropriate with the outside lawyers, would be concerned with drafting the mandate letter to the lead manager, checking that any information memorandum that is prepared by the managers contains accurate information and ensuring that all domestic legal requirements, including the authority of the agency concerned to borrow, have been fulfilled, in order to ensure that there are no unexpected legal hitches after the business deal has been agreed.

There is a danger that if the borrower's lawyers are not involved until after the basic arrangements have been concluded, terms may be agreed in principle before their legal consequences have been considered or even identified. At the same time, it has to be recognised that a number of commercial, economic and political factors will condition and determine not only the commercial terms of the loan but also what can be negotiated in legal terms and how far lenders could be expected to accommodate in the loan agreement the particular requirements of the borrower concerned. Indeed, it was pointed out earlier that the legal negotiations often take place after the business terms with regard to maturity, interest, commissions, etc., have been settled by an entirely different set of people (see Kalderén, p. 39). This is particularly likely to be the case with sovereign borrowers of the Third World, with whom the availability of finance at a given time and the cost of obtaining such finance will often weigh more heavily than what might appear simply to be legal details. This is not to say that legal issues are any less significant for these borrowers but only to stress that their lawyers might face more than the usual difficulties in performing their role to the fullest extent possible.

Moreover, general market conditions, as distinct from the particular circumstances of any individual loan, will have a profound impact on what a borrower might have to accept or, alternatively, could hope to negotiate in both legal and commercial terms. Exceptional events, for example those concerning the Iranian dispute or the more recent Mexican problems, can have a far reaching effect on legal negotiations for all borrowers. It is generally recognised that the growing perception of increased risk in lending to sovereign borrowers has led lenders to seek to strengthen their legal protection. This has important implications which borrowers' lawyers must take into account with a view to avoiding the inclusion of cumbersome details and safeguarding against what might be undue protection for lenders at the expense of the necessary flexibility for borrowers in discharging their normal functions.

'External' economic and commercial conditions lead lenders from time to time to alter their approach on the inclusion of various protective provisions. Apart from such conditions, it is a basic requirement of lenders to ensure that the loan agreement is valid and legally binding in all respects and that there is as little scope as possible for argument as to its interpretation. Borrowers should not expect lenders to accept any real uncertainty as to the validity and binding effect of documentation which is the only evidence of substantial investments by them. It is partly to obtain this certainty of effect and interpretation that lenders in the Eurocurrency market usually prefer to select one of two municipal laws, English law and New York law, to govern the loan agreement. Such laws are also preferred because of their relatively strict attitudes to breach of contract and their relative willingness to enforce the bargain agreed on by the parties. The borrower's lawyers, as will be seen later, will generally have little scope (whatever the standing of the borrower) to obtain a governing law for the documentation which is not that of either England or New York.

In a sense, a Eurocurrency loan agreement, being geared primarily to provide safeguards from the point of view of the lenders, is an 'unequal' contract which appears to offer little opportunity to the borrower's lawyers to take the initiative in promoting the interests of the borrower. It is unlikely that even under European legal systems, which take into account the degree of blameworthiness in determining a breach of contract, the main objective of the contract could be other than to protect the lenders' investment. The role of the borrower's lawyers is nevertheless an extremely important one: they must ensure that the commercial transaction, which the loan agreement is supposed to represent, proceeds successfully by providing the necessary assurances to the lenders but without unduly constraining the ability of the borrower to undertake the normal functions it has to perform. This latter requirement is particularly important in the case of a sovereign borrower, which cannot legitimately be expected to be prejudiced in its functioning as a sovereign or be compromised in terms of its dignity and prestige by undertakings given to lenders, even though it cannot expect to enjoy special privileges such as complete immunity when it has come to transact commercial rather than sovereign business.

As the borrower's lawyers have to adopt what might be considered as essentially a 'defensive' approach, it might be more useful for them to focus selectively on those elements in any particular loan negotiations which are the most important from the borrower's point of view and avoid the temptation of trying to modify in the borrower's favour as many provisions of the loan agreement as possible. A selective approach might, in any case, be inevitable for a number of Third World countries, where it would not be very productive for the scarce skilled manpower resources to be applied in considering every possible legal detail or permutation. Such an approach, however, is subject to two important qualifications. First, it has to be kept in mind that what is considered to be important in a given set of circumstances need not be so under different circumstances and, conversely, what is found to be non-negotiable at any particular time might well become open to compromise following a change in market conditions or in the borrower's importance to particular lenders. Secondly, the suggested selectivity needs to be exercised on the basis of objective criteria and should not be subject merely to perceptions of random changes in circumstances.

A typical Eurocurrency loan agreement could be divided, from the point of view of relative importance to the interests of the borrower, into three main parts:

1. Operational clauses intended to spell out as clearly as possible the parties to the agreement (including the provisions as to assignment); what sums of money, including interest, fees and expenses, are due to be paid at any particular time; how they are to be paid and by whom; and also to ensure that the normal working of the transaction is as smooth as possible. Only some of these would require close attention by the borrower's lawyers. The more important operational clauses to which a borrower's lawyers should give thought are the provisions relating to the definition of the interest rate and optional interest rates; funds for payments; availability and conditions of lending (so that the borrower obtains the loan at the time and in the conditions foreseen by the borrower); fees, commissions and expenses; optional currencies, if any; and assignment.

2. Protective clauses for the lenders, generally grouped under the following headings: (a) representations and warranties by the borrower; (b) covenants by the borrower; and (c) events of default; it is in this area that the borrower's lawyers will need to be most concerned, in the nature of things, to avoid undue restrictions or undue risk of acceleration of the loan.

3. 'Change in circumstances' clauses which seek to compensate the lenders or release them from participation in the loan in certain specified events: these are also important from the borrower's point of view but there will be less scope for change in the borrower's favour here since the lenders will rarely give way on certain protections that have become 'standard' in the market.

Within this general framework, the following pages provide a checklist of some of the most essential points in a loan agreement which, in the present state of the borrower/lender relationship in the Euromarkets, require particular attention from a sovereign borrower's lawyers.

Parties to the loan agreement

It is important for the borrower to choose the lender or lenders with great care if it is to obtain the best possible terms and a number of commercial and practical considerations will determine this choice. Apart from the commercial terms they might offer, banks vary considerably in their approach to legal documentation and the attitudes of their lawyers could be relevant.

Moreover, where more than one lender is involved, as in a syndicated loan, the borrower has to be particularly concerned about certain key banks, e.g. the managing or lead banks and the agent bank, which play a special role in negotiating and/or administering the loan. Also, the borrower has to pay attention not only to its own relationship with the different lenders in the syndicate but also to the relationship between the lenders themselves (as regulated in the documentation), with a view to guarding against problems between the lenders affecting the smooth running of the transaction.

The usual technique of syndication is for the borrower to authorise a single bank (or a small group of two or three banks) to organise the loan on its behalf. The outline of the financial terms is then settled with this bank, often called the lead manager, and included in a 'mandate letter', authorising it to arrange the loan accordingly. The mandate letter also specifies the governing law and principal forum (see Choice of law and jurisdiction, pp. 52–54) and sketches out briefly the usual clauses for that type of loan. The mandate letter is usually intended to be a purely commercial proposal, often including such phrases as 'subject to contract' and without the force of a legal commitment. However, within this legal framework details can vary widely. Some lead managers may merely undertake to use their best efforts to arrange a loan of a given amount, while others will in effect guarantee (subject, of course, to agreement on documentation) the amount whether as a result of their own commitment or that of a small 'club' of co-lenders. Because the mandate inevitably precedes the detailed loan documentation and lenders will not finally commit to lend until documentation is agreed, the nature of the 'obligations' undertaken by the lead manager in the mandate will almost always fall short of a binding commitment but, subject to that, a borrower should seek to make the lead manager's offer as firm as possible, particularly when there is more than one group of potential lenders.

After receiving the mandate letter, the lead manager proceeds to solicit participation by other banks and, possibly, to form a larger management group to help with the syndication. An information memorandum is usually prepared for the purpose of syndication, providing financial and other information about the borrower (see Kalderén, pp. 31 and 35–36). In most commercial jurisdictions, information memoranda for syndicated loans will not fall within the usually stringent requirements covering prospectuses for issues of securities to the public. The lead manager will usually prepare the information memorandum itself and will present it to the borrower for approval. There will often be a representation in the loan documentation as to the accuracy and completeness of the information memorandum and the borrower should guard against inadvertent default arising in this way. The borrower should exclude from any such representation any part of the information memorandum which relates to the lending group or participation arrangements and any other parts over which it has no control or which it is unable to verify. The lead manager will usually circulate the information memorandum on terms that it does not accept responsibility therefor, or for complying with local securities laws, and therefore the borrower cannot usually leave it to the lead manager to protect it from infringements of relevant local laws, while at the same time the borrower cannot readily control the circulation of the memorandum. Moreover, although the borrower should not give express indemnities in respect of the information memorandum, the representation referred to above usually entails potential liability on the part of the borrower for any defects in such memorandum.

Apart from choosing the lead manager, the borrower should also take particular interest in the appointment of an agent bank. While the agent is an agent of the banks and not of the borrower, the functions it performs are essential to the administration of the loan and the borrower will find it useful if the agent is a bank with which it can work harmoniously. Perhaps the potentially most important function of the agent which concerns the borrower is the exercise of discretionary powers to accelerate the loan on the occurrence of an event of default (see p. 61), to call for financial and other information and to grant waivers. It is often a matter of great delicacy how a technical or inadvertent default known to the agent should be notified to the syndicate. While the banks would expect the agent to exercise diligence and skill in protecting their interests, the borrower would wish to see that the agent uses its powers in a reasonable manner. It is, therefore, essential that the agent should be of high standing, with a reputation to protect and thus willing and able to take into account the interests of both the lenders and the borrower.

The borrower's lawyers should also bear in mind that (i) agency clauses increasingly permit the syndicate to remove the agent, as well as resignation by the agent, and the borrower should insist at least on consultation with it before a new agent is appointed, and (ii) it may be worth seeking a provision requiring notification to the borrower, before general notification to all lenders, of an event of default so as to ensure that the borrower has an opportunity of curing any misunderstanding or at least of giving to the lenders generally any reasonable explanation which there may be if an event of default does arise. In practice, agents will usually act with great circumspection once events of default arise so as not to make a delicate situation worse by precipitate action. Whilst an agent may wish to act quickly if default and non-payment threaten, it will at the same time often be reluctant to take the first step against a borrower which may trigger defaults in other documentation and may result in bad debt provisions on the lenders' balance sheets and searching inspection by bank examiners. It should also be noted that the exercise of the agent's discretionary powers is in many cases controlled by the vote of a specified majority of the banks and in some matters the agent may not exercise its discretion unless it obtains the prior approval of all the banks: this demonstrates the importance of choosing all the lenders with care.

The borrower is concerned not merely with the identity of the managers and agent but also with that of all the lenders for the additional reason that on this may turn the question of the jurisdictions in which the borrower may be sued (and for a sovereign borrower this involves possibly hostile countries having a relationship through loan documentation); the impact of increased costs and tax grossing-up clauses; and control over syndicate decisions generally, particularly when default arises. Concern with the lenders is not limited solely to looking at the syndicate (over which a borrower should at least expect to be consulted and perhaps also to have some right of veto) but also at the assignment provisions of the loan agreement. In this context, the borrower should seek to insist that no assignment is made without its written consent, at least if such assignment is to genuine outsiders and not, for example, to banks in the same group as that of an initial lender, although even this kind of assignment should be limited so as not to involve the borrower in any greater costs than would have existed if no such assignment had been made. (See Chronnell and Watson, pp. 240–242.)

Assignment involves a direct legal relationship between the borrower and the assignee. This relationship does not arise where a lender enters into some kind of sub-loan or back-to-back arrangement with a participant whose existence is not notified to the borrower. In practice a borrower need not concern itself to any great extent with such non-direct arrangements, which may be necessary for a variety of reasons (e.g. to overcome regulatory ceilings or money lending/usury restrictions).

Other operational clauses

Although the choice of banks and control of assignment involve, as discussed above, a number of legal and other considerations with which the borrower must concern itself, the clauses which describe the parties to the agreement and govern assignment do not usually give rise to major legal difficulties and can be treated as operational clauses.

Other operational clauses deal with the following: (i) definitions; (ii) the loan amount, its drawdown and currency options (if any); (iii) purpose of the loan; (iv) availability (conditions precedent); (v) interest; (vi) repayment; (vii) prepayment and cancellation; (viii) payments (e.g. to be made in dollars in funds for same day settlement in the New York Clearing House Interbank Payments System ('CHIPS')); (ix) expenses, fees, commissions; (x) counterparts; (xi) applications of monies; (xii) waivers, remedies cumulative; (xiii) partial invalidity; and (xiv) notices.

It is reasonable to assume that the legal documentation produced by the lead manager will include all the necessary operational clauses. However, it would be prudent for the borrower's lawyers to check that they are in accordance with any terms previously agreed. In particular, since in the absence of express provisions the borrower would have a right to prepay when it wishes and to decide how any prepayment is to be applied, it should look carefully at the restrictions on prepayment which will usually be suggested by the lenders. Because of the funding methods for Eurocurrency loans, a prepayment could result in a loss for the banks, who would wish to postpone prepayment until an appropriate time (e.g. the end of an interest period) or to require a premium (sometimes on a sliding scale) to compensate for any such loss. Similarly, it is normal banking practice to require that voluntary prepayments of part of the loan be applied in such a way as to shorten the life of the loan rather than reduce the interim instalments. If the borrower has negotiated variations to these terms, it should check that these variations are specified in the loan agreement.

Choice of law and jurisdiction

An international loan agreement inevitably involves the laws of more than one country, particularly in the case of a syndicated loan made available by banks located in and operating from several countries. However, it is the general practice in Eurocurrency loan agreements for the parties to make an express choice of the law to govern the agreement in the agreement itself, instead of leaving the question to be resolved by courts according to local rules on conflicts of laws.* These rules can be extremely complex and vary from country to country and, if no express choice were made in the agreement as to its governing law, they could lead to a great deal of uncertainty for both the lenders and the borrower.

Moreover, as the banks feel that once they have parted with money it is they who need the greatest protection, they usually insist, particularly in the case of sovereign lendings, that the governing law should be external to that of the borrower's country so as to insulate the agreement from retroactive legal changes in such country. As mentioned earlier, the law chosen by the banks tends to be either English law or New York law, which are the laws of the markets with which lenders are most familiar. Banks feel particularly safe with these two systems which do not require, unlike the civil codes in Europe and elsewhere, the borrower to be at fault for a breach of contract to occur; non-performance by the borrower in terms of the agreement will enable the banks to accelerate the loan even if the borrower has done all it could reasonably do to prevent the event of default.

A related question is the choice of forum. In addition to choosing an external system of law, banks generally wish to protect the advantages of such a system by including a clause conferring jurisdiction on external courts which might otherwise have lacked competence to entertain an action on the loan agreement. They choose as a forum the courts of the jurisdiction whose law is chosen as the governing law, in order to produce predictable results as far as possible. At the same time, lenders feel that remedies for default should not be limited to the courts of a particular country and they do not usually agree to exclusive jurisdiction.

Although it is usual for a borrower to be required to submit expressly to the non-exclusive jurisdiction of the courts of the jurisdiction of the governing law, the borrower should keep in mind that an express submission to such non-exclusive jurisdiction does not provide for complete predictability as to the location of proceedings, as the lenders remain free

---

* It should be noted that the choice of a governing law does not completely exclude the relevance of other laws for certain specific matters, e.g. the status of the borrower and the capacity of the parties will generally be determined with reference to the law of their respective domiciles.

to bring actions in courts, which the borrower may feel are not impartial and which may even be hostile, other than those specified in the loan agreement. Such other courts may have jurisdiction only by virtue of their 'long-arm' rules, at least some of which are based on an insubstantial connection with one of the parties or the transaction. (See Chronnell and Watson, pp. 242–246.)

It seems clear that the current market practice, reflecting the superior bargaining power of lenders before a contract is signed, is to choose the governing law and forum in accordance with the wishes of the lenders. While sovereign borrowers resist—from considerations of sovereignty, prestige and practical convenience—submitting to foreign laws and courts, particularly those preferred by the lenders, exceptions are only made in favour of a very few industrialised country borrowers which have greater bargaining power and enjoy the political confidence of the lenders. Most other sovereign borrowers accept these clauses as 'operational' in nature (partly because they feel that enforcement is extremely unlikely and, in any case, they do not expect defaults to arise), though 'exclusive' jurisdiction has been negotiated in a number of cases. There are, of course, those countries, particularly in Latin America, which apply some form of Calvo doctrine and have constitutional objections to foreign governing laws and submission to foreign courts. But even substantial borrowers in the market (e.g. Venezuela and Argentina) have been constrained to find some constitutional exceptions or other means of permitting submission to external laws and foreign courts, so as to avoid inhibiting the flow of foreign commercial finance.* Indeed, the need for and the availability of finance from particular banks would probably be the most critical factors, as far as the borrower is concerned, in determining the choice of the governing law and the forum. (For choice of law and jurisdiction generally, see Venkatachari, pp. 101–105 and Wood, pp. 123–128.)

Waivers of sovereign immunity

For essentially the same reasons that lenders require an external law to be the governing law for the loan agreement and an express submission by

---

* Venezuela, for example, makes an exception where jurisdiction by Venezuelan courts would be 'inappropriate due to the nature of the contract'; Argentina allows a submission to foreign courts if the executive decrees the loan to be in the national interest and there is some point of contact with the forum concerned.

the borrower to the jurisdiction of a foreign court, they also require that sovereign borrowers waive their immunities from jurisdiction and enforcement of judgment (see chapter by Tudor John, and Chronnell and Watson, pp. 242–246). Under English law, a submission by a sovereign borrower to the jurisdiction of the English courts amounts to a waiver of immunity from jurisdiction, but the borrower will be required specifically to waive any immunity from enforcement and certain other remedies and, under the Foreign Sovereign Immunities Act of 1976 of the United States of America, waivers in certain specific respects are also necessary. In any case, most commercial jurisdictions now accept a restricted view of sovereign immunity which is based on the doctrine that 'if the sovereign descends to the market place he must accept the sanctions of the market place'[1]; but the degree to which immunity has been restricted varies greatly between jurisdictions.

As far as the sovereign borrower is concerned, the objections to waiver of immunity are the same as for the acceptance of a foreign law and submission to foreign courts. In view of what has been said above in this regard, the lawyers of a sovereign borrower would need to consider the following:

1. Whether the immunity can be waived under the borrower's own laws and constitution.
2. The extent to which such waiver can be legally given, as the constitutions of some countries allow waivers in respect of jurisdiction but not in respect of enforcement against certain types of public assets.
3. The extent to which immunity which can legally be waived nevertheless will not be waived on political grounds even if it meant that the loan agreement might not be concluded.

Another consideration for the borrower to bear in mind is that, under both English law and New York law, the property of central banks is specifically immune from enforcement unless there is an express waiver. This special immunity, however, applies only to property which is held by the central bank or monetary authority as a separate entity, on its own account, and not for the account of the state itself.

Representations and warranties

The purpose of warranties (which expression includes both representations and warranties for the present purpose) is to set out a number of legal and commercial undertakings and assurances on the basis of which the loan is made available, and to provide a legal remedy if these were to prove incorrect. It is usually expressly provided that any breach of a warranty is to be an event of default entitling the lenders to cancel their commitments and/or to accelerate the loan. The borrower's lawyers must therefore give special attention to the following:

1. Sovereign borrowers will not be required to give warranties as to their precise financial condition as at a given date, since there is no balance sheet relating to the country as a whole to which specific reference can be made. On the other hand, the information memorandum will certainly include some financial statistics (and these may be quite extensive) and the warranty as to the accuracy and completeness of the information memorandum will accordingly cover such statistics. Litigation is another area where a sovereign borrower may not be expected to give very precise warranties but the extent of any such warranty which is sought should be carefully considered against the background not only of the sovereign borrowing entity but also of governmental departments and other agencies. It is not unusual for warranties by sovereign borrowers as to legal status and the binding effect of the documentation to be subject to such appropriate qualifications, reservations and observations as may be contained in the legal opinions where such warranties are, in effect, repeated. Financial and other factual warranties, where given, may be qualified by exceptions set out in ancillary documents or disclosure letters.

2. All warranties should be checked thoroughly with regard to both domestic law and the facts of the situation so that inadvertent default is avoided.

3. It is becoming increasingly common to require that legal warranties should remain true throughout the term of the loan so as to protect the lenders against subsequent or retroactive legal changes. However, where commercial warranties are given, it must be stressed that it is altogether unreasonable to expect in most situations that such warranties should remain true throughout the term of the loan or even be repeated periodically and great care should be taken to avoid, where possible, such 'evergreen' warranties. (For representations and warranties generally, see Venkatachari, pp. 86−91 and Wood[2].)

Covenants

A borrower is invariably asked to give a number of covenants to ensure continued soundness of the credit and, in the case of a commercial borrower, to provide for the lenders to have a right to certain information on, and a measure of control over, the business of the borrower (see Venkatachari, pp. 91–94). For reasons already mentioned, the covenants for a sovereign borrower are generally less stringent than those for commercial borrowers; the covenants are also much less extensive for a general term loan than for a project loan (see Carroll, pp. 216–218). For a sovereign borrower, the covenants in a general term loan should normally be restricted to those concerning the following:

1. The ranking of the borrower's obligations, which aims to ensure that the loan will rank '*pari passu*' with all other present or future unsecured and unsubordinated indebtedness of the borrower; this is likely to have little practical significance in the case of a sovereign borrower, where there may not be an occasion for a forced distribution of the assets to unsecured claimants following the bankruptcy, insolvency or liquidation of the borrower, and it is sometimes restricted to external indebtedness of the borrower.

2. The negative pledge.

3. The disclosure of information about events of default (see Venkatachari, p. 93).

The most important covenant, particularly for a sovereign borrower, is undoubtedly the negative pledge.

Negative pledge

A negative pledge clause can have many different forms but it will be along the lines of the borrower undertaking that it will not, without the prior written consent of the lenders, permit (a) any security interest by the borrower or any government agency to subsist, arise or be created or extended over all or any of their respective present or future assets, rights or revenues to secure any present or future external indebtedness of the borrower or any government agency or other person, or (b) any external indebtedness of the borrower or any government agency to be guaranteed or otherwise assured against financial loss by any person other than the borrower or any government agency unless such security interest or the benefit of such guarantee or other assurance, or such other security or guarantee or other assurance as the lenders consider equivalent thereto, is at the same time extended equally and rateably to the obligations of the borrower under the loan agreement to the satisfaction of the lenders.

The main function of the negative pledge clause is to restrict the borrower from creating security rights and interests in favour of other lenders so as to ensure that the present and expected assets of the borrower will still be available to the lender for satisfying any outstanding claims under the loan agreement concerned in the event of the borrower defaulting. Lenders also feel that, as the granting of security could indicate that the borrower was in financial difficulties and unable to obtain funds on an unsecured basis, a negative pledge deters the borrower from incurring more indebtedness than it can safely cover. On the other hand, the borrower, particularly a sovereign borrower, will find that, unless the clause is suitably qualified, it will unduly restrict its business or force it to obtain more expensive finance in future than might otherwise be the case; this could eventually be detrimental to the interests of the lenders themselves. It is usual, therefore, for the negative pledge to be qualified, depending on particular circumstances, by a number of stated exceptions and agreed definitions of certain key elements of the clause. (For negative pledge generally, see chapter by Harris.)

The lawyers of a sovereign borrower should generally regard the negative pledge clause as a trap for the unwary and should pay particular attention to the following:

1. Since the borrower undertakes that it will not permit any security interest to 'subsist' (and it may also be asked to represent that it has no secured indebtedness), it should check that none is in existence at the date of the loan agreement.

2. The definition of a 'government agency' should not include any corporation whose equity share capital is controlled by the state but which is carrying on purely commercial activities, unless such corporation is particularly relevant to the financing or to the borrower's general creditworthiness. These corporations are particularly important in most Third World countries and it should be possible in the agreement to identify those corporations on which restrictions are not to be imposed or are to be imposed only to a limited extent.

3. The term 'security interest' should not extend to include off-balance sheet financing, for example where goods are acquired on terms that the

supplier retains title in the goods until payment, payment often being deferred as part of the normal commercial terms of acquisition; this will be specially relevant where the loan is intended to finance a construction project for which materials and equipment will have to be purchased.

4. Indebtedness should be defined in terms of 'borrowed money' so as not to place an unjustified constraint on the borrower's normal business activities. It should also be restricted to refer to external indebtedness only, which in turn should be defined in terms of indebtedness denominated or payable or optionally payable in a currency other than the domestic currency of the borrower so as to leave it free to arrange its domestic finance on whatever basis it considers in its best interests. Where it is found necessary to define external indebtedness with regard to the person to whom such indebtedness is payable (irrespective of the currency), it should be provided that such indebtedness would be considered external indebtedness only if it is booked to an account outside the domestic jurisdiction of the borrower; this is essential to ensure that the borrower would be able to deal with the branches of foreign banks in its jurisdiction on the same basis as purely domestic banks.

5. In order to provide for greater flexibility, the negative pledge should permit an alternative security acceptable to the lenders to be provided instead of the same security as is extended to the other lenders. Any attempts to provide for security to be automatically created in the event of the clause being breached should be resisted as impractical and, possibly, unenforceable in jurisdictions which require registration of security on creation or within certain time limits.

6. Liens arising by 'operation of law' must be excluded; attempts to require other liens to be discharged within a specific period unless being contested in good faith should be resisted as they are likely to arise in such a variety of circumstances as to make a common period for their discharge inappropriate.

7. Eurocurrency loan agreements frequently include clauses relating to set-off. Some of these do not extend the rights of set-off which arise under the general law and merely state the rights that would be available in any case. However, certain set-off clauses do go further and create contractual rights, in addition to those rights available in law, in favour of the lenders over deposits which they may hold at any time on behalf of the borrower. Such contractual rights (particularly where they entitle one lender to set off against deposits held by it sums owing from the borrower to another

lender) may amount to charges or other security interests which are prohibited not only by the negative pledge clause in the agreement under negotiation but also by negative pledge clauses in other loan agreements to which the borrower is a party. Obviously such extensive set-off clauses should be resisted but, if accepted, an appropriate exception to the negative pledge clause may be required to avoid breach thereof (although this will obviously not cure any breach of negative pledge clauses in other loan agreements). If the borrower is a banking agency or development bank which has deposits with other banks which also act as lenders to it the problem may be particularly acute; it is all the more important for such a borrower to refuse to grant a wide set-off clause which extends the rights otherwise available at law.

8. In order not to fetter the ordinary business and other operations of the borrower, exceptions to the negative pledge should be provided for (i) loans secured on goods purchased; (ii) short-term bank financing, limited, if necessary, to some specific activity (for example, refinancing receivables); and (iii) at least some degree of secured financing which would still leave sufficient unencumbered assets for the purposes of the unsecured loan.

9. Depending on the business activities of the borrower, both actual and those likely to be undertaken in the future, exceptions should also be provided to the negative pledge in respect of the following: (i) security interests, existing at the time of purchase, on assets purchased by the borrower in the future or on assets and revenues of companies that become subsidiaries of the borrower, so as not to prejudice its normal commercial policies with regard to acquisition—in some cases, this exception might have to be limited to real property (i.e. land and buildings) up to a maximum amount; (ii) regular financing of the purchase of assets through the creation of security; (iii) financing of trading activities through or by reference to guarantees given by national credit institutions which often require, as counter-security, charges over the documents of title relating to the goods sold; and (iv) forward financing trading activities through security on sales contracts and documents of title.

10. Because of the complexities of the negative pledge and the administrative difficulties which many countries encounter in monitoring the activities of all related departments and agencies, a provision allowing the borrower to correct or cure an inadvertent breach that may result from new financing arrangements should be sought. By the same token, all

departments and agencies concerned need to be fully alerted to the restrictions accepted under any negative pledge.

Events of default and rescheduling

The main purpose of the events of default clause is to enable the lenders to cancel any undrawn commitments and to demand repayment of the loan before the date for repayment originally envisaged, in circumstances which the borrower and the lenders agree in advance would constitute a threat to the lenders. (For event of default generally, see chapter by Youard, and Venkatachari, pp. 94–99.) The demand for early repayment is known as 'acceleration'. It should be noted that cancellation and acceleration do not take place automatically but the lenders must make a decision specifically to set them in motion. This places upon the agent, when it has the power to operate the clause on its own, a sometimes unwelcome responsibility, which could involve considerable expense and adversely affect its standing in the market, since it will usually have to take the decision to act or not to act against the background of conflicting interests and views, not only between the borrower and the lenders, but also between the lenders themselves.

The fact that the lenders have these powers does not, of course, mean that they will exercise them and, even if a default is called, the lenders may not be very likely to press for legal enforcement, partly because of the difficulties that will be encountered in such an enforcement against a sovereign borrower. The more likely outcome will be requests for information and discussion which, in the great majority of sovereign default situations, would be followed by renegotiation. In practical terms, renegotiation always means concessions on the part of the lenders and improvements in certain terms for the borrower as compared with the original loan, but the borrower may well have to pay a higher rate of interest for an extended loan period as well as substantial renegotiation fees. It is the prospect of such concessions and improvements which makes lenders unlikely to accept the inclusion at the outset of a clause providing for the lenders and the borrower to renegotiate in the event of a default arising. It is in the interests of neither the lenders nor the borrower to envisage the rescheduling of a loan from the beginning.

The practical limitations on the freedom of action on the part of lenders does not, however, mean that the borrower should not be concerned with improving the events of default clause from its point of view, though this concern should not be such as to lead the lenders to believe that a default is a real possibility and that the borrower knows this to be the case. The borrower should ensure that its freedom of action during the life of the loan is not unnecessarily restricted by the clause and, to this end, every paragraph of the lenders' draft should be examined with a view to (i) deleting any paragraph that is not relevant to the lenders' particular situation; and (ii) qualifying any paragraph that, although dealing with an event which could threaten the lenders' position, does not really do so to any significant extent (see Chronnell and Watson, pp. 231–237).

Many events of default can be qualified by including (i) a grace/remedial period and/or (ii) a materiality test, which can take many forms, including a threshold figure (e.g. no default if the event involves less than US . . million). It is important that materiality tests should be simple and factual so as not to give rise to any uncertainty as to whether a default has occurred. It will not be practical to leave it to the courts to decide whether the event concerned was material or not. In view of what has been said earlier about the possibility of adverse publicity and the choice of the agent and the banks, it is not necessarily undesirable to leave this decision to the agent or the majority banks; this will to some extent act as a restraint on unduly hasty action by the lenders (see Youard, pp. 181–182).

Another important point in relation to the events of default clause, as in the case of the negative pledge clause, is the desirability of narrowing the definitions of indebtedness and government agencies. As in the case of the negative pledge, this is essential to preserve a reasonable degree of freedom of operation for the borrower. Third World borrowers should give particular attention to the position of government agencies which might come within the ambit of the clause. While it is unlikely that a government-controlled corporation which is the source of most or a large proportion of the country's wealth, or which is closely connected with the development of a particular project being financed, could be excluded, the borrower should make sure that if it can reasonably be argued that a default on the part of an agency does not reflect on the general credit of the borrower that agency is excluded.

Specifically, the lawyers of a sovereign borrower should be concerned with the following:

1. A reasonable number of days of grace (say 5 to 10 days) should be

included for the payment of interest (or any sum, if possible), so as to avoid administrative errors and delays causing a default (see Andrén and Kärde, pp. 252 and 253–254); lenders are unlikely to agree to a very long period of grace which might enable other creditors to take action which would give them an advantage.

2. Any undertakings or obligations in the agreement breach of which would not threaten the lenders' position should be excluded; if possible, a 'remedy period' (of, say, 14 to 30 days) should also be included in respect of any breach or omission that is capable of being remedied.

3. An appropriate materiality test should be included with respect to representations and warranties.

4. In addition to narrowing the definitions of indebtedness and government agencies, as mentioned above, the cross-default provision should not enable the lender to accelerate its loan if another lender is entitled to accelerate its loan but decides not to do so; in other words, other loans should actually be accelerated and not simply be capable of acceleration before they affect the loan in question. If possible, a threshold figure should also be included to ensure materiality and avoid defaults in respect of relatively minor transactions affecting a more significant loan.

5. While a number of events (e.g. moratorium on debt; enforcement of encumbrances on, and attachments of, assets; liquidation of a government agency; etc.) are regarded by lenders as indications of financial difficulties for borrowers and, therefore, included under the events of default clause, it should be possible to include a materiality test in some cases.

6. Any restrictions on disposal or transfer of assets by a government agency with a substantial commercial undertaking should allow sufficient flexibility for transactions and reorganisations which are likely to occur during the life of the loan.

7. In view of the great uncertainty that results from the 'material adverse change' clause, which is included to cover an undefined situation which might threaten the position of lenders, every effort should be made to exclude such a provision but, if such a provision is included, reference to an 'extraordinary situation', which could be an accumulation of several small events over a long period, should be avoided if possible (see Youard, pp. 184 and 188). Reference to an 'extraordinary event' is less objectionable from the borrower's point of view.

It was mentioned earlier that, when a sovereign state encounters difficulties in meeting its foreign currency liabilities, the course of action usually followed is to arrange a rescheduling rather than acceleration under the events of default clause. A rescheduling agreement is an extremely complex document and, apart from involving considerable costs in management and other fees, it has a number of consequences, legal and otherwise, for the borrower. The agreement reschedules, under the 'short-leash' approach adopted in most debt rescheduling agreements, the arrears of principal in respect of an agreed proportion (e.g. 80 to 90 per cent) of specified debt outstanding on a pre-announced cut-off date plus payments falling due over, say, the next 6 to 18 months so that, if necessary, future arrears will have to be rescheduled separately in the future. This is considered essential by the creditors in order to encourage the debtor state to adopt austerity programmes and to avoid an 'over-easy' approach to debt rescheduling.

As for the legal content of the rescheduling agreement between a sovereign state and commercial lenders, a number of clauses are more complex and stringent than they are in an ordinary syndicated loan agreement. These generally include clauses concerning applicable law and jurisdiction, waiver of immunity, negative pledge, disclosure requirements, obligations as to the administration of the foreign reserves of the state and events of default. Creditors also seek to make the state, its central bank, and other economically significant government agencies joint and several obligors for the rescheduled debt so as to enhance set-off against bank deposits which might not otherwise have been available because of the absence of mutuality. The overall effect of these provisions is a significant increase in the exposure of the state's external assets to foreign attachments in the event of a default under the rescheduling agreement.

Moreover, in commercial bank rescheduling, it is generally a condition precedent to the coming into force of the rescheduling agreement that the debtor enters into comparable agreements with regard to its other debt. There may also be a requirement that other comparable debt will not be paid on more favourable terms and the provision may extend to trade debt and bond issues. Apart from being complex, these and the other clauses mentioned above could cause considerable difficulty for the borrower, not only in its relations with other creditors but also in its commercial and financial dealings generally. That the borrower generally finds itself obliged to accept most of these provisions simply reflects the fact that a rescheduling agreement is concluded at a time of financial difficulties for the borrower and when the creditors feel most in need of added protection. The importance of building an experienced and capable negotiating team and of obtaining competent professional advice at both the legal and the commercial level, stressed earlier in connection with negotiating loan agreements, is even greater for rescheduling agreements. (For rescheduling generally, see Wood, pp. 134−148.)

Change in circumstances

Because of the particular funding and operational methods involved, Eurocurrency term loan agreements invariably contain special clauses which aim to protect the banks against changes in circumstances which amount to *force majeure* or result in an increase in their costs which is beyond their control (see Wood, pp. 131−134). While the borrower is not likely to be able to exclude altogether any of the following clauses, some variations are possible and its lawyers will need to be concerned with a number of points.

1. *Substitute basis clause.* In agreements where the rate of interest is determined as a spread or margin over LIBOR or other rate reflecting the cost of funds in a particular market, provisions need to be made for the eventuality that the market may become distorted or even cease to exist. In order to avoid the loan being frustrated altogether or, alternatively, the rate being fixed by a court, the clause should provide that on the occurrence of certain specified events (e.g. non-availability of deposits in a particular market), the parties will negotiate with a view to determining an alternative basis for continuing the loan. If the parties are unable to agree, each of the lenders should be required to certify its own substitute terms which the borrower is free to accept or reject: the borrower might be placed in a more difficult situation if the lenders were able to cancel the loan automatically in the event that all the parties were not able to agree to any single alternative basis.

2. *Illegality clause.* This provides that if it becomes illegal for any lender to make available its commitment or maintain or fund its portion of the loan, then its commitment is cancelled and the borrower must prepay that lender's portion of the loan, even if the lender is still technically committed by the law governing the contract. While the lender obviously cannot be expected to commit an offence under its law, the borrower should try to work in a grace period for any prepayment and, in any case, the lender

should be required, where possible, to take mitigating action, such as switching to another jurisdiction. (See Chronnell and Watson, pp. 237–238.)

3. *Increased costs clause.* This aims to compensate a bank if the result of any law, regulation or official directive (e.g. those requiring it to place interest-free deposits with the central bank or other monetary authorities) is to increase the cost to that bank of maintaining the loan or to reduce the net return. The borrower should limit this clause to changes in law etc. after the date of the loan agreement, and ensure that (i) the eventualities to be so covered are clearly specified; (ii) the increase in costs is such that it is unlikely to be reflected in the variable interest rates, e.g. LIBOR, and, therefore, necessitates some adjustment being made; and (iii) increases are excluded to the extent that they are attributable to an assignment or a change of lending office by a bank.

4. *Tax clause.* This provides for the making of payments by the borrower free of taxes unless taxes are required by law to be deducted, and for grossing-up payments from which taxes are so required to be deducted, so as to protect the lenders against any reduction in net yield through deductions at source. It is, of course, possible to induce the banks to absorb taxes by offering them higher interest, but the tax clause is, in practice, fairly standard, particularly as the banks do not want to be subject to tax changes in the borrower's country. The borrower should see that (a) taxes in other jurisdictions (e.g. where payment has to be made) are excluded; (b) taxes unconnected with the transaction are not covered; (c) taxes on the banks' overall net income which are not deducted from payment are excluded; and (d) no grossing-up is required to the extent that the relevant deduction is attributable to an assignment or a change of lending office by a bank. (See Chronnell and Watson, pp. 228–231 and 240–242.)

In the event that the borrower becomes liable to pay interest on a substitute basis or if the increased costs clause or tax grossing-up clause becomes operative, the borrower should have the right to prepay, if it chooses, the loan or the portion thereof attributable to the relevant lender.

Special aspects of bond issues

This chapter has dealt so far only with the negotiation and documentation of Eurocurrency loans, which are indeed the most common form of international commercial borrowing for Third World countries. However, these borrowers often prefer fixed rate bond issues, which are usually of a longer term than bank finance and protect borrowers against volatile interest rates.* While, for a variety of reasons, their access to bond markets is limited, an increasing number of Third World countries are issuing bonds, particularly the more flexible Eurobonds. (For bond issues generally, see chapter by Wilson.)

Bonds issued in international markets are essentially of two types: (i) those termed Eurobonds, which are underwritten and sold in more than one market simultaneously by a managing group of banks and can be denominated in any single currency (usually the US dollar or certain other major currencies) or composite currency units, and (ii) 'foreign' bonds (e.g. Bulldog, Yankee and Samurai bonds) which are issued by a foreign entity on a single national market and denominated in the currency of that market.

While a basic advantage of Eurobonds is that they are largely free from national regulation, foreign bond markets are highly regulated in almost all industrialised countries.** Partly because many Third World borrowers find it difficult to comply with these regulations and partly because of the unfamiliarity of individual investors with these borrowers, the latter have not been particularly successful in tapping these markets. The following paragraphs, therefore, deal only with Eurobonds.

Even for Eurobonds, every market has its own issue procedures. For instance, a London Eurobond issue would involve the following documents: (i) a prospectus; (ii) a subscription agreement between the managers and the issuer ('underwriting agreement' in American terminology); (iii) an underwriting agreement between the managers (as agents for the issuer) and the underwriters; (iv) selling group agreements between the

---

* It should be noted, however, that a bond issue involves much more complex documentation and greater expense than a bank loan. Moreover, bonds are not suitable in certain circumstances, e.g. when the borrower requires a revolving credit, a standby facility or a multi-currency option; they are also more difficult to reschedule.

** Broadly speaking, these regulations concern (a) issue of securities by non-residents; (b) purchase of foreign securities by residents; (c) disclosure and listing of securities; and (d) taxation.

managers and the selling group members dealing in the bonds;* (v) a managers' agreement between the managers delegating the organisation of the issue to the lead manager; (vi) a trust deed between a financial institution or a trust corporation and the issuer; (vii) a paying agency agreement between the issuer and the banks acting as paying agents in various international centres; and (viii) the bonds themselves.

It is suggested that the borrower (i.e. the issuer of bonds) should pay particular attention to the following points with regard to Eurobond issues:

1. While generally enjoying exemptions from prospectus legislation, a Eurobond prospectus should nevertheless be subjected to a higher degree of verification than an information memorandum, partly because of the possibility of civil liability to a wide variety of investors and partly as a result of stock exchange regulation.

2. While trading of Eurobonds on stock exchanges is only minimal, listing is obtained (usually on the London and/or Luxembourg Stock Exchange) in order to enhance the marketability of bonds amongst investors; cost comparisons (which may be relevant in determining the stock exchange on which the listing is effected) should be made not only with regard to the initial listing fees but over the expected life of the bonds.

3. Selling group agreements should include provisions necessary to comply with restrictions on the sale of the securities; in particular, as the Securities Act of 1933 of the United States of America prohibits the purchase by US nationals or purchases within the US of 'unregistered' securities, a Eurobond issue would need to be a transaction 'not involving a public offering' (i.e. offers being made only to a limited number of 'sophisticated institutional investors'), which does not require registration.

4. Any stabilisation or over-allotment (to counteract any downward pressures on prices in the secondary market) should be done by the managers for their own account or for the account of the underwriters; it should not be paid for by the borrower.

5. If a *force majeure* clause is included in the subscription agreement, a sovereign borrower (as distinct from a corporation) should be involved in the determination as to whether *force majeure* exists; in US underwriting

---

* In New York, the underwriters purchase the securities and the managers then re-sell them on behalf of the underwriters.

agreements, any sizeable group of underwriters (rather than the managers) effectively have a unilateral power to terminate the underwriting agreement and a traditional European *force majeure* clause should not, therefore, be included as well.

6. An important difference between Eurocurrency syndicated agreements and Eurobonds concerns the negative pledge clause. Unlike loan agreements, Eurobonds customarily require a negative pledge which only prohibits the creation or continuance of listed secured indebtedness denominated or payable in a currency other than the domestic currency of the borrower.

7. Cross-default clauses in bond issues can also be limited to external indebtedness in some cases.

8. Under the tax grossing-up clause, the borrower should not assume responsibility for any taxes imposed in the place of payment; the payments clause should provide that payments will be made 'subject to applicable laws and regulations'.

9. While it is not usual for a sovereign borrower to enter into a trust deed constituting its external debt, some observers suggest that it is better to have a trustee representing the bondholders, who will be the only person, in normal circumstances, entitled to take action to enforce the borrower's obligations and to whom the borrower can turn in order to resolve difficulties (e.g. waiver of a technical breach), rather than to risk the consequences of an individual bondholder seeking to accelerate his bond and thereby also prejudicing other debt of the borrower.

10. Under the paying agency agreement, the principal paying agent should not be able to require payments by the borrower to be made to it any earlier than the day before the due date; the costs involved in making payment even one day early could be substantial.

11. Clearing houses such as Euroclear and Cedel lessen the security risk and costs involved in moving large volumes of bearer documents. Furthermore, costs to borrowers of physical presentation can be reduced by the use of 'sealed bond arrangements' where the bonds are kept by a clearing house in sealed packages throughout the life of the issue and interest is disbursed to its account holders without cutting off the relevant coupons and against an indemnity in favour of the borrower for any loss occasioned by the misappropriation of uncut coupons. Problems of physical presentation of bonds may also be avoided by use of the procedures for converting bearer bonds into bonds in registered form, which procedures

result from the Tax Equity and Fiscal Responsibility Act of 1982 of the United States of America (known as 'TEFRA').

Special features of project financing

Another borrowing technique which has not been utilised to any large extent in the Third World is project financing (as distinct from financing for projects), although it has considerable potential in many countries, particularly those with large natural resource projects to develop. These projects (e.g. LNG plants and mining and smelter projects) are so large and complex, requiring enormous amounts of capital and long construction and gestation periods, that no borrowing entity in the country concerned is likely to be considered sufficiently creditworthy by lenders and investors. Instead, lenders and investors agree to rely on the assets and cash flows of the project being financed to repay their capital. In practical terms, this means that the financing and consequently the legal structure of the project are put together in such a way that any cash flows from the project go in the initial years to repay the lenders. However, the borrower has the advantage of having projects financed which would not be financed otherwise and, if successful, they should produce financial returns to the borrower over a long period, well after the lenders have been repaid. There might also be considerable employment and other advantages to the host country, including during the construction period.

It is the large size and complex nature of projects and the long construction and gestation periods over which commercial and non-commercial risks have to be borne by numerous parties which cause most of the problems in project financing. For example, the risk of over-runs in construction and equipment costs cannot be effectively eliminated by entering into 'fixed price' contracts with the contractors, who are unlikely to agree to construct a major facility on this basis or, if they do agree, may simply abandon the project in case of difficulties rather than absorb losses of the magnitude involved.

Similarly, long-term contracts for the sale of project output and long-term energy and raw material supply contracts (which are critical for the viability of projects and the former of which provide, through assignment of sales proceeds to a trustee, the principal security available to lenders in most cases) give rise to many difficulties in devising appropriate pricing formulae. While recent experience of exceptionally wide price fluctuations in ocean transport and basic raw materials makes it essential for both buyers and sellers to retain flexibility over the long period involved (e.g. 10 to 20 years), these formulae also have to provide sufficient certainty to satisfy project lenders.

In most cases, these problems are not 'legal' in the sense of being amenable to a solution by the lawyers themselves; the role of the lawyers is mainly to provide legal structures for the solutions and packages agreed to on commercial and technical grounds. However, there are a number of areas, similar to those relating to loan agreements considered earlier in this chapter, where the borrower's lawyers could play a specific role in resisting or modifying provisions proposed by lenders in the documentation.

These provisions might include warranties with regard to the accuracy of feasibility studies; a negative pledge; covenants that material changes in the scope, nature or status of the project or amendments to any of the agreements that make up the total project package are not made without the prior approval of the lender (which may of course 'hamstring' the borrower); and certain events of default such as changes in the relationship between the borrower and the host government or political or other events which render unlikely the successful completion of the project.

The most distinguishing feature of project financing, is, however, that solutions to legal as well as other problems will vary considerably from project to project. The type of project that is suitable for 'project finance' treatment is so large, so complex and so rare in any particular country that it is not feasible to provide guidelines similar to those for, say, syndicated Euroloans for balance of payments purposes, which might be of fairly general applicability.

A general description of some of the techniques and documentation involved is given in these Guidelines in J. Speed Carroll's chapter on the subject; a select bibliography is also provided by him which might be useful in building up the negotiating capability of the borrower's negotiating team. In effect, working on project financing is a large team effort, involving engineers, businessmen, economists, lawyers, bankers, etc., and the important thing is to assemble as efficient a team as possible and to supplement its capabilities from outside sources, including consultants and independent agencies such as the Technical Assistance Group (TAG) of the Commonwealth Fund for Technical Cooperation.

72

Notes

1. Wood, Philip, *Law and Practice of International Finance,* Sweet & Maxwell Ltd., London, 1980, p. 94.
2. Ibid., pp. 240−243.

The Eurocurrency Loan: Role and Content of the Contract

BY K. VENKATACHARI

The main objectives of this chapter are to provide a general overview of a Eurocurrency term loan agreement, and to explain the construction and the inter-relationships between the various provisions therein. It should be noted, however, that the law and practices involved, and the practices as to drafting, are not static but constantly changing. It should, therefore, be borne in mind that the clauses set out in this chapter are only illustrative and should not be considered as 'standard' or model clauses. Consequently, the provisions dealt with will not reflect all possible variations.

I *Role of the Contract*

Introduction

The growth of international financing and investment has been phenomenal in recent years, in size, importance—and complexity. Legal problems arising out of international financing and investment are also complicated. International financial law embraces within its domains not merely international and domestic law but international trade, commerce, business, economics and even politics. Any international contract, especially a contract relating to a Eurocurrency loan, bristles with legal difficulties to be overcome; for it brings into one fold parties of several nationalities with differing interests and objectives and is at the same time affected by multifarious legal systems. An international contract in respect of a Eurocurrency loan transaction has necessarily to be evolved in the light of, and on many occasions despite, the economic and financial laws of various countries, particularly the laws relating to mercantile and commercial matters, regulation and control of banking, lending and investment, exchange controls, securities' regulations, taxation, monopolies and trade practices, trusts and similar. The legal problems are so vast and numerous that they have been described as terrifying. Naturally, the more terrifying they are, the better it is for legal experts. Perhaps the fact that international financial law is 'an exotic and esoteric field' [1] explains why expertise in this subject is the close preserve of a select and erudite few. Even so, the more adventurous pioneers have brought into existence a few international Eurocurrency loan contracts which seem at least to overcome a number of impediments and pitfalls on the way, and to make the terrain not quite as dangerous as it was. Although it cannot yet be stated with full confidence that the law in the matter of Eurocurrency contracts has been cleared of all doubts and travails, it should not be too difficult to give an overall view of the contract of an international Eurocurrency loan transaction as it stands at present. This chapter seeks to do exactly that.

Eurocurrency and diverse forms of Eurocurrency loan transactions
Eurocurrency is money deposited with and payable at a bank outside the country where that money is legal tender. For example, when a US dollar is deposited in a bank in a country other than the United States of America and is payable by that bank in that country or in any country other than the United States, it is referred to as a Eurodollar. Although the term 'Euro' would appear to indicate that the currency is deposited and is available in any European country, it is not so, and a currency is 'Eurocurrency' even if it is deposited and payable in any country outside Europe, for example Japan, Singapore or Hong Kong. A loan of such a currency in whatever form it is made is a Eurocurrency loan.

Eurocurrency loans may be raised by a note or bond issue, or under a term loan agreement. While raising money by a public issue of notes or bonds in the Eurocurrency market is a common mode resorted to by many borrowers, a very large proportion of Eurocurrency loans is raised under term loan agreements entered into directly between the borrowers and the lenders. A substantial part of these loans is raised by syndicated agreements often involving a large number of lending banks. Since most loan transactions in the Eurocurrency market are very large in size, any one financial institution may not have the capacity or the will to risk absorbing the entire loan requirement of the borrower in that particular Eurocurrency loan transaction. A syndicated loan is the natural consequence, and a group of lenders participate in the lending under a single loan agreement between the syndicate of lenders and the borrower. The purpose of any one loan transaction could be to augment the finances generally of the borrower or to enable the borrower to finance a particular project. If the funds generated by the project are to be applied against the repayment of the loan, the transaction is referred to as 'project finance'. The Eurocurrency loan may be secured or unsecured. If secured, it may be by means of charges over specific assets of the borrower or by means of a guarantee of a third party. In view of these and other diverse practices and features of loan transactions in the Eurocurrency market, the terms in which contracts come to be ultimately spelt out are numerous.

Purpose and scope of this chapter

Amidst these various forms of Eurocurrency note and bond issues, term loan agreements, project finance, etc., there are certain basic features common to all. These are, for convenience, referred to here as the Eurocurrency loan contract. The purpose of this chapter is to give a general overall view and idea of the provisions of the Eurocurrency loan contract. Its scope is limited to dealing with unsecured and unguaranteed Eurocurrency loan transactions and contracts relating thereto which are subject to English law.

Legal issues and the need to take care of them

Complexities of the legal issues

As stated earlier, the legal difficulties and problems likely to arise in an international Eurocurrency transaction are many and complex. By the very nature of the transaction, the lender or the multiple lenders, on the one side, and the borrower, on the other, normally belong to different countries; and so all the legal complications of cross-border transactions need to be resolved. The status of the borrower has a very considerable bearing on the settlement of many of the terms of the contract. By 'status' we mean that the borrower may be an unincorporated body, a trust or a corporation, or may be a state, a government, a government authority or body, or a government-owned corporate entity. Certain limitations and restrictions may pertain to the borrower depending on its particular status and suitable provisions will need to be agreed upon between the parties in order to surmount these limitations or to comply with the restrictions. It is obvious that parties may also adhere to different legal systems; namely, the common law, civil code, socialist and Islamic systems. Limitations and restrictions under these various systems will need to be properly understood and necessary agreement to be arrived at in order to steer clear of the inhibitions. Exchange control laws of the different countries involved will need to be looked into and complied with. Thus, deep and close consideration of legal issues is necessary not only for documenting the contract but also for negotiating its various terms and conditions.

The necessity for, and the manner of, taking care of legal issues
It goes without saying that the resolution of the legal issues, the anticipation of any legal problems likely to arise and the making of the necessary provisions to meet and/or resolve them, as well as the documentation of the contract, have necessarily to be done by legal experts, more specifically by Euromarket lawyers. The selection of the lawyers, both by the lender or multiple lenders and the borrower, no doubt depends upon the traditional ties and relationships between the lawyers and the clients, as well as various other factors. It should, however, be mentioned that it would be useful to select lawyers who have had previous experience of the borrower's or the lender's methods of operation, whichever the case may be.

A Eurocurrency loan contract is not the same as the document for a domestic loan transaction. It is an international contract and the details in regard to each and every term of the contract have to be worked out by the lawyers with a very clear understanding of the discussions between and the conclusions of the financial experts. Very frequently, even conclusions concerning the financial and credit aspects have to be shaped in the light of the various legal possibilities. Persons familiar with Eurocurrency transactions are aware that soon after the initial discussions between the borrower and the lender, the latter would give to the former an offer or commitment letter outlining the basic terms of the loan. In syndicated transactions, even before the lenders come into the picture, the borrower issues to the manager a mandate letter which would *inter alia* contain the principal features of the loan requirements. These letters may specifically be made 'subject to negotiations', 'subject to contract', 'subject to formal documentation' or 'without prejudice'. Despite these precautions, controversies as to what extent these represent the terms of the contract may arise and create complications. It is therefore desirable to involve legal experts from the outset.

Most of the parties who lend and borrow in the Euromarket will have their own in-house law officers and legal experts. These experts may have considerable experience and may undoubtedly be useful for dealing with queries that may be raised in regard to minute details of the position regarding the lender or borrower. It is also possible that the time and money which may have to be spent could be reduced by the involvement of these in-house specialists. Even so, such specialists can only supplement and not supplant the outside specialists, who have a much greater breadth of experience of Eurocurrency transactions. It is necessary on the lender's side for the documentation to be given the seal of approval, in the form of a written legal opinion, of outside specialists acting for the lenders, but it is also important to the borrower for it to have outside specialists looking at the documentation specifically from its point of view.

Purpose of the contract

The legal documentation in a Eurocurrency loan transaction may be spread over a large number of documents, depending on the nature, form and mode of the borrowing. In the case of a term loan facility, whether by a single lender or multiple lenders in a syndicated loan, the document which will contain the basic contract is the term loan agreement. The rest will be the various ancillary documents. Structuring the main contract, namely the loan agreement, would involve developing with precision, and setting out, the terms and provisions that have been negotiated. It should, besides setting out the terms of the loan, also provide the ground rules, procedures and mechanisms for the fulfilment, performance and enforcement of the different provisions of the contract. It should, as far as possible, anticipate and assess the various legal difficulties and problems that may arise and provide suitably for meeting or surmounting the difficulties and for finding solutions to, or steering clear of, the problems.

As has been indicated earlier in this connection, it should be borne in mind that international financial law is closely related to and vastly affected by international economic law. International finance and investment cannot stand in isolation but will largely be governed by international trade, commerce, business and economics. Politics and political conditions, particularly of the different countries whose nationals or currencies are involved in the transaction, could have a great, and possibly even a shattering, impact on the contract. It is necessary to structure the provisions of the contract so as to minimise the potential impact of economic and political changes and upheavals.

Objective and principal concern of the contract

As with all loan transactions—domestic or international—documentation of the Eurocurrency loan transaction seeks to provide all the safeguards that would be necessary from the point of view of the lender. The objective and prime concern of the lender has come to stay as the objective and prime concern of the loan agreement as well; this is to ensure that there shall be no legal problem in the repayment of the loan or the enforcement thereof. As one author effectively put it, '... "front-end" legal considerations affecting the structure of the loan ... are directly related to collectibility because the sanction for failure to structure a loan correctly is noncollectibility'.[2] Thus, failure to ensure by documentation that the interest of the lender is fully safeguarded is to defeat the very purpose and aim of the documentation. Of course, there cannot, and should not, be an issue raised on this objective—for the lender who lays out the money has got to recoup the same.

However, over-anxiety to cover all possible situations that may exist or arise can lead to the making of some rigorous provisions which are onerous to the borrower: these may become self-defeating and backfire on the lender because they may not be enforceable. Examples could be provisions for a higher rate of interest or for penalties in the event of default. Even if the borrower agrees, the former may not be effective because of usury laws that may affect the transaction and the latter may be unenforceable because of penalties being invalid under the law in some jurisdictions.

It has, at the same time, to be ensured that some fundamental features of a Eurocurrency loan transaction, which are of very great concern to the lender, are fully taken care of. In this connection one may refer to the funding requirements of a lender in the Eurocurrency market: the various provisions in the agreement have to be structured to suit the funding practices of the market and the lender. Philip Wood puts it succinctly thus: 'Typically the eurocurrency loan agreement is a more complex document than the normal term loan contract by reason of the additional mechanics flowing from the funding method and the special banking risks peculiar to the market.'³

The sophisticated devices adopted in a typical agreement to meet this funding requirement will be seen later when referring to provisions relating to interest calculations, scheduled repayments and voluntary prepayments, alternative (or substitute) basis for continuing the loan, changes in market conditions and political and economic circumstances, optional currencies, etc.

While the lender's interest has necessarily to be considered in the structuring of the contract, it is equally essential to take into account the borrower's difficulties, particularly the limitations and restrictions to which his operations are subject. The borrower may also be affected by changes in the market and in political and economic conditions, and provisions such as currency options, prepayment, etc., may have to be made in his favour as well. Thus, while the major objective could continue to be the safeguarding of the lender's interests, particularly in regard to repayment and enforcement thereof, there is a great need to balance his interests with those of the borrower when drawing up the terms of the contract.

In short, therefore, the objective and principal concern of the Euromarket lawyers in structuring the Eurocurrency loan contract should be to strike a balance between the interests of the lender and those of the borrower and at the same time to have due regard to the conditions of the market and also the political and economic conditions of the different countries involved.

II *Content of the Contract*

Introduction

It is now proposed to set out the contents of a Eurocurrency term loan agreement and wherever necessary explain the functions, operation and significance thereof.

Instead of dealing with the contents in the order *seriatim* in which the various clauses generally appear in a typical loan agreement, the presentation will be in an order which will facilitate an understanding of the different provisions and their inter-relationships. The proposed order will be as follows: basic minima of a loan agreement; matters which are universally dealt with; matters which are typically dealt with; miscellaneous provisions; and ancillary documents.

Basic minima of a loan agreement

Identification, description and representation of the parties
Borrower. A borrower may be a corporation or company with an autonomous and separate juristic personality. Here all that would be necessary is to ascertain its status and describe it in the document in the name in which the corporation or company can sue and be sued under its charter or constitution and under the laws of the country of its incorporation. Where the borrower is a sovereign state or a government it is particularly important for its borrowing powers to be ascertained and it will be necessary to identify the actual authority which can borrow and the name in which contracts of the state or government have to be entered into.

Lenders. Usually lenders are banks or financial institutions and there should be no difficulty in identifying or describing them in the document. In the case of syndicated loans it is the general practice to name them in an annexure or exhibit to the contract and refer to them in the body of the document as banks/financial institutions.

Managers. In syndications it is customary to identify the manager. The manager is appointed by the borrower to syndicate the credit. The borrower looks to the manager for advice and assistance in this matter. The legal position is that the manager negotiates the terms and conditions of the loan with the lenders on behalf of the borrower. Where there is more than one manager, it is not unusual to specify one or more of them as co-manager or lead manager. In practice, the manager is also generally a lender.

Agent bank. Similarly, as a syndication involves many lenders, one or more of the lending banks are appointed as the agent bank or agent banks. The agent bank represents the lenders and acts for them.

Lead bank. This is another expression often used (although not actually appearing in the loan agreement) to describe the bank carrying out the functions, as outlined above, of the manager (or lead manager).

It is not within the scope of this chapter to define and discuss the specific duties and responsibilities of the managers, agent bank and lead bank.

Execution by representatives. It has to be ensured that an authorised representative of the borrower executes the document on behalf of the borrower, notwithstanding an assurance in this regard having been included in the legal warranties and legal opinions.

The loan, its drawdown and currency options

The loan. It goes without saying that the quantum of the loan will be specified in the agreement. Unlike the case of a bond issue, under a term loan agreement the loan can be made available to the borrower by the lender not only on one specified date, but in instalments on different dates. The agreement will specify the currency and the place and the account of the bank at which the loan or the tranches of the loan will be made available. In Eurocurrency loan agreements a typical provision made in this regard is that the lender will make the loan, or the various instalments, available in US dollars and in funds for same day settlement in the New York Clearing House Interbank Payments System (known in the market as 'CHIPS') not later than the time specified in the agreement at the stipulated office of a bank in New York City or any other bank as may be specified by the borrower at one time or from time to time. In a syndicated loan, each participating bank will agree to make the advance to the borrower through its office identified in the agreement or through such other office which may be specified by such bank in accordance with the agreement. It is also usual to specify that each participating bank will provide the necessary funds to the agent bank in the currency and to the account specified in the agreement. Where there is more than one lender, the agreement will provide that the obligations, interests and rights of each lender under the agreement are several and certainly not joint. Failure of one of the lenders to carry out its obligations under the agreement shall not relieve any other lender, the agent or the borrower of any of its obligations under the agreement, nor will any one lender be responsible for the obligations of any other. In addition the obligations of the borrower will not in any way be conditional upon the performance or observance of the contract by any one of the lenders and not be affected by any other claim that one of the parties may have against another party.

Drawdown. A term loan agreement will provide for the loan to be made available by the lender or the lenders to the borrower either on a date specified or in instalments, in each case in compliance with the stipulated conditions precedent; and the details in regard to such drawings will be provided in the agreement under a head entitled 'Drawdown'. The agreement may provide for drawdown of the loan within a specified period as and when funds are required by the borrower; such period is referred to as the 'commitment period'. It may even provide for a 'revolving' credit, i.e. the borrower may operate a line of credit by drawing, repaying and again drawing, but such drawings and repayments will be subject to the overall limits of the loan, both as to time and amount.

The procedure for drawdown will also be specified in detail in the agreement. Usually, it will provide that drawdowns will be permitted to be made by the borrower subject to the following:

1. A request is to be made by the borrower by means of a notice, the form for which is also generally provided in an annexure or exhibit to the agreement.

2. The notice of drawdown shall be given to the lender or the agent bank, in the case of syndication, not less than the number of days (usually business days) specified in the agreement before the date of drawing.

3. The notice should also specify: (i) the date on which it is proposed to draw down; (ii) the amount of the drawdown (either the whole amount or, in case of an instalment loan, the specified amount of the instalment); (iii) the currency in which the loan is required in a case where there are provisions in the agreement for giving the loan in alternative or multi-currencies; and (iv) if, on any drawdown date, fees and expenses are payable to the lender, the quantum of such fees and expenses.

4. Compliance with the various provisions in regard to representations, guarantees, legal opinions, etc. which require to be complied with before each drawdown, as conditions precedent.

The amounts to be made available to the borrower by the lender or lenders shall be made available in such currency and to such account as may be specified. If it is a syndicated loan, the lending banks will make funds available to the agent bank, which will make available the funds to the borrower in the manner stipulated in the agreement. Once given, a notice of drawdown is irrevocable.

Currency options. The loan agreement can also provide for an option to the borrower to convert the loan into a currency other than the one first or previously specified or even multi-currencies. Interest and principal may then be denominated in the new currency or currencies opted for. Where this is the intention of the parties, specific provision will be made in the agreement to provide for the notice of drawdown or notice of conversion to contain a specification of the currency in which the drawdown is required or into which the loan or relevant part thereof is to be converted and the conversion rates agreed upon by the parties and also some specification in regard to the time: for example, the interest period during which the borrower shall be entitled to denominate the loan or the relevant part thereof in the alternative currency or multi-currencies. Furthermore, where such provisions are made for multi-currencies or alternative currencies, corresponding provisions will have to be made for the benefit of the lenders in regard to changes in circumstances or funding requirements. It perhaps used to involve somewhat complex drafting to make the provisions concerning currency availability, calculation of exchange rates and the manner of exercising currency option, etc. However, a sufficient number of near standard clauses is now available and the drafting of the necessary provisions is comparatively easy.

Interest
Rate of interest and basis for fixation. The rate of interest in Eurocurrency loans is generally a floating, rather than a fixed, rate. The rate is calculated with reference to the particular method of funding by the lending banks and financial institutions in the Eurocurrency market, and the special financial risks undertaken by such lenders which are peculiar to that market. The interest rates on these loans are based on the cost of funds to the lender, a fact accepted as a basic and fundamental feature of Eurocurrency loan contracts. This feature will be reflected not only in the terms as to interest rate but in the other provisions of the contract. The cost of funds to the lender is naturally based on the rate of interest that it has to pay on the matching deposits that it has to take from other banks in the market to fund the loan during the relevant period. These funding deposits are for short terms such as 3, 6, 9 or 12 months. It is the general practice of the Eurocurrency market that the floating rate of interest on Eurocurrency loans is related to what is known as the London Interbank Offered Rate, referred to as LIBOR. In a single-lender transaction,

LIBOR for each period for which interest is payable (such period being referred to as an 'interest period') is usually described as being the rate at which the lending bank is able in accordance with its normal practices to acquire deposits of the relevant currency in amounts comparable with the loan (or the relevant part thereof) in the London Interbank Eurocurrency market at or about 11.00 a.m. (London time) on the second business day before the beginning of each interest period. In a syndicated transaction, the principal London offices of certain of the lending banks are chosen as 'reference banks' and LIBOR is usually described here as being the average (rounded upwards to the nearest one sixteenth of one per cent) of the rates quoted by each reference bank to the agent bank at the request of the agent bank as the rate at which such reference bank was able in accordance with its normal practices to acquire deposits of the relevant currency in amounts comparable with its participation in the loan (or the relevant part thereof) in the London Interbank Eurocurrency market at or about 11.00 a.m. (London time) on the second business day before the beginning of the relevant interest period. The rate of interest applicable to the loan for each interest period is LIBOR for such interest period plus a margin that will be agreed upon between the parties.

The margin could be a varying margin, i.e. it may be different in respect of different interest periods. It may be mentioned that Eurocurrency loans are sometimes based on other methods of fixation of the interest rates such as the US Prime Rate.

While the rate of interest is ascertained at the commencement of each interest period, interest is payable at the end of each interest period, although it is usual to provide for interim payments of interest in the case of interest periods of over six months.

Interest periods. Interest periods are usually of 3 or 6 months' duration, but not infrequently periods of 1, 9 and 12 months are included and occasionally other periods may be specified. The duration of interest periods within the predetermined range is generally left to the option of the borrower, although the lenders will usually have certain rights to veto the borrower's selection. The normal rules relating to interest periods are:
1. If an interest period ends on a day which is not a banking day, the interest period shall be extended to the next succeeding banking day, if such banking day falls within the same calendar month, otherwise the interest period shall end on the immediately preceding banking day.

2. If an interest period commences on the last banking day in a calendar month, it shall end on the last banking day in a calendar month.

3. Interest periods in respect of separate drawings shall, as far as possible, be co-terminous and, for this purpose, the first interest period relative to each drawing shall end on the same day as the then current interest period relating to the first drawing and subsequent interest periods for all the drawings shall end on the same day.

4. The lender or the agent bank in the case of syndication can specify that an interest period or interest periods relative to a drawing or drawings shall be such period as the lender or the agent bank may designate, if such designation is necessary to ensure that the last dates of interest periods coincide with the repayment dates in relation to the principal amount.

Default interest. Generally, Eurocurrency loan agreements also provide for payment of default interest, as failure to provide for default interest may mean that interest shall continue to be calculated at the contractual rate or even a lesser rate. Courts of many countries award interest on overdue debts but the rate of interest may differ depending on the laws of each country. In making a provision for default interest, care will have to be taken that the higher interest rate provided on default is not considered by courts as a penalty but as just, fair and reasonable compensation for the defaulted loan. Whether default interest can be compounded is a debatable question. There would, however, be no objection to providing therefor, if the parties so agree.

Repayment and prepayment
Repayment. It is obvious that any loan agreement has to provide for the repayment of the loan and also the date or dates of such repayment. Usually, Eurocurrency loans are repayable in instalments over a period of time as such repayment will suit the lenders and also the borrower. The amounts of instalments may be required by the agreement to be equal or as nearly equal as possible given the figures involved; alternatively instalments may be a stated percentage of the loan (the aggregate obviously being 100 per cent of the loan) or specified unequal amounts. The three most common ways of fixing repayment dates are: (i) by specifying precise dates; (ii) by reference to the date of the agreement (e.g. 'each of the dates falling 36, 42, 48 and 54 months after the date of this Agreement'); and (iii) by reference to the date of the first drawing (e.g. 'each of the

dates falling 36, 42, 48 and 54 months after the date of the first drawing'). As mentioned above, provision will be made to align repayment dates with the end of interest periods.

Prepayment. It is also necessary to make provision for the conditions subject to which, and according to which alone, a prepayment of the loan could be made. In the absence of a prepayment provision, it may be open to the borrower to prepay the loan whenever it wishes. Such a pre-payment may cause loss to the lender bank as it may have to incur additional costs in having to make the necessary adjustments in its own funding operations. The following provisions are usually made:

1. Prepayment may be made only after due notice to the lender or, in the case of syndicated loans, to the agent bank.

2. The prepayment could be of any part of the loan so long as such part is not less than a specified minimum amount, or integral multiples thereof.

3. The prepayment will have to be made on an interest date relative to the loan or to the part of the loan being prepaid.

4. The prepayment will have to be applied against outstanding repayment instalments in reverse order of maturity.

5. Notice of prepayment shall be irrevocable and the borrower shall be bound to prepay in accordance with such notice.

6. Prepayment should be made together with all accrued interest and all fees and other amounts payable under the agreement.

7. Amounts prepaid cannot be borrowed again.

8. No prepayment shall be made, except in accordance with the conditions stipulated in the agreement.

Matters universally dealt with in a loan agreement

Representations and warranties

Categories of warranties. A typical term loan agreement contains representations and warranties given by the borrower. Representations are statements made, and warranties are assurances given by the borrower on the basis of which the lender makes the credit available. In many loan agreements, both the representations and warranties are narrated under the head 'Warranties' only. Warranties can be classified broadly under two heads: legal warranties, and commercial and financial warranties. The former are generally in regard to the due establishment or organisation of the borrower; its authority to engage in business and to enter into borrowing arrangements; the absence of any contravention of its charter or constitution and applicable law and regulations and other agreements to which the borrower is a party; the obtaining of all governmental licences and approvals for the performance of the loan agreement and material ancillary agreements; and the validity and binding nature of the loan agreement. Commercial and financial warranties would relate to the borrower's financial condition, business operation and contingent liabilities as well as its title to assets, any material litigation and disputes in which the borrower may be involved, the absence of defaults under the loan agreement, encumbrances on the borrower's assets and the like.

A summary of typical provisions on warranties. Anyone attempting to summarise the usual provisions made in respect of the two categories of warranties, cannot do better than to quote Philip Wood:

Legal warranties usually include the following:

Status. A statement as to the status of the borrower, *e.g.* that it is duly incorporated, validly existing and in good standing and is legally qualified to do business in every jurisdiction where such qualification is necessary.

Powers, authority and due execution. A statement that the borrower has the necessary constitutional power to enter into and perform the loan agreement, and that the loan agreement has been authorised by the appropriate constitutional procedures and has been duly executed.

No conflict with laws, etc. A statement that the making and performance of the loan agreement do not and will not contravene any law, regulation or court order or the constitutional documents of the borrower or any contract or mortgage binding on the borrower or affecting its assets.

Legally binding and enforceable. A statement that the loan agreement is the valid and legally binding obligation of the borrower enforceable in accordance with its terms.

Official consents. A statement that all necessary governmental and official consents for the making and performance of the loan agreement by the borrower have been obtained, including any consents necessary to enable the borrower to acquire foreign currency and transmit it abroad.

Filings. A statement that no filings, recordings, or registrations with any public or official body or agency are necessary or desirable in relation to the making, performance, validity or enforceability of the loan agreement.

Commercial transaction. In loans to states or state-related institutions, a statement that the loan is a private and commercial act of the borrower as opposed to a public or governmental act and that the borrower is subject to civil and commercial law in respect of its obligations under the loan agreement.

Other legal warranties. There also may be other legal warranties as to the absence of withholding taxes, as to the enforceability of foreign judgments in the courts of the borrower's country in respect of the loan agreement, as to the absence of stamp duties, that no adverse legal consequences would arise to the lender as a result of the loan agreement, that the agreement is in proper legal form for enforcement in the courts of the lender's country, and as to the use of proceeds.

Warranties as to the commercial position of the borrower would generally cover the following:

Financial condition. A statement that the most recent audited financial statements of the borrower show a true and fair view of the financial condition of the borrower as at their date and the results of the operation of the borrower for the financial period ending on that date; that the borrower has no material liabilities not disclosed in those accounts and that there has been no material adverse change in the financial condition of the borrower since that date.

Litigation. A statement that the borrower is not involved in any litigation or administrative proceeding and that no such litigation or proceeding is, to the knowledge of the borrower, threatened which might have a material adverse effect on the business or financial condition of the borrower.

Contracts. A statement that the borrower is not in default under any contract, instrument or mortgage affecting it or its assets and no event of default (or event which with the giving of notice, lapse of time or other condition may constitute an event of default) has occurred or is continuing.

Warranties as to financial condition and litigation would not usually appear in sovereign loans.[4]

Qualification of warranties. Although qualified warranties may not generally be acceptable, it is not unusual to qualify the legal warranties as being subject to the specific qualifications, reservations and observations contained in the legal opinions, and some of the financial warranties as being subject to the specific exceptions contained in any one of the ancillary documents or in a separate communication generally referred to as a disclosure letter or a disclosure document. The latter is particularly true in the case of sovereign borrowers: while it is the case, as mentioned above, that sovereign borrowers do not give warranties as to financial condition in the sense of referring to a set of financial statements, financial information is usually given to lenders in an information memorandum and the borrower would usually have to give a warranty as to the accuracy and completeness of that information. In my opinion, these cannot be stated to qualify the warranties as such, but only make the statements and assurances under the warranties more precise than they may appear to be.

Warranties to continue to subsist. It is not uncommon for lenders to require that some of the warranties, besides existing at the time of the agreement, would continue to be in existence at the time of the actual borrowing or, if there are several borrowings, at the time of each drawdown. Some agreements may require these warranties to be repeated periodically. Such warranties as are required by the lenders to remain subsisting throughout the term of the loan agreement are suitably called 'evergreen warranties'.[5]

Purpose of the warranties. It is of interest to examine the purpose that is sought to be served by these representations and warranties.

1. Remedies for misrepresentation: The lender may have a remedy by way of an action for damages or, in some circumstances, even rescission of the contract in the event of an inaccuracy in the representations and warranties.

2. Estoppel: As these representations and warranties are made before the lender agrees to give the loan and as they also form the basis for the lender agreeing to give the loan, they will constitute estoppel against the borrower. It is well known that if any person makes a false representation to another and the other acts upon that false representation, the person who made the representation shall not be allowed to set up later that the representation was false. Such an estoppel can avail against the borrower only in respect of statements of fact or, at best, of mixed law and fact. Thus most of the warranties in respect of the commercial and financial position of the borrower cannot be rebutted by the borrower later. Even here, namely warranties in respect of financial and commercial matters, if the damage has already been done, reliance on estoppel against the borrower cannot be of much help. In regard to legal warranties, estoppel may not be of much advantage to the lender, for there cannot be an estoppel in respect of a misrepresentation of the law. In other words, even after the borrower had represented that he had the necessary powers to borrow but in fact did not have the power to borrow, the loan would be void, regardless of the misrepresentation.

3. Checklist of things to be attended to: It has also been stated that representations and warranties have a practical value, in that they more or

less constitute a checklist for a responsible borrower. Its specific attention is being drawn to the fact that the various matters in respect of which it gives warranties require to be complied with. They also serve the lender's monitoring process.

4. Condition precedent: The loan agreement generally provides as a condition precedent to each drawdown that some of the representations and warranties continue to be effective on an updated basis.

5. Event of default: There will also be a provision that if any of the representations and warranties should turn out to be untrue, it will be an event of default enabling the lender to cancel the commitment and to accelerate the outstanding loan.

Special warranties where the borrower is a sovereign or a state. Where the borrower in a Eurocurrency loan is a sovereign or a state, certain special warranties are included in the loan agreement. Such warranties would generally be on the following lines:

1. The borrower is subject to civil and commercial law with respect to its obligations under the agreement.

2. The borrowings by the borrower under the agreement and the execution, delivery and performance of the agreement by the borrower constitute private and commercial acts.

3. Neither the borrower nor any of its revenues or assets enjoy any right of immunity from set-off, suit or execution in respect of its obligations under the agreement, save as may be extended by any competent court in respect of commercial transactions by a sovereign state.

4. The waivers by the borrower contained in the agreement of any right or immunity are irrevocably binding on the borrower.

Warranties of this kind seek to ensure that the borrower, notwithstanding that it is a sovereign or a state, will be estopped from pleading that it is an independent and autonomous sovereign or state and that the various provisions in the agreement relating to its borrowing and agreement on the governing law and jurisdiction of the chosen fora are not binding because of its immunity from suit, set-off, attachment, execution, etc.

Such a warranty is necessary for whatever its worth, as a sovereign state has been for quite a long time a privileged subject under international law and no action could be taken against it in its own courts or in any foreign court. The immunity in its own courts is because the courts are its own creations and the immunity in foreign courts is on grounds of diplomatic privilege and reciprocity between autonomous states. Nowadays, however, it has come to be recognised that a sovereign state would have its privileges only in its functions as a sovereign and cannot be allowed to enjoy special privileges when it has come to transact commercial business. Trade and commerce are surely not sovereign functions. Those who indulge in such functions cannot claim special privileges thereunder. As Philip Wood puts it: 'Most commercially significant jurisdictions now hold that if the sovereign descends to the market place he must accept the sanctions of the market place'.[6]

Covenants (including the negative pledge)
In general. Any typical loan agreement invariably contains certain undertakings which are referred to generally as covenants and are required to be complied with by the borrower. It is stated that the function of covenants is to ensure the continued soundness of the credit. They also entitle the lender to have certain inside information on, and limited control over, the business of the borrower. Covenants are by and large detailed more extensively in project loans than in term loan agreements. In the latter, mainly more important covenants such as the ranking of the borrower's obligations, the negative pledge and the disclosure of information about events of default, are included. Such undertakings and covenants are not generally made very incisive or pervasive in loans to sovereign states, for covenants of control of operation are viewed with suspicion and also as affecting the prestige and dignity of the borrowing state or government. It is also very frequently stressed that the executive of a state cannot be prejudiced in its functioning by undertakings and covenants given to lenders.

Objectives of covenants. Dealing with objectives of covenants, Philip Wood observes:

The range and purpose of covenants naturally depends upon the circumstances. The primary functions of covenants for a corporate commercial borrower might include the following:
To preserve the *identity* of the borrower (merger restrictions, maintenance of corporate existence, payment of franchise taxes and the renewal of corporate charters).
To preserve the *equal ranking* of a claim against the assets and to prohibit subordination or discrimination (negative pledge and pari passu clause).

To preserve or test *asset quantity* (financial ratios, restrictions on disposals, on distributions to shareholders, on contingent liabilities and on borrowings).

To preserve or test *asset quality* so as to protect earnings potential and break-up value (covenants to repair and insure, restrictions on leases, on investments, on the making of loans and on capital expenditures, and various financial ratios).

To test the *liquid assets* out of which the obligations can be serviced without resort to the sale of capital assets on which the earning power is based (restrictions on borrowings and on contingent liabilities, minimum working capital and current or quick ratios).

To control an excessively *rapid growth* which cannot be sustained by financial resources or management availability (restrictions on mergers, investments, borrowings, capital expenditures and changes of business).

To enable the lender to *monitor* the condition of the borrower and the terms of the loan (the provision of financial information and compliance certificates).[7]

Usual covenants. The following are by and large the usual covenants:

1. Ranking of obligations: The borrower has to undertake that the loans will constitute direct, unconditional and general obligations of, and will rank at least *pari passu* with all other unsecured indebtedness from time to time outstanding, issued, created or assumed by, the borrower. A provision in this regard is referred to as the '*pari passu* clause'. A clause of this kind in the case of a corporate borrower is directed towards ensuring that other unsecured creditors are not given rights of priority of payment over the lender, leaving, perhaps, insufficient assets available to satisfy the claims of the lender either in full or, in the event of bankruptcy, insolvency, liquidation or forced distribution of assets of the borrower, to the same extent as all other unsecured creditors. In the case of a sovereign borrower the clause is intended to prevent the borrower giving preference to certain creditors by, say, giving them first bite at its foreign currency reserves or its revenues. Often in the case of a sovereign borrower the covenant is limited to the External Borrowings (see definition below) of the borrower. This kind of clause catches arrangements which merely give a right of priority of payment; it is not concerned with arrangements as to creation of security over the assets of the borrower (or others)—that will be provided for in the negative pledge clause.

2. Negative pledge: A negative pledge clause is intended as a restriction on the creation of security rights and interests in favour of creditors other than the lenders under the Eurocurrency loan agreement. A typical

negative pledge clause, without providing for exceptions, could be as follows:

So long as any part of the loan or any other amount under the agreement remains outstanding, the borrower will not create or permit to subsist any mortgage, charge, pledge, lien or any other form of encumbrance on any of its assets to secure any present or future indebtedness of the borrower or any other person.

It will be noticed that this is too broad a provision and will restrict the borrower's business very considerably. It is also not unusual to restrict a negative pledge to only the external indebtedness of the borrower. Also, certain specified encumbrances or certain categories of encumbrances are generally excluded. Creation or assumption of obligations in the ordinary course of business are also generally exempt. To be more specific, an undertaking in regard to a negative pledge is generally not applicable to: (i) liens arising solely by operation of law and in the ordinary course of the borrower's operation; (ii) any security to be created on any assets acquired or developed by the borrower after the date of the loan agreement for the sole purpose of financing or refinancing such acquisition or development; (iii) any present or future charge, pledge or lien over goods arising or created in the ordinary course of trade; and (iv) any other security created or outstanding with the prior consent of the lender.

Another prevalent practice of making exceptions to a negative pledge is to permit the creation of encumbrances provided that: (i) the lender at the same time and in a manner acceptable to it, is secured equally and rateably in respect of the loans made and/or to be made to the borrower and all other sums outstanding under the agreement; or (ii) the lender is secured by security equivalent in value to the security encumbered to third parties; or (iii) the security in favour of the third party will also automatically stand secured to the lender.

3. Notification of events of default: The borrower will covenant to notify the lender, or the agent bank in the case of syndication, of any event of default under the agreement immediately upon becoming aware of it and will from time to time, on request, deliver to the lender or the agent bank a certificate confirming that no event of default has occurred and if it has occurred give details thereof together with the action taken or proposed to be taken to remedy it.

4. Undertaking regarding financial accounts: The borrower will covenant

to deliver to the lender its audited accounts and balance sheet as at the end of every financial year, together with copies of the annual reports and other documents circulated generally, whether to shareholders or otherwise.

5. Ratio of liabilities to assets: The borrower may undertake to maintain a specified ratio of current liabilities to current assets and also to maintain a specified liquidity ratio.

6. Restriction on distribution of profits: There may be also financial covenants restraining the distribution of profits and depletion of cash resources.

7. Information about pending litigation: The borrower will also undertake to furnish promptly to the lender all information about any litigation, arbitration or administrative proceedings which to the knowledge of the borrower are pending or threatened and also any other information about the financial condition and operation of the borrower which the lender may from time to time reasonably request.

It is pertinent to close these observations on covenants with the following statement which summarises the purpose they serve:

The function of a majority of the covenants normally employed in term loan agreements is to set guidelines and limits, relevant to the continued soundness of the credit, within which the borrower is expected to operate over the life of the loan, and to provide standards for measurement of the status of the credit and the borrower which, if not met, serve as warning signals of impending or present difficulties.[8]

Events of default
Purpose of specific provisions on events of default. One of the provisions always made in a Eurocurrency loan agreement relates to what will constitute default by the borrower in the performance of the agreement. The relevant provision is termed as 'Events of Default'. A borrower may default in the performance of the agreement directly, that is, fail to make payments on the due date or to comply with the other provisions of the agreement, or it may be in breach of and not be in a position to perform the agreement by supervening circumstances, such as suspension of payment of debts by the borrower. Unless there is an express provision as to what would constitute an event of default it would become largely a matter of interpretation and dispute as to whether a particular event

should be construed as the borrower having defaulted in the performance of the agreement. To get over the possible contentions in this regard, the loan agreement will itself provide as to what would constitute events of default and also provide for remedies for the lender in case any such event of default should occur.

Balancing the interests of the lender and borrower. While making these provisions, an amount of circumspection may be necessary to strike a balance between the anxiety of a lender to make the provisions rather rigorous and the borrower's genuine difficulties in a possible situation of the lender being cantankerous and seeking to invoke the remedial measures even in respect of very technical or trivial defaults. It is, therefore, usual that each event of default is considered with some care and modified, where necessary, to relieve the borrower's difficulties. For example, where there are events of default on grounds of breach of warranty or failure to adhere to a covenant, provision is generally made that the breach should be in a material respect, or opportunity should be given to the borrower to rectify the breach within a reasonable period. Another modification would be the introduction of a grace period in respect of certain payments by the borrower. On the other hand, the lender's interests should not be unduly prejudiced where its loans are unsecured and it may have to take expeditious steps if a default has really occurred.

Usual provisions in regard to events of default
1. In general: The specific provisions in regard to events of default are normally preceded by a statement that the events specified will be construed as events of default if any of them occurs at any time during the continuance of the agreement for any reason whether within or beyond the control of the parties.
2. Non-payment: Failure of the borrower to pay, in the manner and in the currency provided in the agreement, the principal, interest or other amounts due on the due dates would amount to an event of default. It is not unusual to provide that the due payments of interest could be made within a specified grace period, for instance three days.
3. Breach of warranty: It would be an event of default if any representation, warranty or statement made or deemed to be made or repeated by or in respect of the borrower in or pursuant to the agreement or in any notice, certificate or statement referred to in or delivered under the

agreement is or proves to have been incorrect in any material respect. Sometimes the borrower is given an opportunity to 'cure' any such incorrectness within a specified number of days of receipt of notice from the lender but it should be noted that it is not usually possible to 'cure' misrepresentations since a representation is made with reference to a particular point in time, at which time the statement is either true or not, and even if action is subsequently taken which enables the statement to be made at a later time and be true at such later time that does not remove the fact that there was a misrepresentation at an earlier date which, under many events of default clauses, will remain available as an event of default.

4. Breach of covenant: If the borrower does not perform or comply with any one or more of its obligations under the undertakings or covenants given by it in the agreement, it would be an event of default.

5. Breach of other obligations: Failure of the borrower to perform or comply with any one or more of the other obligations under the agreement, unless the default is capable of remedy and is remedied within a certain number of days of notice (generally 30 days) by the lender, would be an event of default.

6. Cross-default: An event of default would also be provided to have occurred if any *other* indebtedness in respect of borrowed money of the borrower is not paid by the borrower on the date when due (as extended by any applicable grace period in any agreement relating to that indebtedness) or such other indebtedness becomes due and payable or capable of being declared due and payable before its normal maturity by reason of default or event of default however described.

It will be noticed that the default under a clause of this nature is not in respect of any obligations undertaken by the borrower under the loan agreement itself. This relates to the borrower's other financial obligations. Such a clause is normally termed in the Eurocurrency market as a 'cross-default clause'. The purpose of this clause is evidently to protect the lender in anticipation because the underlying intention is to deal with deterioration in the financial position of the borrower, but the borrower should be aware that acceleration of other indebtedness for borrowed money may result from circumstances which do not reflect financial deterioration. Furthermore, it is possible that the concerned creditor in the other transaction where the borrower has defaulted may commence action against the borrower and this would affect the interest of the lender in the realisation of its loan. In particular, if the other is an unsecured obligation, it may become necessary for the lender to expedite steps to ensure that it does not lose its *pari passu* claim in respect of the borrower's assets.

Notwithstanding that there is such an obvious risk to the lender, the actual working of the clause may present practical difficulties. Although a cross-default clause generally confines itself to specified financial obligations of the borrower (i.e. borrowed money) and not to all its liabilities, crystallising the cross-default clause could be difficult. Recently a controversy has arisen over whether the cross-default clause in an Eurocurrency loan should not be generally done away with. On the other hand, there is the view that the difficulty of crystallising the default cannot be surmounted merely by doing away with the cross-default clause. For where the financial position of a borrower has really weakened, it would in any event be necessary for the lender to review the position to see whether it is in its own interest to continue the loan transaction or to put an end to it. On the whole, it would appear that it would suffice the purpose if borrowers seek relaxation in the application of the clause.[9]

7. Insolvency: It would be an event of default if (i) the borrower becomes insolvent or is unable to pay its debts as they fall due; (ii) the borrower stops, suspends or threatens to stop or suspend the payment of all or a material part of its debts; (iii) the borrower begins negotiations or takes any proceeding or other steps with a view to readjustment, rescheduling or deferral of its indebtedness; (iv) the borrower proposes or makes a general assignment or arrangement or composition with or for the benefit of its creditors; (v) a moratorium is agreed or declared in respect of or affecting all or a material part of the indebtedness of the borrower.

It will be seen that the essence of a clause on the above lines is that where there is an admission of inability to pay debts as they fall due, it will be an event of default.

8. Enforcement proceedings: An event of default would be provided to have occurred if there is a distress, attachment, execution or other legal process levied, enforced or sued out on or against the whole assets of the borrower or any part thereof reasonably considered by the lender to be substantial in the context of the loan and such is not discharged or stayed within a specified number of days, say 30 days.

It may be queried whether such attachments should always be considered as indicative of financial weakness; if not, would there not be a case for a substantially longer grace period being provided?

9. Winding up or dissolution of the borrower: If an order is made or resolution passed for the winding-up or dissolution of the borrower, it will also be an event of default. Here again, it is not unusual to provide a grace period in a case where the threatened dissolution is not a voluntary one.

10. Illegality: It will be an event of default if it becomes unlawful for the borrower to perform or comply with any one of its obligations under the agreement.

11. Seizure of assets: In the case of a non state-owned borrower, it would be an event of default if all or a material part of the undertaking, assets or revenues of the borrower were seized, nationalised, expropriated or compulsorily acquired by or under the authority of any government.

12. Material adverse change: It would be an event of default if any event occurs or circumstance arises which in the opinion of the lender gives reasonable grounds for believing that the borrower is unlikely to perform or comply with any one or more of its obligations which is reasonably considered by the lender to be material under the agreement.

Implementation of a clause of this nature may be difficult as, while the lender may consider the circumstance as material, however reasonable his conclusions may be, the borrower may also have equally good reasons to consider that it is not an adverse circumstance. It would, therefore, be better if the lender's decision about the adverseness of the circumstance is provided to be taken in consultation with the borrower.

Remedies on occurrence of an event of default. Typical remedies provided for the occurrence of an event of default in respect of which the lender decides to take action are: (i) cancellation of all further available commitments under the loan agreement; and (ii) all loans, accrued interest thereon and any other sums which are payable under the agreement would become immediately due and payable. This is generally known as 'acceleration'.

It is also not unusual to provide a clause for default interest and this has been dealt with above (see p. 85).

Waivers. It would be open to a lender to waive a default. Where such a waiver is given, it is to be by means of writing. It is possible that an event of default may have occurred, but mere occurrence of an event of default would not compel the lender to resort to the remedies available. Notwithstanding the default, the credit may continue to be sound and the lender may not be prejudiced. The lender may even desire the continuance of the credit in its own interest for other reasons; for example it may be that the loan may be difficult to realise at that time. On the other hand, it may be prudent in the circumstances not to treat it as an event of default. Or the lender may desire a renegotiation. In such circumstances, it would not be necessary for it to cancel the further commitment or accelerate the payments due under the agreement. On the question of whether a waiver has to be in writing or could be implied, Philip Wood makes the following observation:

Preferred practice is to deal with waivers specifically in writing where breaches occur since waivers by conduct may raise difficult questions as to the extent of the waiver. If there is, say, a breach of the negative pledge clause, there could be uncertainties as to whether only the particular breach is waived or whether the whole clause and the accompanying event of default are lost.[10]

Changes in circumstances

The basic and fundamental nature of the contract may change under certain circumstances. Such changes in respect of a Eurocurrency loan contract may be due to: (i) changes in law; (ii) increased costs to the lender; and (iii) changes in market conditions. The change in circumstances due to these reasons may necessitate a substitute basis for working out the rate of interest, indemnity by the borrower for the increased costs, and/or prepayment of the loan by the borrower. To this end, it is standard to make detailed provisions in the loan agreement. It is interesting to note the following observations by Francis D. Logan in the volume edited by Rendell:

A significant portion of any Eurodollar loan agreement, in length and in potential importance (although infrequently invoked in practice to date), consists of provisions which reflect the nature of the Eurodollar markets. These are (a) indemnification provisions designed to protect the lender's anticipated yield by shifting the burden of increased costs (due to taxes, reserve or other regulatory requirements, and the like) to the borrower; (b) provision for alternative interest rate bases and/or alternative currencies should Eurodollars cease to be available to the lender in the requisite amounts and tenor; and (c) clauses protecting the lender from changes in law which would render the making, funding or maintaining of the loan illegal.[11]

Changes in law. If as a result of any change in the interpretation or application of any law or the issue of any directive by a competent authority, it becomes illegal for the lender to allow the whole or any part of the commitment to make loans to remain outstanding or make available further funds and/or to continue to allow or remain outstanding the whole or any part of the loan or to fund its participation in the loan, it shall be open to the lender to notify the borrower who shall, on the next interest payment date relating to the loan or within the number of days specified in the agreement, say 30 days, or on an earlier date, prepay the loan.

Increased costs. The borrower shall indemnify the lender against increased cost or reduction in sums receivable under the agreement if, after the date of the loan agreement, as a result of any change of any law or regulation or the imposition of any taxes (other than taxes on the overall net income of the lender), the cost to the lender of maintaining or funding the loan is increased or any sum receivable under the agreement is reduced.

As against a provision of this type, there will be a provision to enable the borrower, if it so chooses, to prepay the loan.

Changes in market conditions. If during the subsistence of the loan agreement the lender determines that (a) by reason of circumstances affecting the London Interbank Eurocurrency market, adequate and fair means do not exist for ascertaining LIBOR in respect of the loan or LIBOR does not reflect the cost to it of funding or maintaining its participation in the loan; or (b) deposits in the denoted currency are not available in the London Interbank Eurocurrency market generally and it is impossible for the lender to fund or to continue to fund its participation, it shall be open to the lender to intimate to the borrower an alternative basis called the 'substitute basis' for calculating the rate of interest. If this is acceptable to the borrower the rate of interest will be changed by negotiation. If it is not acceptable to the borrower, it will have to prepay the loan.

As has been observed earlier, precise and very detailed provisions setting out the procedure for ascertaining cost, giving notices, holding negotiations etc., are usually made in the loan agreement in respect of the above matters. In view of the need to condense the narration, only the essential features have been set out above.

Jurisdiction

Choice of forum. It is necessary to determine and provide in the contract the legal forum before which disputes in regard to the contract and its enforcement will have to be settled. In present day international loan contracts, such a clause in regard to the forum normally contains provisions in respect of the following:

1. Submission by the borrower to the non-exclusive jurisdiction of courts of the jurisdiction of choice (such a jurisdiction is generally England or New York).

2. A person (for example, in the case of a state, the consul or the ambassador) is appointed in the jurisdiction of choice to receive the service of process etc., with a suitable addition that such service shall be deemed as a proper service on the borrower.

3. There will be a complementary clause waiving any objection in regard to the venue of legal proceedings in the court of the jurisdiction of choice; and any inconvenience that the borrower may have by the lender commencing legal proceedings in the jurisdiction of choice even though it may be inconvenient to him. Such a clause has the following objectives: (i) it confers an effective jurisdiction upon the desired courts; (ii) it ensures the validity of an independent forum for resolution of disputes; (iii) such an express submission enhances the eligibility of a judgment of the chosen courts for recognition and enforcement in foreign jurisdictions; (iv) arguments on the basis of the doctrine of *forum non conveniens* could be eschewed; and (v) laws of foreign jurisdictions may require a specific acceptance conferring jurisdiction on courts. A provision on the above lines may also comply with such a requirement.

Normally, there will be no controversies as to the acceptance by the borrower of a clause in regard to this matter, except where the borrower is a sovereign or government.

Sovereign immunity and its waiver. Where a sovereign or a state is a borrower, it is very usual for a special jurisdiction clause to be included in the agreement, reading as below:

The borrower agrees that should the lender bring legal action or proceedings against it or its assets in relation to any matter arising out of this agreement, no immunity from such legal action or proceedings (which shall be deemed to include, without limitation, suit, attachments prior to judgment, other attachments, the obtaining of judgment, execution or other enforcement) shall be claimed by or on behalf of the borrower or with respect to its assets. The borrower hereby irrevocably waives any such rights of immunity which it or its assets now has or may hereafter acquire.

Such a jurisdiction waiver is considered necessary as a protection against the risk of making loans to a sovereign, familiarly known as sovereign risk. The basic feature of such a risk is that a sovereign or state is normally immune from judicial proceedings. On this issue, the following observations may be quoted:

And loans to governments are the perfect illustration of my basic point: that the lender should concentrate on collectibility. When a private debtor defaults, he is dragged to the courthouse. But when a government defaults, it is already in the courthouse; it owns the courthouse. Therefore, in the case of a loan to a government or its instrumentality, the lender's prime concern is twofold: to get the debtor before a court that *will* give a fair judgment and that *can* provide an effective remedy. It's not easy.[12]

These observations stem from the fact that for centuries, sovereigns and governments always had a privileged position. In modern times, the situation is not as alarming as is stated. In the domestic courts of the state in question it has come to be recognised that actions can be brought by private citizens against the state or the government. There may be differences between different jurisdictions in regard to the matters in respect of which action could be commenced or the assets against which judgments and decrees could be executed. In respect of actions against foreign sovereigns, it should be stated that while sovereign immunity as a principle is accepted even in modern times, there has been considerable erosion of the doctrine in many jurisdictions by means of exceptions to the immunity either statutorily or by court pronouncements. The statutes pertinent to the subject are the Foreign Sovereign Immunities Act, 1976, in the United States of America, and the State Immunity Act, 1978, in the United Kingdom. These two acts confirm the general rule that a foreign state shall be entitled to immunity, but provide substantial exceptions in regard to jurisdiction and execution against the foreign state or government. A similar position obtains in many jurisdictions. Details vary from state to state but as a broad generalisation it could be said that submission to jurisdiction and a declaration that the immunity will not obtain in respect of commercial transactions are the general requirements of the exceptions. The risk involved in a loan made to a sovereign state or government could, therefore, be safeguarded as indicated earlier by: (i) a waiver of immunity from jurisdiction and an express submission thereto; (ii) the appointment of an agent for service of process within the jurisdiction; and (iii) waiver of immunity in respect of, and submission to, all proceedings including attachment and execution.

It may be that in some jurisdictions mere submission to jurisdiction may be sufficient and express waivers as to other proceedings may not be necessary. These are, however, details with which one may be concerned when drawing up the jurisdiction and immunity clauses in any particular loan agreement.

Governing law

Market practice. Whatever may be the position with regard to the validity or usefulness of a provision with regard to the choice of law that would govern the contract in respect of *domestic* contracts, the need for a provision in an *international* contract has come to be recognised. The enforcement of a provision with regard to the choice of law in an international contract may also present considerable difficulty as will be referred to below. However, it is sensible to assume that specification of the governing law has necessarily to be made.

Normally in Eurocurrency loan contracts the experience has been to specify that English law or New York law shall govern the contracts. In some contracts, particularly those where a government is the borrower, the law of the borrower's country has also come to be specified.

Freedom of choice of law. The freedom to choose the law that will govern the contract, known as 'party autonomy', is not entirely unrestricted. According to Philip Wood:

The merits of party autonomy are obvious. The rule confers a degree of certainty on an essential term of the contract and does not leave the parties in suspense until a decision of the courts where the action may be brought .... Further it allows the parties freedom to choose a law for their own good reasons, *e.g.* because they have confidence in it or it is a neutral law or they are familiar with it.[13]

He also adds:

Nevertheless there is no such comforting unanimity when one comes to the limitations that various jurisdictions place upon this initial freedom.[14]

Ground rules for making a choice of law. First, there should be a substantial relationship between the transaction and the jurisdiction whose law is chosen. This means that the law to be chosen should be the law where the contract is negotiated or executed or where the lender or the borrower is located or where the funding market is situate or where the contract is to be performed by payment. The following passage from Harfield explains in a forthright manner what the result would be if there were no such substantial relationship. 'If a bank in East Dakota lends Eurodollars, repayable in London, to a jute exporter in Bangladesh, the credit agreement may say that New York law is to govern. However, no court in New York or elsewhere is bound to act on agreements.' [15]

A reasonable justification for departing from this rule could, however, be the desire of the parties to subject their loan to a neutral law or a favourable legal system in which they have confidence.

The choice of law should also be such that the courts of a particular jurisdiction, particularly the courts in the jurisdiction selected by the parties as the appropriate forum or jurisdiction, will apply a foreign proper law. Such a situation may arise if the forum selected should view the foreign law chosen as in conflict with the local law or policy or accepted moral doctrine.

Another limitation on the choice of law could be that certain countries may have prohibited their borrowers from entering into contracts choosing a foreign law. Such a restriction would apply more forcefully in respect of governmental borrowing. Governments may have a mandatory provision that contracts should be governed by the law of that country and that country only.

It is also possible that the choice of a particular law may become bad if the choice is made, as Philip Wood puts it, 'with a view to evading a mandatory rule of law which would have applied to the contract if the "objectively connected" proper law had been chosen'.[16] It is said that parties are not permitted to abuse the freedom of choice by selecting a law in order to validate a loan which would be void under the legal system which would otherwise have applied.

While the above would be the various considerations that would influence the choice of the governing law for the contract, it is not unusual for a lender to seek to have the law of its state designated in the contract as the law in accordance with which the contract shall be construed and governed. This situation arises because the lender cannot properly assess the risks that may have to be taken in accepting the laws of the country of the borrower. The borrower usually agrees more or less with this, unless there are special circumstances, such as the statutes of its own country, which prevent it. Notwithstanding all these limitations, as has been stated earlier, generally English or New York law is accepted. In this connection, the following passage by Logan may be quoted:

In multi-lender syndicated Eurodollar transactions, one frequently sees the laws of New York or the laws of England selected for this purpose. Lenders are familiar with, and experienced in, working under the laws of their own jurisdictions; and in the case of both New York law and English law, there is a substantial body of law, precedent, experience and sophistication in dealing with complex international financial and commercial matters, rendering the predictability of outcome more certain than might be the case in the absence of such factors.[17]

Effect of choice of law. Where a law has been chosen as the governing law for the contract, unless there is anything specifically stated it should be assumed that the chosen law will apply with regard to interpretation and performance of the contract. With regard to the making of the contract, however, namely its execution, the necessary authorisations have to be governed by the laws of the country of the borrower or the lender or any other party, as the case may be. It has been stated that in recent times international contracts occasionally come to provide that the governing law shall be the chosen law 'except in the event proceedings are brought in the courts of borrower's country'. It goes without saying that such provisions are fraught with difficulties and should be avoided.

Where no specific choice of law is made. Where the contract fails to provide the law that shall govern it (which is neither generally done nor feasible to do), there are many complications in ascertaining the law that should be applied in the interpretation and performance of contract. In such circumstances, an attempt is usually made by the courts to see whether there is any provision in the contract from which it could be inferred or interpreted that the law of a particular country has been tacitly chosen by the parties. When no such tacit understanding can be deduced from the contract, various theories have been tried out and each case will have to be considered on its merits by the judicial forum. It is beyond the scope of this paper to consider a matter which is not contained in a contract.

Matters which are typically dealt with

Definitions
Defining the various terms used in an agreement and wherever necessary giving certain phrases a due interpretation or construction, are normal and typical features of any agreement. A provision for definitions is, therefore, generally found in Eurocurrency loan agreements as well. It does not appear necessary to refer here to all the terms that are normally defined. However, certain terms are special to these agreements and it would be worthwhile referring to these.

Banking Day is defined to mean a day which is both a Business Day and a day on which banks are open for business in New York or any other place where a payment is required to be made for any of the purposes under the agreement.

Business Day means a day on which the relevant London financial markets are open for the transaction of the business contemplated in the agreement.
    These two definitions are particularly necessary to make specific provision with regard to computation of interest, drawdowns, payments, repayments and prepayments.

Commitment: Commitment in relation to the lender would mean the obligation of the lender to make the loans under the agreement up to the aggregate principal amount agreed upon.

Commitment Period means the period from the date of the agreement until close of business on the day on which the last instalment of the loan could be drawn by the borrower.

Commitment Termination Date is also defined where a commitment period is not, and this is defined with reference to a specific date.
    These definitions would be necessary to specify in the agreement the available commitment of the loan facility by the lender to the borrower and also the period and the last date up to which such commitment would be available to the borrower. In syndicated loans, these definitions are suitably amplified to indicate the commitment of each lender bank. It is

not unusual to specify the amounts of commitment opposite the names of the various banks in an appropriate annexure or exhibit.

Indebtedness is defined to include any obligation (whether present or future, actual or contingent, secured or unsecured as principal or surety or otherwise) for the payment or repayment of money.

Borrowings is defined to mean Indebtedness incurred in respect of (i) money borrowed or raised, (ii) any bond, note, loan stock, debenture or similar instrument, (iii) acceptance or documentary credit facilities, (iv) the deferred payment for assets or services acquired, (v) rental payments under leases entered into primarily as a method of raising finance or of financing the acquisition of the asset leased and (vi) guarantees or other assurances against financial loss in respect of Borrowings of any person.

External Borrowings is defined to mean Borrowings denominated or payable, or payable at the option of the debtor or the creditor in, or calculated by reference to, a currency other than the legal currency of the borrower's country or owed to any person not resident in, or whose principal or lending office is situate outside, the borrower's country.

These definitions would be of use in the *pari passu* clause and the negative pledge clause while the covenants of the borrower are drafted. Considerable flexibility is practised in defining these terms depending on the actual circumstances or situation of the borrower. Very frequently the restrictions by way of these clauses on the borrower will apply only to the External Borrowings of the borrower.

LIBOR means the London Interbank Offered Rate and has been suitably defined earlier in this chapter under the heading Interest. For the purpose of ascertaining LIBOR, the definition of reference banks would be necessary (see pp. 83–84.)

Reference Banks would mean the principal London offices of banks specified in the agreement itself, or which may be decided on subsequently, the procedure for which will be set out in the agreement.

Loan is defined to mean in relation to each lender that part of the advances or loans which is owing to such lender. This definition may also be amplified as meaning the principal amount of each borrowing by the borrower under the agreement or each amount treated as a separate loan by virtue of provisions of the agreement or the principal amount from time to time outstanding and all collectively referred to as the 'Loans'.

Dollars. Where the loan is denominated in dollars or where dollar payments are to be made, dollars are defined as the lawful currency of the United States of America and, in respect of all payments to be made under the agreement, funds for same day settlement in the New York Clearing House Interbank Payments System (or such other US dollar funds as may at the relevant time be customary for the settlement of international banking transactions denominated in US dollars).

Fees, commissions and expenses
In a single-lender loan agreement, there would be provision only for commitment fee, charges and expenses, and expenses on enforcement. In a syndicated loan, it may also be necessary to provide for a management fee and an agency fee.

Commitment fee: A normal provision in regard to a commitment fee is that the borrower will pay to the lender or, in the case of a syndicated loan, to the agent for distribution to the lenders, a commitment fee in dollars or any other specified currency computed at the rate agreed upon on the daily undrawn amount of the total commitments during the period commencing and ending on the dates specified or during the commitment period. Provision will also be made for the accrued commitment fee to be payable, usually quarterly in arrear. It is also usual to provide that the commitment fee shall accrue from day to day and be calculated on the basis of a year of 360 days and the actual number of days elapsed.

It is also not unusual to provide different rates of commitment fee for different sub-periods within the commitment period and specify the rates with reference to the available facility for each commitment sub-period.

Management fee: In a syndicated loan the borrower shall pay to the agent, for the account of the managers, a management fee at an agreed percentage of the total commitments. Normally, the fee is payable either on the first borrowing date or before a specified date, whichever is earlier.

Agency fee: In addition, in a syndicated loan the borrower will pay to the agent, in the specified currency, for the agent's sole benefit, an agency fee, which fee is to cover only normal administration of the loans. The agency fee is usually payable annually or semi-annually as per the agreement.

Charges and expenses: The borrower also agrees to reimburse the lender or, in a syndicated loan, the agent all charges and expenses (including but not limited to the fees and expenses of its legal advisers) incurred by the lender or the agent in connection with the negotiations, preparation, syndication, execution and advertising of the agreement up to a specified agreed amount which may be treated as maximum. These charges and expenses will also be deducted from the first borrowing under the agreement or paid before a specified date, whichever is earlier.

Stamp duties: The borrower shall pay or shall indemnify the lender and all other parties to the agreement against any or all stamp, registration and similar taxes, levies or charges imposed by law or any authority of the country where the agreement is executed or of the borrower's country, if such charges are payable or determined to be payable in connection with the execution, delivery or performance of the agreement or any other ancillary document. The borrower shall also indemnify the other parties for such charges if they become payable at the time of the enforcement of the agreement or any of the ancillary documents.

Expenses on enforcement: The borrower shall also bind himself to pay on demand all costs and expenses (including taxes thereon and legal fees) incurred by the lender or any other party in protecting or enforcing any rights against the borrower under the agreement or any ancillary document.

Waivers—remedies cumulative

A specific provision is also made to the effect that (i) no failure on the part of the lender, or the agent or manager or bank in the case of syndication, to exercise, and no delay on its part in exercising, any right or remedy under the agreement will operate as a waiver thereof, nor will any single or partial exercise of any right or remedy preclude any other or further exercise thereof or the exercise of any other right or remedy and

(ii) the rights and remedies provided in the agreement are cumulative and not exclusive of any rights or remedies provided by law. The lender may, of course, agree with the borrower to amend, or waive compliance by the borrower with, any provision of the agreement and, in the case of a syndicated loan, the agent bank usually has the power to amend (with the agreement of the borrower) or to waive any provision of the agreement, in each case with the prior authority of the majority of the banks, although there are certain provisions which are excepted from this where the prior authority of all the banks is required. Sometimes it is also expressed in the agreement that a waiver may be given subject to any condition which the person giving it thinks fit and that it shall be effective only in the instance and for the purpose for which it is given.

Assignments
Benefit and burden of the agreement: There will be a specific provision that the agreement shall benefit and be binding on the parties, their respective successors and any permitted assignee or transferee of some or all of the parties' rights or obligations under the agreement. Any reference in the agreement to any party shall be construed accordingly.

Borrower: The borrower shall not assign or transfer all or any part of its rights or obligations under the agreement without the prior consent of all the other parties.

Lender or banks in syndication: Any lender or any bank in a syndication may assign all or part of its rights and obligations under the agreement with the prior written consent of the borrower which shall not be unreasonably withheld.

The assignment by a lender or bank may be effective only after the assignee has given an undertaking to be bound by the agreement and to perform the obligations (if any) transferred to it.

Notices and communications
All notices and communications under the agreement shall be made by telex or otherwise in writing. Each notice, communication or document to be delivered to any party under the agreement shall be sent to that party at the telex number or address and marked for the attention of the person (if any) from time to time designated by that party for the purpose of the agreement.

The initial telex number, address and person (if any) so designated by each party shall initially be set out in the agreement. It is also usual to provide that in a syndication any notice or communication or document from or to the borrower shall be sent to, by or through the agent.

It is also not unusual to provide that any notice or communication from the borrower shall be irrevocable and shall not become effective until received by the lender.

There will also be a need for making a provision for service of process. The borrower will be required to appoint a person to receive process in London or New York, as the case may be, and to maintain such an appointment throughout the loan period. Any delivery of the process to him shall be deemed as a complete service.

Counterparts

The agreement may be signed in any number of counterparts, all of which taken together and when delivered to the lender or the agent, in the case of syndication, shall constitute one and the same instrument. Any party may enter into the agreement by signing any such counterpart.

Miscellaneous provisions

In general

There are some matters in respect of which provisions are not made universally or typically in a Eurocurrency loan agreement and it is possible that standard provisions in respect of these matters have not yet been developed. Even so, provisions with regard to such matters are either made or sought to be made. It is proposed to deal with some of them in this section.

Defaults beyond the control of the borrower

At times a clause on the following lines is sought to be provided:

A default which will be an event of default under the agreement shall be an event of default notwithstanding that the reason for its occurrence is beyond the control of the borrower or whether the default is voluntary or involuntary or has occurred as a consequence of any law, rule, regulation, direction or order of a statutory agency or a court or otherwise.

The obvious intention of a clause of this type is to get over any argument that may be open to the borrower that the contract has become frustrated because of subsequent illegality or supervening impossibility or frustrated by reasons including *force majeure*. How far such a clause will be effective is not beyond doubt.

Severance clause

Term loan agreements may contain a severance clause on the following lines:

If any provision of the agreement shall be invalid or unenforceable for any reason in any jurisdiction, the validity and enforceability of such provision in other jurisdictions shall not be impaired or be affected thereby nor shall the validity and enforceability of other provisions of the agreement be impaired or affected thereby.

There is also an element of doubt about the enforceability of a provision of this nature. It is possible that a court may say that if any provision of an agreement is unenforceable and invalid in law, the agreement has to be invalid in all respects and cannot be allowed to be enforced only in some areas.

Purpose and application of monies

The purpose for which a Eurocurrency loan is made and the application of the monies would be relevant in any agreement dealing with project finance. The Eurocurrency market has become a highly important source of finance for major industrial and natural resource projects in the world. Such lending could be *for* a project or even *to* a project. In the former case, loans may be made to a state or government or a company or corporation to enable such a borrower to finance a project. In the latter case, financing *to* a project, the lender makes the finance available to the project itself and looks to repayment from the success of the project. Almost all loans that are made are of the former category. There would be various legal, commercial and political considerations to be taken into account in financing parties for a project. The possible completion of the project may depend on various factors such as cost overruns, delays in the infrastructure, technical difficulties, labour troubles, etc. After the project has been completed, there could be further problems in its operation such as the availability of raw materials, the possibility of break-downs, product marketability, etc. There would also be political risks: the possibility of cancellation of royalties, concessions and licences, regulations in regard to pricing, export, import or exchange controls, etc. The safeguards that would be necessary from the lender's point of view to take care of these aspects are to be provided for in the agreement. Some of the provisions that would require to be specially looked into from this aspect would be the definitions, payments, drawdowns, warranties and covenants. Certain special provisions would also require to be made. For example, it may be necessary to provide as a condition precedent to the making of the loan that the various contracts, concessions, licences, etc. concerning the project should have been completed. There should be a provision for the borrower undertaking to use the entire proceeds of the loan towards financing the project, without any obligation on the part of the lender to check on the use of the loan. There may also be a special provision for the loan amount being directly paid by the lender to the contractors of the project. Such a provision would ensure the use or the application of the monies. Otherwise, suitable undertakings by the borrower as to the application of the monies may have to be provided for.

Language

It is generally provided that all notices, communications and documents shall either be in English or accompanied by a certified translation into English by a translator acceptable to the parties. If there is a conflict, the English translation shall prevail over the original language version.

Arbitration

Arbitration is a matter not generally provided for. A provision for reference of disputes to arbitration is normally found in a commercial contract. Normally, arbitration is preferred to court proceedings as being an expeditious remedy and also as giving finality to a matter, as an arbitration award is not usually subject to an appeal. Also, unlike in the case of court proceedings, arbitration may ensure privacy and confidentiality to the hearing of the dispute. However, in contrast to the case with commercial contracts, there has been a disinclination of the lenders in the Eurocurrency market to agree to provide for submission of a dispute to arbitration. Perhaps some of the reasons for this attitude lie in a lack of confidence in arbitration and a feeling that arbitrators are prone to give compromise awards—and compromises in loan agreements are harmful. In many arbitrations, the rules of evidence and procedure may not be as highly developed as in court proceedings. Although these reasons do not appear to be convincing, a provision for arbitration is not normally made in an

Eurocurrency loan agreement. It may, however, be mentioned that international institutions, such as the World Bank, do make a compulsory provision in regard to arbitration. Perhaps, with the passage of time, arbitration may come into vogue in the Eurocurrency market as well.

Ancillary documents

Security documents and comfort letters
Besides the term loan agreement, there are also certain other documents which are taken and they are referred to as ancillary documents. Broadly speaking, these documents could be of two types. They may be in the nature of affording security to the loan transaction such as documents creating mortgages, charges, etc., or guarantees executed by the government of the borrower's country of domicile or a third party, and/or undertakings or assurances issued by such parties in favour of the lender. Whenever mortgages or guarantees are taken, the text of the mortgage or the guarantee is also settled in advance and the agreed text is provided for in the loan agreement as a schedule or annexure. Their execution in the forms settled would be provided for as a condition precedent to the availability by the loan. Wherever specific guarantees are not insisted upon by the lender, it is possible that third parties supporting the loan transaction may be required to give comfort letters in the forms agreed upon and the object of these documents would not be the creation of any security as such, but would be to provide support for the financing by the government of the borrower's country or by any parent company, if the borrower is a subsidiary.

In addition to these support documents, in syndicated or consortium loans intercreditor agreements would also be required.

Legal opinions
As a rule, in all Eurocurrency transactions legal opinions also form part of the documentation in respect of the loan transaction. Lawyers of the borrower's domicile are called upon to provide formal legal opinions on various points in the transaction. The furnishing of these legal opinions is also made a condition precedent to the availability of the loan. The borrower's lawyers are generally required to give a legal opinion to the effect that:
1. The borrower, for example if it is a corporation, has been duly incorpo-

rated, is validly existing and is in good standing under the laws of the country of the borrower.

2. The borrower is qualified to do business and has the corporate powers to enter into and perform the various obligations undertaken under the agreement.

3. The agreement has been duly authorised, executed and delivered and is legally binding on, and is enforceable against, the borrower.

4. All the official consents of government and statutory agencies required in the borrower's domicile have been obtained.

5. The agreement and/or its performance do not and will not conflict with the laws of the borrower's domicile.

6. There is no pending or threatened litigation or any legal proceeding against the borrower which would materially affect its financial position.

7. The judgment of the forum chosen in respect of the agreement would be enforced by the courts of the country of the borrower.

8. The borrower is not entitled to immunity from suit or enforcement of judgment on grounds of sovereignty or otherwise in the courts of the country of the borrower.

9. The choice of the governing law by the borrower will be upheld by the courts of the country of the borrower's domicile.

While the above are matters which a legal opinion is generally required to cover, there will be other matters on which the opinion of the lawyers may be required with special reference to the loan.

The opinions of the lawyers do not give any security or guarantee or indemnity to the lender. They are only assurances in respect of the specific matters and points covered by the opinions.

III *Summary*

1. An international contract in respect of a Eurocurrency loan transaction has necessarily to be evolved in the light of, and on many occasions despite, the economic and financial laws of various countries. Although it cannot yet be stated with full confidence that the law in the matter of Eurocurrency loan contracts has been cleared of all doubts and difficulties, it should not be too problematic to give an overall view of the

contract of an international Eurocurrency loan transaction as it stands at present (pp. 73–74).

2. Eurocurrency is money deposited with and payable at a bank outside the country where that money is legal tender. Currency is Eurocurrency even if it is deposited and payable in a country outside Europe.

Eurocurrency loans may be raised by a note or a bond issue or under a term loan agreement. Such loans may be made by a single lender or a group of lenders and in the latter event it is a syndicated loan (pp. 74–75).

3. The scope of this chapter is limited to dealing with unsecured and unguaranteed Eurocurrency loan transactions and contracts which are subject to English law (p. 75).

4. Deep and close consideration of legal issues is necessary not only for documenting the contract but also for negotiating the various terms and conditions of the contract (pp. 75–76).

5. Resolution of legal issues, anticipation of legal problems likely to arise and the making of the provisions required to meet and/or resolve them has necessarily to be done by legal experts, particularly Euromarket lawyers. It is desirable to involve legal experts from the outset as well as during negotiations. Although in-house specialists (local counsel) may be involved, it remains desirable to employ outside specialists (pp. 76–77).

6. The Eurocurrency loan agreement should, besides setting out the terms of the loan, also provide the ground rules, procedures and mechanisms for the fulfilment, performance and enforcement of the different provisions of the contract. The contract should be structured so as to minimise the impact of any changes in the political conditions of the different countries involved (pp. 77–78).

7. The major objective of the contract should be to safeguard the lender's interests, particularly with regard to the repayment and enforcement of the loan. The contract should strike a balance between the interests of the lender and those of the borrower and also have due regard to the conditions of the market and the political and economic conditions of the different countries involved (pp. 78–79).

8. Identification, description and representation of the parties is one of the basic minima of a loan agreement. Where the borrower is a sovereign state or a government it is particularly important for its borrowing powers

to be ascertained and it would be necessary to identify the actual authority who can borrow and the name of the authority in which the contract is to be entered into. In syndicated loans the manager(s) (including, if any, co-managers and lead managers), agent bank(s) (and lead banks) will have to be identified and described. It has to be ensured that an authorised representative of the borrower executes the documents on behalf of the borrower (pp. 80−81).

9. In a term loan agreement, the loan can be made available to the borrower by the lender not only on one specified date but in tranches on different dates. Where there is more than one lender the agreement will provide that the obligations, interests and rights of each lender are several and also not conditional upon the performance of the contract by any one of the lenders. The agreement will make the necessary provisions subject to which the borrower may draw the loan. The drawdown of the loan may be in one shot or in tranches. The loan could also be by means of a revolving credit, i.e. the borrower may operate a line of credit by drawing, repaying and drawing again.

The agreement may also provide for the borrower having the option to draw in specified or even multi-currencies. Detailed provisions will need to be made in regard to currency availability, calculation of exchange rates and the manner of exercising currency options (pp. 81−83).

10. Interest is generally not at a fixed rate. The interest rate is fixed with reference to the method of funding peculiar to the Eurocurrency market. In Eurocurrency loans it is accepted as a basic and fundamental feature that the contract has to take full note of, and make the necessary provisions on the basis of, the cost of funds to the lender.

Interest on Eurocurrency loans is generally related to what is known as the London Interbank Offered Rate (LIBOR). LIBOR is ascertained with reference to the average of the rates offered by chosen reference banks to leading banks in the London Interbank Eurocurrency market in respect of deposits for corresponding periods. Interest is also sometimes based on other methods of fixation of interest rates such US Prime Rate.

Periods for calculation of interest, known as interest periods, are fixed at the option of the borrower but subject to rights of veto by the lenders. A provision for payment of default interest is usually made (pp. 83—85).

11. Provisions will be made in any term loan agreement for the repayment of the loan and also the date(s) of such repayment. If repayment is to be

made in instalments suitable provisions are also made to align the instalments with interest periods.

Provisions for circumstances in which the borrower can prepay the loan will also require to be made. If no such provision is made, the borrower will be entitled to prepay the loan at any time, which may affect the cost to the lender (pp. 85−86).

12. A typical loan agreement will contain provisions on representations and warranties given by the borrower.

These warranties may be legal warranties or commercial warranties. Legal warranties usually include matters relating to the status of the borrower, its powers and authority to borrow, due execution of the contract, the conformity of the contract with the laws of the country of the borrower, the legal validity and enforceability of the contract, the obtention and subsistence of official consents, and the private and commercial nature of the act of borrowing. Commercial warranties will include statements about the business and financial condition of the borrower.

Legal warranties may be qualified as being subject to the qualifications, reservations and observations contained in legal opinions. Some agreements may require warranties to be repeated periodically so that they remain subsisting throughout the life of the agreement.

The purpose sought to be served by the warranties is to provide estoppel against the borrower; to afford a checklist of items to be attended to by the borrower; to make representations and warranties conditions precedent to drawdowns; and to make any failure to comply with representations and warranties an event of default (pp. 86−91).

13. The borrower is required to give certain undertakings which are referred to generally as covenants. These covenants relate largely to ranking of obligations, giving of a negative pledge, responsibility for notifying an event of default, furnishing of information relating to the business or financial position of the borrower, maintenance of a certain ratio of liabilities to assets and so on (pp. 91−94).

14. A borrower may default in the performance of the agreement directly, that is, by failure to make payments on the due date and to comply with other provisions of the agreement, or it may commit anticipatory breach of the contract such as suspension of payments by the borrower. It is necessary that, where there is an anticipatory breach by supervening

circumstances, there should be a provision in the contract constituting it as an event of default. Besides non-payment of the loan, usual events of default are breach of warranty, breach of covenant and breach of material obligations under the contract. It is also provided that if the borrower fails to honour its indebtedness in respect of transactions other than the relevant Eurocurrency loan, such failure would also amount to an event of default. This is known as cross-default. There may be other events of default such as insolvency, distress, attachment, execution or other legal process against the borrower, and the winding up or dissolution of the borrower.

If it becomes unlawful for the borrower to perform or comply with any one of its obligations and agreements, it will also be an event of default.

On the occurrence of an event of default, the remedies available to the lender are cancellation of all further available commitments and acceleration of the repayment of the loan. It would be open to a lender to waive a default (pp. 94–99).

15. The basic and fundamental nature of the contract may change under certain circumstances. Such changes may be due to: (i) changes in law; (ii) increased costs to the lender; and (iii) changes in market conditions. These changes will require a substitute basis for working out the rate of interest, indemnity by the borrower for increased costs, and/or prepayment of the loan by the borrower.

If, by a change in law, it becomes illegal for the lender to continue its obligations under the contract in any manner, it may notify the borrower and require prepayment of the loan. If for any reason the cost of funding the loan increases or the sums receivable under the agreement get reduced, the borrower has to undertake to indemnify the lender against such increased costs or reduction in sums receivable. Similarly, if due to a change in market conditions adequate and fair means do not exist for ascertaining LIBOR or any other formula forming the basis of ascertaining interest, or deposits in the denoted currency are not available to the lender, the lender may notify the borrower of a substitute basis for calculating interest. If it is not acceptable to the borrower it will have to prepay the loan (pp. 99–100).

16. It is necessary to provide in the contract the legal forum before which disputes in regard to the contract and its enforcement will have to be

settled. For this purpose the borrower will have to submit to the jurisdiction of the courts of the jurisdiction of choice, nominate a person to receive service of process, and also waive objection to jurisdiction on any ground.

In this context, where a sovereign or a state is a borrower there should be provisions to waive sovereign immunity and such provisions will have to be in compliance with the statutory law involved, for example, the Foreign Sovereign Immunities Act, 1976, in the United States of America and the State Immunity Act, 1978, in the United Kingdom (pp. 101–103).

17. The law that shall govern the contract with regard to interpretation, performance and enforcement thereof has to be chosen and set out in the agreement. Where no choice of law has been made there will be complications in ascertaining the law and interpreting the contract (pp. 103–105).

18. Definitions of various terms used in the agreement are also typical parts of the contract. The following terms are very special to the Eurocurrency loan agreement and it would be worthwhile to define them: (i) banking day; (ii) business day; (iii) commitment; (iv) commitment period; (v) commitment termination date; (vi) indebtedness; (vii) borrowings; (viii) external borrowings; (ix) LIBOR; (x) reference banks; (xi) loan; (xii) dollars (pp. 106–108).

19. The various fees, commissions and expenses which require to be ascertained and provided for are: (i) commitment fee; (ii) management fee; (iii) agency fee; (iv) charges and expenses; (v) stamp duties; (vi) expenses on enforcement (pp. 108–109).

20. It would be necessary to provide that the rights and remedies under the agreement are cumulative and not exclusive of any rights or remedies provided by law.

There should also be a provision for waivers of rights and remedies to be in writing. It should also be provided that any waiver or consent shall be effective only in the instance and for the purpose for which it is given (pp. 109–110).

21. There will be a specific provision that the agreement shall benefit and be binding on the successors and assignees of rights and obligations of the parties under the agreement. The borrower can assign only by prior consent of other parties. Once any consents required from the borrower

are obtained, the assignment of obligations by a lender will only be effective when the assignee has agreed to perform such obligations (p. 110).

22. All notices and communications shall be made by telex or otherwise in writing. The addresses of parties to receive notices and communications should be specified (pp. 110–111).

23. The agreement may be signed in counterparts (p. 111).

24. At times provision is made to get over a plea by the borrower that the contract has become frustrated because of subsequent impossibility or has become frustrated by circumstances beyond the control of the borrower, including by *force majeure* (pp. 111–112).

25. There may also be a provision that if a part of the agreement becomes illegal or unenforceable the part which is legal and enforceable will continue to have effect (p. 112).

26. The purpose for which the loan is made and the application of the monies are normally provided in an agreement related to project finance. To ensure application of monies to the project, suitable provisions are included in the agreement (pp. 112–113).

27. All notices and documents shall be in English or accompanied by a certified translation into English. In any conflict, the English translation shall prevail (p. 113).

28. Normally no provision for arbitration is made in a Eurocurrency loan agreement. Perhaps with the passing of time arbitration may come into vogue in the Eurocurrency market (pp. 113–114).

29. Besides the term loan agreement there are also other documents known as ancillary documents. These are mainly security documents and comfort letters (p. 114).

30. Legal opinions from the in-house legal specialists of the borrower and outside lawyers of the borrower's country are also documents taken and treated as ancillary documents (pp. 114–115).

Notes

1. Baxter, R.R., 'Introduction' to Rendell, Robert S., (ed.), *International Financial Law: Lending, capital transfers and institutions,* Euromoney Publications Ltd., London, 1980, p. 7.
2. Harfield, Henry, 'Legal Aspects of International Lending' in Mathis, F. John, (ed.), *Offshore Lending by U.S.Commercial Banks,* Bankers' Association for Foreign Trade and Robert Morris Associates, Washington and Philadelphia, 1975, p. 82.
3. Wood, Philip, *Law and Practice of International Finance,* Sweet & Maxwell Ltd., London, 1980, p. 252.
4. Ibid., pp. 242–243.
5. Ibid., p. 242.
6. Ibid., p. 94.
7. Ibid., p. 145.
8. Logan, Francis D., 'Term loan agreements' in Rendell, op. cit., p. 15.
9. See Carroll, J. Speed, 'The Worst Clause in the Euromarkets', *Euromoney,* June 1981, p. 90, and Youard, R.G.A., 'Why the Cross-Default Clause Won't Go Away', *Euromoney,* July 1981, pp. 170–171.
10. Wood, op. cit., p. 173.
11. Logan, op. cit., p. 19.
12. Harfield, op. cit., p. 86.
13. Wood, op. cit., p. 8.
14. Ibid.
15. Harfield, op. cit., p. 83.
16. Wood, op. cit., p. 9.
17. Logan, op. cit., p. 17.

Selected Aspects of International Loan Documentation and Rescheduling

By PHILIP WOOD

This chapter deals with a rag-bag of selected topics which are nevertheless of great significance in international loan agreements. They are often controversial. I propose to suggest some approaches from the point of view of the borrower. I appreciate, however, that one solution does not necessarily suit everybody.

International loan contracts are complex. In 1916 Scrutton LJ considered a loan agreement in the case of *Horwood v Millers Timber Trading Company Limited* and said 'I have seen a good deal of the ways of moneylenders but it had not entered my wildest imagination that any of them could have concocted a document of the nature of that which we have before us in this case, and I am glad that at last the court has an opportunity of pronouncing an opinion on it, to which, from my experience of moneylenders, I do not suppose they will pay any attention whatever'.

The learned judge was commenting upon a contract imposed by a loan shark but his reaction may not be altogether different from that of a first-time sovereign borrower faced with the standard syndicated Euro-dollar loan agreement.

Choice of Law

Every contract has to have a governing law. It cannot itself set out all the rules, nor can it exist in a vacuum or be a law unto itself.

If the parties do not select a governing law, the court will select it for them. The manner of determining the governing law where there is no express choice varies from jurisdiction to jurisdiction. In many common law countries such as England, the courts look for evidence of implied intention, e.g. a choice of local courts for hearing disputes. If no implied intention can be found then they determine the system of law with which the agreement is most closely connected. Some other countries, in the absence of a tacit choice, apply various presumptions such as the law of the residence of both parties, or if there is none, the law of the place of performance or contracting.

Express choice of law

Usually the loan contract makes an express choice of governing law. What systems of law are available? In theory, practically any law can be chosen so far as the English courts are concerned, subject to rules about capricious or evasive choices of law. In practice, there are basically three available options: the law of the lender's country, the law of a particular market (especially in syndicated credits with lenders from all over the world) or the law of the borrower's country. The parties can choose public international law or, more appropriately, the general principles of law recognised by civilised nations (which is generally regarded as being one of the sources of public international law). The World Bank maintains that their governing law clause amounts to an effective choice of public international law. This is the law which applies between states and is theoretically the same everywhere. Municipal law, on the other hand, is a domestic system of law and differs from jurisdiction to jurisdiction. Note that a governing law is not necessarily that of a country since many countries have several different systems of law. There are seven distinct systems of law in the British Isles and as many different systems of law as there are states in federal countries such as the United States and Australia. France, on the other hand, has a unitary system of law.

Insulation

It is almost invariably the case that commercial banks require an external system of law. The reason, and this is very important from their point of view, is that the choice of an external system of law helps to insulate the contract from legal changes in the borrower's country. The point is illustrated by two English cases.

The first is *Re Helbert Wagg & Co Limited* [1956] Ch. 323. An English company had made a loan in sterling to a German company under a loan agreement governed by German law. Payments of principal and interest were to be made in sterling in London. In 1933 a German moratorium law was passed that required the German borrower to make the agreed payment to a government agency in Berlin in German marks instead of in sterling. By the end of the war, the borrower had paid the full equivalent of the whole loan in marks to the government agency with the result that under the moratorium law it was discharged from all further liability. The English court held that since the loan agreement was governed by German law, German law decided whether or not the contract was discharged by payments to the local German agency. As the moratorium law was a German law, the lender had no further claim.

The contrasting case is *National Bank of Greece and Athens S.A. v Metliss* [1958] A.C. 509. In 1927 the National Mortgage Bank of Greece issued sterling mortgage bonds guaranteed by the National Bank of Greece. The bonds were governed by English law. A Greek decree imposed a moratorium suspending all obligations and rights of action upon the bonds. In an action brought by one of the bondholders for recovery of arrears of interest, the court held that since the obligation to pay interest was governed by English law, the moratorium law, being a Greek law, was to be disregarded and the defendant bank was liable to pay the arrears. It followed that the choice of an external system of law insulated the contract from the local moratorium law.

There are numerous cases in other jurisdictions tending to the same result. The result is that where a loan contract is not governed by an external system of law, the contract can be changed unilaterally by the borrower's country and the change may be recognised by the courts of the lender's country.

Attitudes to foreign law

From the borrower's point of view, an external system of law plainly inhibits freedom of action in the event of national emergencies where the public interest may require that payments be delayed or where the borrower needs a breathing space. Hence, any rescheduling has to be agreed with the foreign lenders and cannot be achieved unilaterally, e.g. by the introduction of exchange controls. On the other hand, legislative changes which defeat the contractual rights of foreign lenders might be provocative and may influence lenders in their future lending policy to the country concerned.

It is true that the external system of law can be changed adversely for the borrowing country in the same way as the law of the borrower's country can be changed adversely for the lender. The proper way to deal with the matter is to make sure that the external system of law is that of a jurisdiction in which the borrower has a reasonable degree of confidence. What is required is a legal system which is likely to be reasonably impartial and stable so as not to defeat legitimate expectations on both sides.

What is the attitude of most sovereign borrowers to the matter of submission to foreign law? I think it is true to say that most countries are willing to contract under an external system of law. They do not regard it as some sort of derogation of sovereignty. This is true of industrialised states which have come to the market (with two notable exceptions) and also of non-industrialised states. In one case (*R v International Trustee* [1937] A.C. 500), the submission to a foreign system of law worked to the advantage of the borrowing country. In this case US dollar bonds issued by the United Kingdom were subject to New York law. The bonds had a gold clause which indexed their value according to gold. In 1931 gold clauses were invalidated in the United States. The question was whether the United Kingdom still had to pay according to the gold clause or whether payment could be made in depreciated paper money. The House of Lords held that since the bonds were governed by New York law and since New York law had removed gold clauses, the gold clause was unenforceable.

A number of countries in South America object to foreign law for historical reasons. The objection is known as the Calvo doctrine after a mid-nineteenth century Argentinian statesman of that name. The doctrine resulted from the alleged interference by European metropolitan powers in the domestic affairs of certain Latin American countries by gunboat diplomacy on the stated pretext of protecting national creditors. Some countries espousing the Calvo doctrine, such as Brazil, have accommodated themselves more or less to the requirements of the international market. Others, the most important of which is Colombia, have not been able to do so.

Notwithstanding the exceptions, the non-acceptance by a sovereign borrower of an external governing law can jeopardise a successful syndication. There have been cases where proposed loans have collapsed on this issue. As always, a state borrower should weigh up the risks involved in this matter.

One may note incidentally that the governing law of a contract does not determine all issues which arise under the contract. For example, under

English conflicts rules, such matters as the status of the borrower (e.g. whether it is a corporation) and its powers (e.g. to borrow or guarantee) are generally determined by the law of the place of incorporation. Rules of private international law in contractual matters are complex and are outside the scope of this paper.

Choice of forum

My second topic, which is closely related to choice of law, is choice of forum, i.e. the courts where disputes will be litigated or the agreement enforced.

The law which applies to a contract and the courts where it is litigated are quite separate. It is true that often the governing law and the courts coincide. However, the courts in most commercial jurisdictions are willing to apply a foreign system of law to a contract. If there is a dispute as to the rules of that foreign system of law, the court simply invites local experts to explain or (in some countries) makes its own investigation.

The reason that commercial bank lenders usually seek an external forum is precisely the same as for choice of law, namely, insulation. If the lender could enforce his contract only in the courts of the borrower's country, then those courts may ignore the foreign system of law or at least apply it only to the extent that it is not inconsistent with local law, e.g. a local moratorium or exchange control.

The usual procedure in international loan contracts is for the borrowing state to submit to the jurisdiction of a particular external court. This is usually done in common law countries by the appointment of a local agent for service of process. The agent can be any person or body, for example an ambassador or a commercial consul or an independent trust corporation. Many lenders prefer an independent trust corporation since there may be state immunity problems with service on an ambassador. The fees of trust corporations for the service are generally nominal.

What are the implications from the point of view of a borrower of a submission to an external jurisdiction? Again, the borrower should have confidence in the chosen courts. He should feel confident of their impartiality and of the likelihood that the borrower will get a fair hearing without undue favour being given to local interests.

Some borrowers ask for arbitration. However, arbitration is not favoured by most commercial bank lenders. A number of syndications have collapsed because of the borrower's insistence upon an arbitration forum. One reason for the objection is that normally loan contracts do not involve the complex factual issues which make the choice of a specially trained arbitrator desirable, e.g. a construction engineer. The courts of many commercial states are well equipped to deal with investment disputes. Another reason is that arbitration is a condition precedent to enforcement, so that there is a likelihood of delays. There are various other objections on the side of lenders to arbitration such as expense, greater difficulties in enforcing the award in municipal courts, inability to obtain a summary judgment and so on.

The World Bank, on the other hand, together with the major development lending institutions, adopts arbitration as a matter of course. These institutions, however, have a different attitude to enforcement. The reason, no doubt, lies in the considerable diplomatic bargaining power which the development banks have in the case of payment difficulties. Their bargaining power is strong enough to enable them to prevent rescheduling of their debt where other creditors must accept a rescheduling.

Syndication

Functions of agent banks

The usual arrangement in a syndicated loan agreement is that the banks appoint one of their number as an agent who acts as a representative of the lenders. The agent acts as a conduit pipe for payments and carries out various administrative duties, such as the review of the legal documentation required as a condition precedent to the making of loans. The agent also acts as the recipient for notices of borrowing, prepayment and the like. The objective is that, as a matter of convenience, the borrower should have to deal only with one bank and not the entire syndicate.

Present market practice is for the agent not to take on any additional managerial duties in relation to the loan. Many agent banks consider that the risks are too great. Members of the syndicate are sufficiently sophisticated to make their own decisions and indeed wish to do so.

Several commitments

As regards the relations between the syndicate and the borrower, it is important to notice that the commitments of the lenders are several. If one bank fails to put up its share, then the other banks do not have to take it up. The banks do not underwrite each other. A borrower controls this risk by making sure that the banks in the syndicate are reputable banks who are likely to be able to carry out their obligations. Some banks will accept a clause which provides that if a bank fails to put up its share, then the managing banks will for, say, thirty days, seek an alternative participant as a substitute. Such a clause does not of course assure the borrower that an alternative participant will be found.

Syndicate democracy

An important aspect of syndication is the degree of democratic control amongst the syndicate. In this respect loan contracts with commercial bank lenders are quite different from bond issues constituted by trust deeds. In bond issues, there may be thousands of investors spread all over the world. Not all of them may be sophisticated. Some may insist on declaring a default when an acceleration of a bond would be against the interests of the creditors as a class. Others may stand in the way of sensible compositions. Furthermore, it is usually impracticable to contact all the holders of bearer bonds in order to secure their agreement to a change. As a result, bond issues are often constituted by trust deeds under which a trustee is appointed to monitor the issue and generally look after the interests of the bondholders. This trustee is quite different from a fiscal agent. A fiscal agent does not carry out any monitoring functions and is the agent of the issuer, not of the bondholders. A fiscal agent is primarily a paying agent who has also various administrative tasks in relation to such matters as replacement of lost bonds and the making of drawings. Where there is a trustee, on the other hand, the trustee can make arrangements for the holding of meetings of bondholders. The required majorities can then impose changes on the minority, subject to the inviolability of certain entrenched rights. Furthermore, the trust deed may contain a 'no action' clause whereby bondholders are not permitted to accelerate the bonds or to take enforcement action unless the trustee, upon being required to do so, has failed to do so within a reasonable time.

In syndicated loan agreements on the other hand, the banks are generally sophisticated institutions who have a substantial investment in the loan. They therefore require that they should have separate and independent rights of enforcement. They also wish to retain the ability to veto changes to the loan agreement.

However, there are a number of areas where the idea of syndicate democracy does seem to have taken hold. Some of these areas are important from the point of view of the borrower.

First, a borrower should look to see that an acceleration of the loan on account of a default should require a majority decision (by amount of participations). Ideally, a two-thirds resolution should be required but certainly a simple majority. Secondly, a borrower should aim for provisions that enable relaxations to be made to certain covenants, such as the negative pledge, by a simple majority of participations so as to override a single bank veto. International loans generally are long-term by comparison to other commercial contracts. Circumstances can change over 7, 10 or 12 years. On the other hand, it is generally impossible to negotiate a clause whereby a majority can change fundamental terms such as the currency, amount and terms of payment.

Pro rata *clauses*

Another exception to the general principle that syndicates like to regard themselves as separate lenders is the *pro rata* clause. Normally payments under the loan agreement are made to the agent bank. The agent bank divides the payment amongst the participants according to their participations. However, there could be cases where one participant obtains a preferential payment. A participant may, for example, hold a deposit from a borrower which, on a default, it is able to use to pay off the whole of its participation.

A *pro rata* clause is introduced to deal with this situation. The effect of this clause is that if one member of the syndicate obtains a payment (whether by set-off, the pursuit of independent legal proceedings, the benefit of security or otherwise) in a greater proportion than the other participants, then the favoured syndicate member must share the benefit of the payment with the rest of the syndicate so as to preserve the *pari passu* principle.

One disadvantage of these clauses from the borrower's point of view is that deposits placed with members of the syndicate are vulnerable to being shared amongst the rest of the syndicate. In other words, the surplus can be eaten up after the bank holding the deposit has been paid out. Normally this surplus would have to be returned to the borrower. The effect is similar to the borrower charging all its deposits with the syndicate to secure the whole loan.

Another objection from the point of view of borrowers is that these clauses, unless they are very carefully drafted, can amount to charges on deposits and other assets, thereby contravening negative pledges.

On the other hand, a possible advantage of a *pro rata* sharing clause is that it may discourage the race to the court-house door if something goes wrong: a bank will not obtain the rewards of being the most diligent if it has to share the proceeds of any action with the rest of the syndicate. I think that this advantage is outweighed by the disadvantages from a borrower's point of view.

Set-off clauses

These *pro rata* clauses must be distinguished from set-off clauses. It is often provided that a bank may set off any moneys it may hold for the borrower against unpaid amounts under the loan agreement. Even without such a clause, many jurisdictions permit set-off in any event. In such a case the clause does not add much to available rights and merely closes up certain uncertainties in the law of set-off, e.g. whether set-off is available across currencies or across international boundaries. Such a set-off clause should not be controversial. However, clauses which greatly extend the general banker's right of set-off should be examined with care since they may create charges in contravention of negative pledges.

Eurodollar market clauses

Eurodollar loan agreements contain a number of somewhat idiosyncratic clauses peculiar to the market. These are the substitute basis clause, the illegality clause and the increased costs clause. They look somewhat alarming since the first two involve a compulsory prepayment by reason of circumstances outside the control of the borrower. The third, the increased costs clause, puts the borrower at risk that there may be an increase in the spread, again because of circumstances outside the control of the borrower.

However, these clauses are a market requirement. It is difficult, if not impossible, to syndicate without them. The increased cost or snatch-back vulnerability is therefore a *quid pro quo* of the advantages of the market, e.g. its enormous availability and rapidity of response.

It is of some comfort to borrowers that, over the past decade or so, there does not seem to be any case—that I have heard of—where the substitute basis clause, the illegality clause or the increased costs clause has been utilised in a general international Eurodollar syndication. This does not mean that they will not be used. It is suggested that the proper method of mitigating the risk is to introduce qualifications which temper the severity of the clauses if a disaster occurs.

Substitute basis clause

A substitute basis clause allows the parties to fix an alternative basis for continuing the loan in the event that the interest rate can no longer be fixed by reference to the chosen market, e.g. the London Interbank market because, say, funding deposits cease to be available.

If indeed the banks were not able to fix an interest rate, e.g. because deposits cease to be available in the London Interbank market, then the legal results would be somewhat unpredictable. One possible result could be that the loan is frustrated, i.e. subject to *force majeure,* in which event, under English law, the loan may become immediately repayable. This would hardly be a satisfactory solution from the borrower's point of view.

Borrowers should aim at introducing two relaxations. The first should limit the events which crystallise the clause to circumstances which generally prevail in the Eurodollar market and not, for example, to circumstances peculiar to a particular bank. Thus, the inability to obtain deposits in the market should be attributable to market circumstances and not, for example, to the financial status of the bidding bank. The market disturbances should also apply to a specified proportion of the banks, not a single bank.

Secondly, the borrower should seek the 'locked-in' version of the clause as opposed to the 'snatch-back' version. Under the snatch-back version, if the market disturbance occurs then the parties negotiate but if they cannot agree then the borrower must prepay. Under this version the lenders do not have to agree: they can withhold agreement at their discretion.

The locked-in version states that if the parties do not agree on the substitute basis, then the lenders must certify the basis upon which they would be willing to continue the loan, e.g. the rate, the currency and so on. The borrower then has the choice to accept or reject each particular participant's substitute basis. If a substitute basis is rejected, then the borrower has to prepay that participant. In other words, while the lenders can choose the terms of the continuance of the loan, the loan has to be continued.

Illegality clause

This clause provides that if it becomes illegal for a bank to make, fund or maintain the loan, then the borrower must compulsorily prepay. Here is another case of a forced prepayment by reason, possibly, of circumstances beyond the control of the borrower.

On the other hand, the circumstances are usually outside the control of the lender as well. If the law changes so that it becomes illegal for a lender to continue with the loan, there is no question of fault on either side. The question is who should carry the risk. The market requires that this risk, such as it is, should be borne by borrowers.

The borrower should endeavour to negotiate grace periods for the prepayment. Many lenders will also agree to a provision that they will take mitigating action in the event of illegality, for example by changing their lending office to another jurisdiction in order to avoid the illegalities. These mitigating clauses usually have few teeth since lenders are often reluctant to commit themselves to a change of jurisdiction: the localisation of a loan has political, taxation and other implications.

Increased costs clause

The increased costs clause provides that if any change in law or regulation is to result in an increase in the underlying cost to the lenders, then the cost is passed on to the borrower. A typical example of a legal change giving rise to an increased cost is the imposition of reserve requirements by a monetary authority. Thus, if a bank is required to deposit 10 per cent of its assets or liabilities with the central bank at a nil interest rate, the cost of making the loan is correspondingly increased. This cost will not necessarily be reflected in the cost of funding deposits.

The objective of the increased costs clause is to provide an adjustment in the margin in the event of changes in the legal background. The costs of deposits may change just as much from legal factors as from market forces. However, it may be observed that increased interest rates resulting from market forces constitute an enormously greater hazard from the point of view of a borrower than margin increases from, say, reserve requirements. Experience in the domestic lending field indicates that the costs attributable to changes in reserves are comparatively small.

Detailed relaxations can be negotiated. For example, increases in costs attributable to taxes should exclude taxes on net income or changes in the rate of tax. A borrower should have the right to prepay a syndicate member who implements the clause. Normally general prepayment clauses require a prepayment of the entire syndicate. It is useful to include a provision that, if the clause is implemented by a lender, that lender will endeavour to move the loan to another jurisdiction where the difficulty does not arise. Unilateral assignments or changes of lending office by a bank should not result in a greater expense to the borrower.

Debt Rescheduling

Introduction
Where a state encounters payments difficulties so that it is no longer in a position to pay its foreign currency liabilities as they fall due, it will be necessary for the state to approach its official and private creditors with a view to arranging a rescheduling.

Creditors invariably require that the state enter into a standby arrangement with the International Monetary Fund (if the state is a member) since creditors take the view that the IMF economic stabilisation programmes are an important contribution to the rehabilitation of the debtor state's credit and an encouragement to continued parallel financing by commercial banks. The IMF encourages states to approach the Fund well before a balance of payments difficulty arises. It is thought that many states are deterred from making an approach to the Fund at an early stage by their view as to the political and economic consequences which might flow from IMF conditionality, i.e. the economic disciplines which are expected to be followed as a condition of the IMF standby. On the other hand, it is probably the case that the conditionality is much harsher if the approach to the IMF is made too late.

Financial terms
Where a state's external position is deteriorating, there is a tendency for the short-term portion of its external obligations to increase markedly as foreign banks and suppliers reduce maturities. A preponderance of short-term debt seriously increases a state's exposure to a sudden panicky withdrawal of confidence and indeed the withdrawal of credit can be very rapid. Where the position is serious, the procedure has been for the state to announce a specific cut-off date upon which it proposes to suspend

payment on its foreign obligations (or the relevant classes of those obligations) accompanied by an announcement of the opening of negotiations to reschedule.

Such an announcement tends to have a stabilising effect since the cut-off is effectively a declaration that the creditors concerned are to be treated equally and there is therefore no point in a disorderly race to the courthouse door. It is as well to remember that nowadays, in many commercial jurisdictions, states do not enjoy immunity from judgment or execution in commercial transactions, so that the attachment of external assets by disgruntled creditors is a serious possibility.

Further, the cut-off enables a distinction to be made between existing arrears which are liable to be rescheduled and new debts. The state may therefore be in a better position to convince fresh sources of credit that debt incurred after the cut-off date will not be subject to rescheduling.

A key feature of many debt relief agreements for very many years, whether negotiated with governments or commercial banks, has been the 'short-leash' approach. Under the short-leash, the amount of debt which is rescheduled is limited to a proportion of the amount of existing or imminent arrears. The rescheduled debt is defined as arrears at the cut-off date plus payments falling due over, say, the next 6 to 18 months so that if credit is not restored then it will be necessary to reschedule future arrears in future years. The short-leash tends to be adopted even though it may be plain that the debtor state will not be able to service future payments when they fall due. Creditors adopt the short-leash approach to debt rescheduling mainly because they apparently think that this is the only way in which they can encourage the debtor state to adopt the necessary austerity programmes and also because they wish to discourage an over-easy debt relief. The matter would have to be negotiated at the time.

It is the usual aim of creditors to reschedule only a proportion of current arrears of principal, e.g. something between 80 and 90 per cent, on the basis that the balance would be paid as a condition of the rescheduling. There is generally also an expectation that interest will be kept current, as well as foreign exchange and immediately reimbursable letter of credit commitments. There is a reluctance to reschedule short-term debt if this can be avoided. Recently arguments have been advanced for ensuring that public bond issue debt should be paid promptly, mainly because of the difficulties of representing the anonymous holders of negotiable securities, the impact on confidence in international bond markets and the desire to protect the small investor. It is also frequently desired to keep trade debt current since the continuance of trade is essential to the preservation of the economic life of the debtor state.

Nevertheless, in all of these cases, if the payments difficulty is cata-strophic, virtually all classes of debt may have to be rescheduled and arrears programmes agreed with suppliers and others. Both commercial banks and official creditors usually take the view in these circumstances that all creditors should be subject to the *pari passu* principle.

Rescheduling of official debt

At the governmental level, the most important consortium engaged in the negotiation of debt relief for foreign states is the Paris Club. This is an *ad hoc* informal consortium of creditor countries, comprising mainly Western industrialised nations, formed first in 1956 under French chairmanship, initially to cope with Argentinian payment difficulties. Subject to excep-tions, the traditional Paris Club approach to debt relief has been that relief will not be granted except in the case of an emergency, that official and other creditors should accept the comparability principle, that debt relief is to be on a short-leash, short-term basis and is not development aid, that the terms of the debt relief are non-concessional and finally, that the debtor state should adopt an IMF stabilisation programme. The proce-dure is for the state to agree with the Paris Club common terms for debt rescheduling and then to enter into bilateral negotiations with each credi-tor state with a view to establishing agreements with the creditor states individually. Each state is expected to observe the commonly-agreed new maturities but differentiation is generally allowed in relation to interest rates to reflect the domestic cost of capital in each country.

Other debt negotiations—notably involving India and Pakistan—have taken place under the auspices of an aid consortium under the chair-manship of the World Bank. Turkish debt in recent times has been renegotiated at meetings of the OECD Consultative Aid Group under arrangements comparable to those of the Paris Club.

Official debt with other countries, e.g. CMEA countries, will generally be rescheduled on a bilateral basis.

Commercial bank reschedulings

The usual procedure is for a steering committee of the leading commercial bank creditors of the state to be established to act as a liaison committee between the debtor state and the body of commercial bank creditors. As a general rule it is not desirable for a state to negotiate with separate committees formed on a national or some other basis since the presence of several bank consortiums tends to lead to competition between creditor banks and therefore greater delay and harder terms. The banks' steering committee does not generally enjoy any formal authority from the banks and is merely a negotiating forum. The steering committee will offer advice but has no mandate to make arrangements binding on a creditor. In practice most banks tend to go along with the solutions which the steering committee requests the debtor state to offer to bank creditors.

Commercial bank rescheduling agreements are extremely complex and the rescheduling is very expensive in terms of management fees to the rescheduling banks and in terms of the costs payable to the banks and their advisers. The debtor state should establish its own negotiating team comprising individuals who have the necessary authority and experience in the international financial markets. Proper professional advice at both the legal and commercial level should be sought.

As a general rule all of the banks participating in the rescheduling will sign the agreement. There may be provision for subsequent accession by eligible creditors. The rescheduling agreement usually comes into force only when the payments required to be made as a condition of the rescheduling have been met, e.g. the unrescheduled portion of principal in arrears, interest and certain other amounts, and when creditors holding a specified threshold of debt eligible for rescheduling have filed claims.

The usual aim of bank creditors is that the state, its central bank and often economically significant state entities should jointly and severally become obligors for the rescheduled debt. The effect is to strip off the veil of incorporation from state entities and to enhance set-off against bank deposits which might not otherwise have been available because of the absence of mutuality. Creditors also expect that the rescheduling agreement will be governed by foreign law, that the debtors will submit to foreign courts and that there will be an extensive waiver of immunity in respect of suit and enforcement. In addition there is generally a requirement for the centralisation of foreign exchange and other international monetary assets with the state's monetary authority. The combination of these factors is generally a significant increase in the exposure of the state's external assets to foreign attachments in the event of a default on the rescheduling agreement.

Nevertheless, experience has shown that acceleration of debt, the calling of defaults and the attachment of assets by bank creditors is extremely rare and has been adopted as a sanction only where the state concerned has evidenced an intention of repudiating debt or otherwise taking hostile measures. It is of vital importance for the orderly rescheduling of external debt that the state should reassure creditors of its willingness to honour its obligations as and when it is in a position to do so.

One of the most difficult clauses is the 'most favoured debt' clause which appears in both official and bank rescheduling agreements. In bank rescheduling agreements it is generally a condition precedent to the coming into force of the rescheduling agreement that the debtor state enters into comparable arrangements with regard to its other debt. Further, there may be a requirement that other comparable debt will not be paid on more favourable terms than the rescheduled bank debt and this provision may extend to trade debt and bond issues.

In addition, the negative pledge, the disclosure requirements, the obligations as to the administration of the foreign reserves of the state and the events of default are considerably more complex and sophisticated that those appearing in ordinary syndicated loan agreements. Special attention should be given to the negative pledge since, if not properly negotiated, it can have a major debilitating effect upon normal trade transactions such as letters of credit.

Note on sources: The recent literature on the subject includes Hardy, *Rescheduling Developing Country Debts, 1956 to 1980, Lessons and Recommendations,* February 1982, Working Paper No. 1, Overseas Development Council; Cizauskas, 'International Debt Renegotiation, Lessons from the Past', *World Development,* Vol. 7, 1979, p. 199; Wood, Philip, *Law and Practice of International Finance,* update to American edition published by Clark Boardman & Co., New York, 1982, Ch. 4. The classic legal work on the subject is Borchard and Wynne, *State Insolvency and Foreign Bondholders,* 2 Vols., Yale University Press, 1951, although this covers only pre-1950 debt adjustment agreements. See also Wood, Philip, 'State Insolvency and Priorities of Debt', *International Financial Law Review,* November 1982.

Questions raised during the Uppsala seminar discussion in November 1981

Question: It seems as if commercial bank lenders are always striving for over-protection. The loan agreements appear completely one-sided. Please would you comment.

Answer: International loan contracts do indeed seem one-way. The lender appears to have all these snatch-back rights, to demand a compulsory prepayment on this or that event, to accelerate on an occurrence of a default, to claim this or that indemnity, to pursue remedies in all courts everywhere and so on. However, I am reminded of Hamlet's remark, 'Methinks, the lady doth protest too much'. A contract of loan is an unusual commercial transaction. It is unusual because one party performs at the beginning and leaves the other party to perform at the end. Many other contracts require concurrent performance. Under the loan contract the lenders part with the funds at the start, and they are left with a piece of paper while the borrower has the funds. The piece of paper must remain a good valid claim for the money over many years. But it is only a claim. The piece of paper protests because it is nowhere near as strong as the possession of the money which it represents.

Question: Is it possible to provide that specified courts will have exclusive jurisdiction?

Answer: It is possible to provide this in theory. The courts of many commercial countries will uphold an exclusivity provision unless there is some overriding reason why they should not, such as unfairness. The reason is that the courts keep the parties to their bargain and also there is no derogation from jurisdiction absolutely, since there is one available court. On the other hand, lenders are usually reluctant to agree to an exclusivity provision. This means that a borrower is exposed to multiple, possibly concurrent, actions in various courts around the world. One reason for the lenders' reluctance is that they are not willing to limit their remedies if there is a default, especially their ability to move quickly to attach assets in the jurisdiction where they happen to be. A compromise sometimes agreed is to limit the courts, not just to those of one country but to the jurisdictions of the parties.

Question: Why is it necessary to submit expressly to the jurisdiction of a particular court when in any event many courts have a long-arm jurisdiction?

Answer: You are quite right that the long-arm jurisdiction is virtually universally available in commercial jurisdictions. For example, in England the English courts can claim jurisdiction over a contract which is signed in England or which is expressly or by implication governed by English law, even without an express submission by the parties. This type of nexus between the contract and the jurisdiction concerned is a frequent basis of jurisdiction in common law countries such as Canada, New Zealand, Australia and the United States. Other states have a different version of the 'excessive' or 'exorbitant' jurisdiction. In France, the French nationality of the plaintiff is enough to confer jurisdiction on the French courts. The position is the same in Luxembourg. In the Netherlands it is understood that the residence of the creditor is sufficient. In Germany the 'tooth-brush' jurisdiction prevails. There, the courts have jurisdiction if the defendant has any assets within the jurisdiction. There is a celebrated Austrian case where that magnificent French skier, Jean-Claude Killy, left behind him a pair of boxer shorts in an Austrian hotel. The Austrian courts were held to have jurisdiction. Tooth-brush jurisdiction applies also in Japan and Scotland, but not England. The nationality of the plaintiff lender is not enough in England or New York.

However, there are a number of reasons why lenders are not willing to rely on a long-arm jurisdiction, among them:

1. In some countries such as England, the exercise of the long-arm jurisdiction is discretionary and is not available as of right. It follows that the availability of the chosen jurisdiction may be unpredictable from the lender's point of view.

2. Express submissions coupled with the appointment of an agent for service of process within the jurisdiction generally improve the likelihood that the judgment will be recognised and enforced in other jurisdictions. The reason is that the foreign enforcing court is less likely to question the basis of jurisdiction of the original court.

Question: The courts to which a borrower is often asked to submit are usually stated to be 'non-exclusive'. Does this mean that a borrower can be sued anywhere and that the borrower is submitting to all the courts in the world?

Answer: The position depends upon the terms used. As a very general rule, a mere submission by the borrower to all courts where a lender may choose to take action is generally not enough to confer jurisdiction upon the chosen courts. One reason is that many courts require certain steps to be carried out before the lender has a claim on their jurisdiction as of right. In England there must be a local agent on whom the writ can be served. In a number of European continental countries, it is understood that there must be an election of local domicile.

However, in this case, as in many other matters pertaining to these loan contracts, one should stand back and evaluate real risks. It is a fact of life that anybody who breaks an international commercial contract, whether it be a sale of goods contract, a contract of carriage or a loan contract, is vulnerable to litigation in somebody else's courts. No doubt many of the clauses in loan contracts give the impression that lenders are constantly ready to pounce if something goes wrong, but experience is different. I believe it to be general experience that court enforcement actions by lenders against sovereign borrowers and their agencies are rare, even where the state is seriously in default. This is certainly the case where the borrower expresses willingness to continue payments even though it may not presently be in a position to meet its debt on schedule. The position is different where a state deliberately repudiates its debt.

Question: You said that syndicate lenders do not underwrite each other. What are a borrower's rights against a syndicate member who fails to make available its proportion of a loan? Failure could be most embarrassing for a borrower, especially in the case of project loans.

Answer: The borrower would normally have a right of damages against the defaulting lender. In English law the damages would be assessed on the basis of normal contractual principles. The damages are those which may fairly and reasonably be regarded as arising naturally from the breach of the contract or as may reasonably be supposed to have been in the contemplation of both parties at the time they made the contract as the probable result of a breach of it. For example, if the borrower can readily obtain another loan in good time, then the damages would normally be the expense of doing so and any increase in the interest rates on the other loan. There could be substantial consequential losses if the defaulting lender should have foreseen, at the time the contract was entered into, that the money would be required for a specific purpose and the borrower is able to prove consequential losses within the contemplation of the parties. But it is not always easy to show that the lender should have been aware of the losses which would result from the non-advance of a loan.

Question: What is the claw-back clause?

Answer: The claw-back clause provides that where the agent pays out the proceeds of a loan to the borrower and it turns out that one member of the syndicate did not put the agent in funds, then the agent has a right to recover that proportion from the borrower or alternatively from the defaulting bank. As a result, the borrower may have to hand back a portion of the proceeds of a loan after its receipt. The reason for the clause arises from the manner in which international payments work. An agent must generally give instructions in advance of the value date at a time when the agent does not know whether or not all the participants have advanced the loan proceeds to the agent's account for disbursement to the borrower. If a bank fails, an agent, which nevertheless makes the payment, will then in effect have underwritten the defaulting bank. Agent banks are not generally willing to take this sort of risk. All that the clause does is to put the risk of default of a member of the syndicate on to the borrower rather than the agent. This is not considered unreasonable. These clauses give rise to more discussion than they deserve. In the first place, it is rare for a bank which is a member of an international syndicate to default. Secondly, the default has to happen between the time that the agent gives instructions for the loan proceeds to be disbursed and the actual disbursement—a somewhat small gap.

Question: Can a lender be stopped by a majority bank clause from taking action on an event of default unless the majority banks agree?

Answer: It is often possible for a borrower to negotiate a provision that there can be no acceleration unless a majority of the lenders so direct. On the other hand, one would not normally find a clause which prevents a lender from taking independent action to recover an unpaid instalment of principle or interest without an acceleration. Similarly, after an acceleration, lenders are able in the usual case to take independent enforcement proceedings. However, syndicates often act together in such situations.

Question: Many loan agreements which I have seen contain a clause that all payments by the borrower are to be made free of taxes and if any taxes must be deducted from a payment then the borrower must pay additional amounts so that the lender receives the full amount provided for. What relaxations can be introduced to reduce the severity of this clause?

Answer: In principle it seems fair that a lender having bargained for 100 cents in the dollar should get 100 cents and not, say, 75. The grossing-up clause is another example of a provision which adjusts the cost of funds if there are changes in the legal environment as opposed to market forces. Suggested relaxations are:
1. A state borrower should seek to limit the clause to the taxes of its own jurisdiction. A state borrower is, of course, in control of its own taxation. But many lenders will look to have protection against taxes arising in other jurisdictions, notably, where payments have to be made.
2. It should be made clear that the clause applies only to deductions from payments at source and not to other taxes, e.g. taxes on the lender's overall net income which are not deducted from payments.
3. A borrower should also have the right to prepay any lender which implements the clause without penalties.
4. It may be possible to negotiate a tax credit clause whereby a lender which receives a grossing-up amount and subsequently obtains a tax credit or benefit in respect of the deduction, must return the compensating benefit to the borrower.

But many lenders resist tax credit clauses. However fair they are in theory, they can give rise to severe practical difficulties.

5. A borrower should also include a provision in the assignment clause to the effect that an assignment or a change of lending office by a bank is not to give rise to greater expense under the tax grossing-up and increased tax clauses.

Sovereign Immunity

BY WILLIAM TUDOR JOHN

Introduction

It had long been a fundamental precept of international law that sovereign governments could not be sued in foreign courts, or in their own courts, without their consent. It was a corollary of this that sovereign governments, even if they consented to be sued, could claim immunity from the execution of any judgment brought against them. The ideas are founded not on technical legal rules, but on broad principles of public policy. Because of the non-legal, even political nature of the doctrine, its application has developed differently in different countries.

During the nineteenth century, US courts, like those in most other countries, adhered to the absolute theory of sovereign immunity, namely, that immunity from suit could be claimed by a sovereign government in respect of *any* of its actions.

As in many countries, the absolute theory began to be eroded in the USA on a gradual basis, the courts there slowly adopting the theory that immunity should not be granted in certain types of cases. The courts were, in fact, pursuing a policy established by the executive, in particular the State Department, and were responding to hints from the executive that there should be a differentiation between the sovereign actions of a government (in respect of which immunity could be claimed) and the trading or commercial actions of a sovereign government (in respect of which immunity should not be allowed).

The application of this restricted theory of sovereign immunity culminated in the State Department Letter of 19th May, 1952—The Tate Letter —wherein the restricted theory was established as a matter of executive policy. The purpose of the letter was to accommodate the interests of individuals doing business with foreign governments in having their legal rights determined by the courts, with the interest of governments in being free to perform political acts without undergoing the embarrassment or hindrance of defending the propriety of such acts before foreign courts.

Thus, as a result of the Tate Letter, the policy of which was pursued by US courts, the position was that a sovereign government could not be sued in US courts unless:

1. It submitted to the jurisdiction expressly (e.g. by entering an appearance in a court action).
2. It submitted to the jurisdiction by implication (e.g. bringing a counterclaim).
3. It expressly waived its immunity.
4. The State Department was asked to intercede and characterised the action giving rise to the claim as a commercial action.
5. The State Department did not intercede and the courts characterised the action as commercial.

While the Tate Letter formally established a policy which had been quietly pursued for some years and helped to clarify the legal situation, difficulties were not entirely eroded. In particular, problems arose in the following areas:

1. The Tate Letter dealt only with immunity from suit and did not cover immunity from execution of judgment. It was not clear, therefore, whether property of a sovereign government would be attached even where immunity from suit was disallowed.
2. No guidelines were established as to how one should characterise the action of a government.
3. It was never made clear, either in the Tate Letter or in subsequent court actions, whether a waiver of immunity by a government would be effective if given at any time other than when suit was brought against that government.

In view of the lack of clarity in the situation, always inherent in situations where courts must rely on previous interpretations of executive policy, the Foreign Sovereign Immunities Act of 1976 was enacted, enshrining the restricted theory of sovereign immunity in statute.

Present sovereign immunity rules in the USA

The essential elements of the US Foreign Sovereign Immunities Act of 1976 are set out below. It should be noted that the Act covers not only foreign governments, but also political sub-divisions of a state, state agencies and state-owned corporations: the term 'foreign state' should be construed accordingly where used below. It should also be noted that the commercial character of an activity will be determined by reference to the transaction itself and the course of its conduct, rather than by reference to its purpose.

Immunity from jurisdiction

A foreign state will normally be immune from the jurisdiction of US courts, unless:

1. An international agreement between the USA and that foreign state states otherwise.
2. The foreign state has expressly or impliedly waived its immunity (and waivers are effective whenever given and cannot be withdrawn).
3. The suit is based upon the commercial activity of the foreign state in or directly affecting the USA.
4. The suit is connected with property taken in violation of international law and that property either is in the USA in connection with a commercial activity or is owned by a state agency or state-owned corporation carrying on commercial activity in the USA.
5. The suit is connected with land in the USA or property in the USA acquired by gift or succession.
6. The suit is an action for damages for personal injuries or death caused by the tortious acts of a foreign state or its officials. (There are some minor exceptions to this.)
7. The suit is an admiralty suit, for which proper notice of action has been given, and is in connection with the enforcement of a maritime lien arising out of the commercial activity of the foreign state.

Immunity from attachment and execution of property

A foreign state's property will normally be immune from attachment, arrest and execution unless the property concerned is used for a commercial activity in the USA and:

1. The foreign state has expressly or impliedly waived such immunity from attachment (and waivers are effective whenever given and cannot be withdrawn); or
2. The suit is based upon the commercial activity of the foreign state and the property is or was used for such activity; or

3. The execution relates to a judgment establishing rights in property taken in violation of international law; or

4. The execution relates to a judgment establishing rights in US land or in property acquired by gift or succession; or

5. The property is an insurance policy or insurance proceeds covering the liability on which the suit is based; or

6. In relation to property owned by a state agency or state-owned corporation, any such property can be attached (whether or not it relates to the suit in question) if the entity concerned is not immune from jurisdiction by virtue of paragraphs 3, 4, 6 or 7 under 'Immunity from jurisdiction'.

Notwithstanding the above, however, the following property will always be immune:

1. Embassies or residence of the head of the embassy.

2. Property of organisations designated by the President of the USA as enjoying the immunities of the International Organisations Immunities Act.

3. Property of a central bank or monetary authority unless such bank or authority or the foreign state has expressly waived immunity in relation thereto.

4. Property is military or is used by a military authority or defence agency.

General

There are various other provisions in the Act relating to service of process and the extent of any liability under any action brought against a foreign state.

The importance of the Act is that it established beyond doubt that the restricted theory of sovereign immunity would be applied by the US courts and that it would be a matter for those courts, not the executive, to determine whether or not in any particular instance sovereign immunity can be claimed. More importantly, the Act established that contractual waivers of immunity, whether in relation to jurisdiction or execution, will be upheld and cannot be withdrawn.

Sovereign immunity in the United Kingdom

The restricted theory of sovereign immunity developed more slowly in the

United Kingdom, where the absolute theory was adhered to for considerably longer than in most other countries. However, during the past decade, developments in English common law (culminating with the Trendtex and Congreso Cases) and legislative changes have seen the adoption in the United Kingdom of the restricted theory. The UK law is described more particularly below.

The State Immunity Act 1978 is the cornerstone of the present law in England on sovereign immunity and embodies in statute the restricted theory. Its principal provisions are as follows:

Immunity from jurisdiction
The Act provides that a state is immune from the jurisdiction of the courts of the United Kingdom except as provided in Part I of the Act. Hence the Act establishes the general principle of immunity but goes on to provide wide exceptions to the general rule.

It should be noted that, as in the USA legislation, the Act distinguishes between immunity from jurisdiction (the right of the English courts to sit in judgment on the claim) and immunity from enforcement (the right to enforce any judgment granted by the English courts).

Exceptions to immunity from jurisdiction
The following represent the exceptions to the general principle of immunity from jurisdiction or suit:

Submission to jurisdiction. Section 2(1) provides that a 'State is not immune as respects proceedings in respect of which it has submitted to the jurisdiction of the courts of the United Kingdom'.

Submission can now arise, by virtue of the Act, by prior written agreement to submit to the jurisdiction; and also arises if:
1. The State has instituted the proceedings; or
2. The State has intervened or taken any steps in the proceedings, except (i) where the intervention or step is taken for the purpose only of claiming immunity or 'asserting an interest in property in circumstances such that the State would have been entitled to immunity if the proceedings had been brought against it' (an example is an action *in rem*), or (ii) where the step is 'taken by the State in ignorance of facts entitling it to immunity if those facts could not reasonably have been ascertained and immunity is claimed as soon as reasonably practicable'. It is difficult to foresee cir

cumstances in which this might apply: note that the ignorance must be of 'facts', not law.

Commercial transactions. Section 3 provides that a state is not immune as regards proceedings relating to a 'commercial transaction entered into by the State'. This provision does not apply in the following cases:

1. It does not apply if the parties to the dispute are states.
2. It does not apply if the parties to the dispute have otherwise agreed in writing.
3. The section does not apply to Admiralty proceedings or proceedings on any claim which could be made the subject of Admiralty proceedings if the state in question is a party to the International Convention for the Unification of Certain Rules Concerning the Immunity of State Owned Ships signed at Brussels on 10th April, 1926, together with the Protocol of 24th May, 1934 ('the Brussels Convention'), and the claim relates to the operation of the ship owned or operated by that state, the carriage of cargo or passengers on any such ship or the carriage of cargo owned by that state on any other ship. (This is to avoid conflict between the Brussels Convention and the Act.)

For the purposes of section 3, a 'commercial transaction' means: (i) Any contract for the supply of goods or services; (ii) any loan or other transaction for the provision of finance and any guarantee or indemnity in respect of any such transaction or of any other financial obligation; and (iii) any other transaction or activity (whether of a commercial, industrial, financial, professional or other similar character) into which a state enters or engages otherwise than in the exercise of sovereign authority.

Contracts to be performed in the United Kingdom. Section 3 further provides that a state is not immune as respects proceedings relating to 'an obligation of the State which by virtue of a contract (whether a commercial transaction or not) falls to be performed wholly or partly in the United Kingdom'. As to place of performance, a contract to pay money is generally performable where the money is to be paid. However, this does not apply in four cases:

1. If the parties to the disputes are states.
2. If the parties to the dispute have otherwise agreed in writing.
3. If the provision mentioned above relating to the Brussels Convention applies.

4. If (i) the contract is not a commercial transaction, and (ii) the contract was made in the territory of the state concerned, and (iii) the obligation in question is governed by its administrative law.

Arbitrations. Section 9 provides that where 'a State has agreed in writing to submit a dispute which has arisen, or may arise, to arbitration, the State is not immune as respects proceedings in the courts of the United Kingdom which relate to the arbitration', e.g. presumably where a dispute arises as to the validity or interpretation of the arbitration agreement, as to the arbitration procedures, or as to the setting aside of the award. However, this does not apply:
1. If there is contrary provision in the arbitration agreement.
2. To any arbitration agreement between states.

Ships used for commercial purposes. Section 10(2) states that a state is not immune as respects an action *in rem* against a ship belonging to that state or an action *in personam* for enforcing a claim in connection with such a ship, if, at the time when the cause of action arose, the ship was in use or intended for use for commercial purposes.

Other cases. There are also special provisions excluding sovereign immunity for proceedings in respect of (among other things):
1. Contracts of employment.
2. Death or personal injury or damage to or loss of tangible property caused by an act or omission in the United Kingdom.
3. Any interest of the state in, or its possession or use of, immovable property in the United Kingdom or any obligation of the state arising out of its interest in, or its possession or use of, any such property, e.g. mortgage actions.
4. The membership of a state in a body corporate, an unincorporated body or a partnership in certain circumstances.

Immunity from enforcement
As regards the matter of enforcement of English court judgments, the general principle of immunity is established by the Act, subject to various exceptions, and, save as provided in the following section, the following remedies are not available against a state:
1. Injunctions.
2. Orders for specific performance.

3. Orders for the recovery of land.

4. Orders for the recovery of other property.

5. All proceedings against property of the state for the enforcement of judgments or arbitration awards.

6. Actions *in rem,* orders for the arrest, detention or sale of the property of the state.

Exceptions to immunity from enforcement

1. Written consent: by section 13(3) any relief may be given or process issued with the written consent of the state concerned. This consent may be given by prior agreement.

2. Commercial property: by section 13(4) the remedies listed in 5. and 6. in the preceding paragraph (and only those remedies) are available against the property of the state used or intended for use for commercial purposes.

State entities

1. Generally, state entities enjoy less immunity protection than states themselves. Separate entities are defined by the Act as any entity 'which is distinct from the executive organs of the government of the State and capable of suing or being sued'.

2. Section 14(2) provides that 'A separate entity is immune from the jurisdiction of the courts of the United Kingdom if, and only if (i) the proceedings relate to anything done by it in the exercise of sovereign authority; and (ii) the circumstances are such that a State (or, in the case of proceedings to which section 10 applies (mainly Admiralty proceedings), a State which is not a party to the Brussels Convention) would have been so immune'.

In other words, generally speaking, a separate entity is immune only where the state itself would have been immune and the separate entity is exercising sovereign authority.

3. Section 14(3) provides that if a separate entity submits to the jurisdiction in respect of proceedings in the case of which it is entitled to immunity by virtue of section 14(2), then it is entitled to the same immunity from enforcement and the other procedural privileges (subject to the same exceptions) as are afforded to states by section 13(1) to (4). This is subject to a special exception in favour of central banks and other monetary authorities, the property of which shall not be regarded as in use or

intended for use for commercial purposes; thus, the property of such entities does not lose its immunity unless written waiver of such immunity is given by the entity in question.

A state's central bank or other monetary authority is given such special favourable treatment as regards enforcement, because, without such immunity, foreign central banks might have been discouraged from depositing foreign reserves in the United Kingdom and hence lost the safe haven afforded by a country traditionally providing that protection.

Diplomatic and taxation immunities

Certain matters are excluded from the Act by section 16. The most important of these are:

1. Diplomatic immunities: Part I of the Act does not affect any immunity or privilege conferred by the Diplomatic Privileges Act 1964 or the Consular Relations Act 1968. These grant immunity to such assets as diplomatic premises and archives.

2. Taxation: Part I of the Act does not apply to any proceedings relating to taxation other than those mentioned in section 11 of the Act (VAT, customs or excise duty, agricultural levies and certain rates).

Effective date of the Act, and common law immunity rules

The Act came into force on 22nd November, 1978 and its provisions affect agreements entered into on or after that date. Agreements entered into before then are therefore covered by English common law principles relating to sovereign immunity. As has already been mentioned, English common law for a long while recognised the absolute theory of sovereign immunity. However, in 1977 the Court of Appeal, in Trendtex Trading Corporation v Central Bank of Nigeria, held by a 2 to 1 majority that sovereign immunity could not be claimed in respect of suits involving commercial acts of a state: the restricted theory thus became part of English common law. The case was, however, weakened by two factors: firstly, its decision conflicted with previous judgments of the highest English appellate tribunal, the House of Lords, and secondly the case involved the Central Bank, a separate legal entity and not an arm of state. The weakness has since been removed by the House of Lords' decision in 1981, in the Congreso case, that the restricted theory of sovereign immunity should prevail. Thus, the Congreso decision, and the restricted theory, will apply in respect of agreements entered into prior to 22nd November, 1978.

Banking practice

Banking institutions are becoming increasingly exposed to 'sovereign risk' situations these days, since the existence of state borrowings has increased dramatically over the past years. In view of their increased exposure, banks have been concerned in the development of the restricted theory of sovereign immunity and have always insisted, wherever possible, that sovereign immunity in relation to jurisdiction and enforcement should be waived in any relevant financial contracts. The law in both the USA and the UK is, of course, protective of the interest of international banks and accordingly it is becoming the rule for banking transactions involving states to be governed by English or New York law and for waivers of immunity to be sought.

Sovereign states must therefore bear in mind that lenders will insist upon waivers of immunity, but in assessing the acceptability of this, each state must consider the following:

1. Can it waive immunity under its own laws?—the constitutions of some countries prohibit waiver (e.g. Colombia).
2. What is the extent to which it can legally waive its immunity?—the constitutions of some countries, while allowing waivers in respect of jurisdiction, do not allow waivers in respect of enforcement against certain types of state property (e.g. Brazil).
3. What is the extent to which it can politically waive its immunity? —military assets, for example, should be protected.

State borrowers, after assessing these questions, can determine the extent of acceptability of the concept of waiver.

The following are alternatives of clauses to be seen in loan agreements, the first relating to a Swedish loan, the second relating to a Brazilian loan, and both containing exceptions from waiver:

1. '(A) The borrower agrees that should any bank bring judicial proceedings against it in relation to any matters arising out of this agreement in the courts and in the circumstances specified in Clause 19(B), no immunity from such judicial proceedings or from execution of judgment shall be claimed by or on behalf of the borrower or with respect to its assets, the borrower hereby irrevocably waiving any such right of immunity which it or its assets now has or may hereafter acquire. The borrower hereby consents generally in respect of any legal action or proceedings in the courts and in the circumstances specified in Clause 19(B) arising out of

or in connection with this agreement to the giving of any relief or the issue of any process in connection with such action or proceedings including, without limitation, the making, enforcement or execution against any property whatsoever (irrespective of its use or intended use but subject as provided by Clause 19(C)) of any order or judgment which may be made or given in such action or proceedings.

(B) The borrower hereby consents to any legal action or proceeding with respect to this agreement being brought in England or the Kingdom of Sweden, hereby irrevocably submits to the jurisdictions of the High Court of Justice in England and the Courts of the Kingdom of Sweden and hereby irrevocably designates His Excellency the Ambassador of the Kingdom of Sweden at the Court of St. James's as its authorised agent for receipt of service of process in the High Court of Justice in England. Additionally, if neither the High Court of Justice in England nor the Courts of the Kingdom of Sweden accept jurisdiction in the legal action or proceeding in question or if only the High Court of Justice in England accepts jurisdiction but it would be impracticable to obtain an order of the Courts of the Kingdom of Sweden enforcing any judgment of the High Court of Justice in England on the legal action or proceeding in question, then the borrower hereby consents to such legal action or proceeding with respect to this agreement being brought in New York, and hereby irrevocably submits to the jurisdiction of any state or federal court in the city of New York and (without prejudice to the foregoing and for the purposes of such submission only) hereby irrevocably designates the Consul General for Sweden in New York as its authorised agent for receipt of service of process in any state or federal court in the city of New York. For the purpose of the foregoing waiver and without prejudice to its generality, the borrower hereby expressly acknowledges that its consent and submission are intended to be irrevocable under New York and United States law and in particular but without limitation, under the Foreign Sovereign Immunities Act of 1976 of the United States and, in addition, hereby expressly waives any objection to the institution of proceedings in New York on the grounds of *forum non conveniens.*

(C)* For the avoidance of doubt it is expressly declared that the consents and waivers by the borrower in Clause 19(A) and 19(B) do not apply to the borrower's title to or possession of property for a diplomatic mission or to the property of Sveriges Riksbank.'

2. 'To the extent that the borrower or any of its property, assets or revenues has or hereafter may acquire, or may acquire the right to claim, any right of immunity from legal proceedings, attachment (whether prior to the entry of or in aid of execution upon a judgment), judgment or execution on the grounds of sovereignty or otherwise, the borrower hereby irrevocably waives such right of immunity in respect of its obligations hereunder

and under the Notes* (except, in so far as it is applicable, for the limitation on the alienation of public property provided for in Article 67 of the Civil Code of Brazil). In so far as concerns any legal action or proceedings in the state courts of or federal courts in the state of New York, the aforesaid waiver shall have effect under and be construed in accordance with the United States Foreign Sovereign Immunities Act of 1976.'

* Exception to waiver

Negative Pledge

BY PAUL I. HARRIS

This chapter examines a typical negative pledge clause, one which is de-liberately drafted in very broad terms, and analyses its intended purpose and function. Next, it looks at the various exceptions often appended to negative pledge clauses and the ways in which the borrower's position can be ameliorated.

The negative pledge clause is a companion to the so-called *pari passu* clause. Whilst the *pari passu* clause contains an obligation on the borrower to maintain parity between its unsecured obligations, the negative pledge clause seeks to control the borrower's ability to create or maintain secured indebtedness. Its main function is to ensure that the present and expected assets of the borrower will still be available for satisfying any outstanding claims of the lender in the event of the borrower defaulting. The lender does not want to find that specific assets of the borrower have been set aside in favour of one secured creditor who is thus preferred to all others and he, the lender, then has to look to any assets remaining for satisfaction of his claim. Furthermore, whilst a secured creditor is under a duty to obtain the best possible price when he realises his security, it is still the case that such a creditor's main interest is to satisfy his own debt and he is less concerned about the impact such a sale may have on the remaining assets of the borrower. This could further reduce the amount available to the lender and the other unsecured creditors.

The lender would also like to ensure that the borrower does not create more indebtedness than he can safely cover, so that in the event of an insolvency there are enough assets to cover his unsecured liability. The negative pledge clause will have established equality between creditors if the assets available to creditors are not sufficient to satisfy all their debts. In this way all creditors lose out to the same percentage, whereas with a system of priorities some lose out altogether while others are paid in full. (There should be mentioned one qualification to this statement, which is that most systems of law provide for a category of preferred creditors who, by operation of law rather than contract, obtain prior rights to assets on a liquidation. These preferred creditors commonly include employees in respect of unpaid salary and state agencies such as the Revenue Departments in respect of unpaid tax.)

A further reason for restricting the ability of the borrower to secure future debt is that it may be an indication that the borrower is in financial difficulties and unable to continue to obtain funds on an unsecured basis. It is in just those circumstances that earlier unsecured lenders would wish to share in the security offered, rather than see assets of the borrower appropriated for the benefit of another class of lenders.

Whilst it may be thought that these considerations apply only in the case of commercial concerns, they are nonetheless applicable to sovereign risk lending. There are many precedents where states have sought to borrow more advantageously on a secured basis or indeed, in some cases, where states have only had access to funds if prepared to grant security. Such security may be in the form of a charge over cash generated from a specific project, or over all or part of the gold or foreign currency reserves of the state. In such circumstances an unsecured lender could find that he had no practicable means of applying pressure to a state reluctant or unable to meet its obligations if, in fact, the viable assets of the state were already encumbered.

A typical negative pledge clause is set out in full in Appendix A. In summary, it provides that the borrower shall not grant security for its other indebtedness without extending the benefit of such security to the lender under the Loan Agreement. This is the simple formulation of the clause. Let us examine some of the key words and phrases:

'shall not create or permit to exist'
The lenders will wish to ensure that not only is the borrower to be restrained from granting security in the future but also that any security previously given and still subsisting should be discharged. The borrower should make enquiry within its organisation to ascertain that it will not be in breach of the agreement at inception, particularly as it is likely that the agreement will contain a warranty by the borrower that it has no secured indebtedness.

'principal subsidiaries, subsidiaries, agency'
The clause extends to restrict not only the borrower but also, in the case of a corporate borrower, its subsidiaries. Although the covenant to repay may be given only by the borrower and, accordingly, a lender only has direct recourse to the assets of such borrower, lenders often wish to restrict the ability of other members of the group in respect of the giving of security. Obviously the lender will not have a direct right of recourse against the assets of such subsidiaries but will only have rights against the value of the borrower's interest in such subsidiaries, that is the amounts left over after the creditors of such subsidiaries have been satisfied. However, lenders often argue that they may be prejudiced if the parent company is restricted but subsidiaries are able to encumber their assets. This may be because of a high level of inter-company trading within the group or because it may affect the value of a loan made to a parent company for other lenders to lend to major subsidiaries on a secured basis. Furthermore, if the subsidiaries of the company borrow on a secured basis it vests in those secured lenders the ability to realise the assets of these subsidiaries in the event of the group falling into financial difficulties. The lenders would wish to see such realisations made for the benefit of the creditors of the group as a whole, when a better price for such assets may be obtained. Likewise it may be possible for the group to be disposed of to a potential purchaser with greater facility if there are no secured creditors. Finally, to restrict the ability of a subsidiary to secure its borrowings does make less acute the need to restrict inter-company transfers of assets and also protects the lenders from new business being deposited in a subsidiary rather than the parent company and assets generated from such business being primarily available for secured creditors of that business rather than creditors generally.

It is common for lenders to accept that this restriction should only be imposed upon principal subsidiaries rather than each member of the group. This is for practical reasons and makes less difficult the process of monitoring the observance of the clause. What subsidiaries are to be regarded as principal subsidiaries is a matter for negotiation but commonly it includes subsidiaries that comprise more than, say, 5 per cent of the group's net worth. Sometimes the ratio is determined not by reference to net worth but by reference to profits generated or gross assets. Likewise, lenders may wish to name particular subsidiaries which, whilst falling below the criteria otherwise necessary, are considered to be of sufficient importance to be subject to the same restraints. Clearly the borrower would wish to set the ratio as high as possible once it has been obliged to consider that its group companies are also to be restricted.

Where the borrower is a holding company, it will be difficult for it to resist the argument of the lenders that its group of companies should be restricted. Where the borrower is an operating company and generates the major part of the business of the group, then, even though it is possible that the borrower may in the future establish new subsidiaries and such new subsidiaries may generate an increasing proportion of the group's business, it should be possible to persuade the lenders that only the borrower should be subject to the restrictions.

Where the borrower is the state or an organ of the state different problems ensue. Lenders will wish to regard the state as comprising not just the government but also the agencies of government. Likewise, if a loan is made to a principal organ of the state, lenders will seek to impose restrictions with regard to the other principal organs of the state including the state itself. The exact construction of the restrictions will depend upon who is the borrower and how, as a matter of domestic law, the different organs of state may be distinguished. Lenders will not wish to advance monies to the state, as borrower, and then find that a major agency of the state borrows on a secured basis. The contrary will also be true and borrowings by principal state agencies will also commonly contain restrictions on the ability of the state itself to create security. Again the parameters of this restriction are subject to negotiation.

A typical definition of 'agency of a state' is contained in Appendix B. The first two paragraphs of such definition are likely to be fairly uncontroversial and contain references to what may be regarded as 'alter egos' of the state. Rather more controversial is the part of the state included in paragraph 3. This makes reference to persons controlled by the state and may include corporations carrying on a conventional commercial activity but whose equity share capital is controlled by the state. Lenders will argue that the fact of control means that the state can dictate its borrowing activities. Lenders will say that where the controlled corporation is profitable and occupies a major influence in the economy of the state then its ability to borrow on a secured basis should be restricted. However, if the paragraph is not qualified, then the state-controlled corporation will be at a disadvantage in the financial marketplace in respect of raising funds when compared to analogous corporations that are not within the state sector. This aspect of the definition should be looked at and lenders are normally prepared to identify those corporations, if any, upon which they would not wish to impose restrictions. It is then open to the state to take issue with the lenders, both as to the concept of restricting the freedom of its agencies but also on the degree to which those particular agencies should be restricted. If the restriction would impose unwarranted and unjustified restraints upon the freedom of such agencies then the definition will need to be narrowed. However, it is unlikely that lenders would be prepared for the definition to be narrowed to a degree which would enable major undertakings, which contribute significantly to the revenues of the state, to borrow on a secured basis, particularly where the balance of payments of such state would be adversely affected by a calling in of such security.

Lenders will need to have regard to the internal realities of the country concerned, so as not to introduce limitations on the state which might otherwise paralyse its commercial activities. Some states have established parastatal corporations which have been deliberately created to enable borrowings to be made for specific purposes on a secured basis. If the clause were to be applied to them, they would not be able to operate, and so the state and the lenders must consider together the implications of such a situation and how it may be accommodated in the loan agreement. If a particular organ of state is set up on the basis that its financing is done only or largely on a secured basis, the lenders would have regard to their assessment of the creditworthiness of the state and the strength and value of its unencumbered assets.

The World Bank has approached this problem by seeking to identify those assets of the borrower that are to remain unencumbered. The result amounts to much the same as is found in covenants contained in commercial bank loans and still requires careful analysis by the borrower to safeguard its freedom of action. A typical World Bank clause is set out below:

The term 'assets of the borrower' as used in this section [and which are subject to the negative pledge] includes assets of the borrower or any of its political subdivisions or of any agency of the borrower [listed below] or of such political subdivision, including the [name of central bank] or any institution performing the functions of a central bank.

It will be seen that the definition does not focus on the type of assets but rather on the organisation owning such assets and, as such, will still call for exceptions to be made in similar fashion to those found in commercial bank agreements (see further below and Appendix C).

'security interest'

The phrase 'security interest' is defined in Appendix B. It cites most of the prevalent forms of security interest and ends with the catch-all phrase 'any other encumbrance', to catch any forms of security interest not specifically mentioned. Obviously different legal systems will have different types of security interest and lenders will seek to include all relevant forms. When dealing with, for example, England, the draftsman will specifically mention 'charges'. A restriction only on liens and pledges might not catch charges or mortgages.

The first set of words in square brackets should be considered very carefully because they seek to regard certain forms of off-balance sheet financing as secured borrowing. In so doing, the words are so widely drawn that they would tend to catch many innocent activities. Most goods are acquired on terms that the supplier retains title in the goods until payment, payment often being deferred as part of the normal commercial terms of acquisition. These would not normally be shown on a balance sheet or be commonly regarded as secured borrowing. The extended definition of security interest should be resisted unless the lenders are able to establish that the borrower engages to a sizeable extent in such financing, in which event some restrictions may be imposed which still enable the borrower to carry out its normal business operations.

Where the borrower is a state agency requiring the funds for a construction project, it should be mindful of this aspect of the clause and have particular regard to the second set of words in square brackets which will go some way to ensuring that it does not inadvertently breach the clause.

The formulation of the clause can have great practical effect. It may be recalled that, in about 1976, a negative pledge clause entered into by Zaire received international attention, due to a proposed payment facility agreement which was to be entered into, whereby certain foreign exchange earnings of Zaire would be placed in a special deposit from which new loans to be advanced would be repaid. The proposed payment facility agreement contained a bold-faced legend to the effect that the agreement did not create, and was not intended to create, any lien or security interest on funds to be deposited in the special account.

Argument centred on whether the words 'lien' and 'encumbrance' in an earlier negative pledge clause should be construed narrowly to mean only security interests created in the classic sense, or more expansively to catch this type of preferential arrangement. In the event the issues were resolved by mutual agreement but it explains why lenders are sensitive to any narrowing down of the defined term.

'assets, revenues or rights to receive income'
Although revenues and rights to receive income, when received, are assets, they are often specifically included in the clause. This may be to ensure that borrowers give thought to the implications of the clause as regards matters such as the forward sale of revenue earnings which may, depending on the structure of the arrangements, be regarded as the equivalent of a secured borrowing.

'present or future'
This is to cater for not only the assets currently available but also future assets that may be available. For example, if a new copper mine or oil field was discovered by a country, the revenues from these would fall within the clause. It stops a borrower from selling existing assets and purchasing new assets which, not being owned at the time of the loan, might not otherwise be covered by the clause.

'any indebtedness'
The next key word in the clause is 'indebtedness'. It will be seen from the definition in Appendix B that any obligation for the payment or repayment of money constitutes indebtedness. Obviously this is a very wide definition and would restrict the borrower from securing any of its monetary obligations. Thus a security given in a purchase obligation in relation to the supply of goods would cause the borrower to be in breach of the negative pledge clause. A borrower may therefore argue that such a wide definition is an unjustified constraint on its normal business activities and that it would find its commercial activities to be unduly hampered thereby and perhaps even made more expensive, to the detriment of its lenders. The lenders, on the other hand, will argue that they are creditors in the same ways as the trade creditors and that trade creditors should not have any priority rights not enjoyed by the lenders. Clearly this is a matter for negotiation, but borrowers will frequently wish to define indebtedness in

terms of 'borrowed money' and a typical definition would read as follows:

> 'borrowed money' includes any indebtedness for or in respect of money borrowed or raised (whether or not for a cash consideration), by whatever means (including acceptances, deposits and leasing), or for the deferred purchase price of assets or services, or guarantees or other assurances against financial loss, including agreements to purchase or to invest and other contracts having a similar effect to a guarantee.

'borrower [or others]'

Lenders will normally wish to ensure that restrictions are imposed on the borrower's ability to charge its assets irrespective of whose indebtedness it is intended to secure. For example, if the borrower has guaranteed the indebtedness of a third party and seeks to secure such guarantee it could only do so by extending the benefit of such security to the lenders.

'which is guaranteed by any [third party] [agency]'

A restriction often imposed as part of the negative pledge clause is one which seeks to prevent the borrower from arranging for its other indebtedness to be guaranteed by some third party. Clearly this does not, as such, affect the remedies available to the bankers against the borrower nor diminish the assets available to the borrower to repay the lenders (unless the subrogation rights of the guarantor give some preferential remedy to the guarantor under local law). Rather the lenders would be concerned to ensure that, if the borrower does not arrange for its obligations to the lenders to be guaranteed, then no other category of lender should be more favourably treated. It relates more to the competitiveness of the loan than a protection against the diminution of the borrower's assets. The lenders may perhaps argue that, in a workout situation, a guaranteed loan has the edge on an unguaranteed loan but this is perhaps more apparent than real.

'other security interest'

It may be that if the borrower becomes obliged to extend a security interest to the lenders, the benefit of that security interest cannot be, or the lenders do not want it to be, extended to them. The clause provides that so long as alternative security acceptable to the lenders is granted there is no breach of the negative pledge clause. This provides a more satisfactory and flexible solution where the negative pledge clause is, or is liable to be, breached.

Attempts have occasionally been made to provide for security to be automatically created in the event of the clause being breached. (This is because the provisions of such a clause, even if couched in positive terms, are not likely to be capable of specific enforcement and calling in the loan may be an insufficient remedy where the general assets of the borrower are not adequate to meet its unsecured obligations. Furthermore, the damage may already have been done in the sense that the prior charge may have already been created to the prejudice of unsecured lenders.) Such attempts are fraught with difficulty as the assets over which the security is to attach may be insufficiently identified and the position of third parties, already entitled to such assets, unclear. Furthermore, many jurisdictions require such security to be registered on creation or within a certain time limit which, if not accomplished, renders the security void.

Some typical exceptions

Some typical exceptions to the negative pledge clause are now to be examined. These are listed in Appendix C. It should be emphasised that many of these exceptions may not be appropriate for inclusion in certain loan agreements. Their incorporation will depend on the circumstances of each transaction. It would also be rare for more than a few of the exceptions to be found in practice in the same clause. Many may not be relevant for state borrowers unless restrictions are sought over their trading agencies. However, the list should be studied carefully by all potential borrowers, for it is unlikely that a borrower will be able to enter into an agreement containing an unqualified negative pledge clause without some of these exceptions being relevant.

The numbering below corresponds to the numbering of the paragraphs in Appendix C.

1. It should be explained that the term 'lien' may have a different meaning under different legal systems. Thus New York law may regard a lien as a fully fledged encumbrance granting to the holder the right to realise the relevant assets in appropriate circumstances. Under English law, on the other hand, a lien is, strictly speaking, only a right to retain an asset pending satisfaction of a debt owed to the holder of such asset, e.g. a car repairer has a lien over a car until he has been paid, a solicitor has a lien over his client's papers until his bill has been settled, a banker has a lien

over a customer's title deeds deposited (otherwise than simply for safe custody) until a loan is discharged and so on.

In order to ensure that the ongoing business operations of the borrower are not to be prejudiced, this exception is essential. The examples just given of liens arising would fall within the exception as they arise 'by operation of law', provided that they are within the ordinary course of the borrower's operations. Often borrowers wish to except *all* liens arising in the ordinary course of business (whether by agreement or operation of law). This is likely to be resisted by lenders on the basis that it could open the door to argument by the borrower that, for example, secured bank finance was 'in the ordinary course of business' because it was a necessary part of financing the ongoing business of the borrower, without which the borrower could not conduct its operations. It is more likely that the lenders would wish to separately identify exceptions to the negative pledge clause so that each may be examined on its merits.

The exception also allows liens to be expressly granted by agreement where the effect is the same as that which arises by operation of law. But the agreement must not go beyond that which would apply in the absence of such agreement.

This is a convenient moment to discuss a real problem which has much exercised lawyers' minds and on which there are differences of opinion.

It is well known that a banker has a right of set-off in respect of accounts maintained for the same customer. This right of set-off is a right to combine accounts by the banker setting-off debit and credit items so as to strike a balance. Accordingly, where a borrower maintains with a bank a current account and enters into a borrowing arrangement with the same bank then, in the absence of a contrary agreement, the bank should be entitled to appropriate the sum in the current account in the event of a default by the borrower in repaying the loan. It is, therefore, arguable that merely by entering into the borrowing arrangements the borrower has allowed a right of set-off to arise over the amounts of any credit balance that it maintains with the lending institution and that this right constitutes a charge over such moneys. It is considered that this view is too extreme, but it is undeniable that a borrower granting to a bank an *express* right to combine accounts should take careful stock of the impact on the negative pledge clause. Such clauses are quite common in loan agreements, particularly one bank agreements, where the loan is provided on the bankers' standard form document.

Whilst a right to set-off arising by operation of law does not in my view constitute a charge, as that term is understood in English law, it is very possible that it does represent a lien by the banker on any credit balance and as such would breach the negative pledge clause without language in the form of the first exception being included. Where an express right of set-off documented in an agreement is granted to a bank which merely restates the right arising by operation of law, the position would be the same both in regard to this exception and also in regard to determining whether the document created a charge (although it does probably restate the banker's right to a lien over such moneys). But an express right of set-off, which confers a right not available in the absence of a contractual stipulation, does amount to the creation of a charge. This perhaps is a consequence not always foreseen. Borrowers should, therefore, have regard to their loan agreements to see whether they have granted to the lending institutions a right to appropriate credit balances in satisfaction of the debt in terms which go beyond that which is provided by operation of law. If this is the case,·then some further exception of the negative pledge clause may be required or the set-off clause should be eliminated from the other loan agreement, the lending institution being told that it must rely upon its pre-existing rights under the general law which, in many cases, will give sufficient protection. There will be no objection to the position as to set-off under the general law being declared under the loan agreement so that the lending institution can see that it has a right of set-off and that such right has not been excluded, so long as the declaration does not provide any additional rights not otherwise arising by operation of law.

Where the borrower is itself a banking institution (as, for example, where the borrower is a development bank), it will continually be placing deposits and taking loans in the interbank market. This being so the problem may well be in a particularly acute form and some fairly specific exception to the negative pledge clause may be required. Thus, wording such as 'any security interest created or arising in the ordinary course of banking business' may be needed to except charges which may commonly be created or allowed to arise in the course of interbank business. Lenders may wish to see that this exception only applies where the banking business is carried on in the ordinary course of its operations, in the place and at the time the charge is created or arises. This limitation would ensure that the borrower needs to establish that it has acted in the ordinary course in the place where the arrangements were concluded

—the effect of the arrangements elsewhere would be disregarded.

Lenders will often seek to limit the exception so that liens arising by operation of law must be discharged within a certain period of time after they arise (unless being contested in good faith). This limitation should be resisted on the basis that the various types of lien that may arise by operation of law (and thus fall within the exception) apply in a variety of different circumstances and that it is not apt to require them to be discharged within a common period of time. It may mean, for example, that the borrower will be restricted from seeking some more advantageous purchase terms in respect of goods to be purchased, simply because by deferring the time of payment a lien may arise over the goods and not be discharged (by payment for the goods) within the period of time stipulated in the loan agreement.

2. The second exception enables ordinary business transactions, financed by loans secured on the goods purchased, to continue. The loans are limited by time and are to be paid off out of the proceeds of resale. But for this exception, a large number of everyday commercial transactions would not be possible.

3 and 4. These except short-term bank loans and secured indebtedness up to a specified percentage of tangible net worth. They recognise a level of secured financing that may be made by the borrower without prejudicing the lender's interests. It would be rare for lenders not to concede some degree of short-term bank financing, although the exception may be limited to some specific activity such as, for example, refinancing receivables. Likewise, lenders may often agree that, provided that there is a certain proportion of unencumbered assets, the balance may be secured without limitation. This may depend on whether the lenders would regard the crystallisation of a security on part of the assets of a borrower as prejudicing the value at which the remaining assets may be realised, particularly where the borrower may only have one business activity in which the assets are used. A factory may only, in book value terms, represent a small proportion of a borrower's net worth, yet its influence on the ongoing business of the borrower may be considerably greater.

5. This permits any security to be created with the prior consent of the lenders. Some criteria for establishing consent may be considered in

advance and provided for in the clause, so that if the application falls within such criteria, the lenders would be unable to withhold consent. This may be difficult for the lenders to agree, but could be applicable to a project already in contemplation, or to business activities in a given jurisdiction where the grant of security was commonplace.

6. This exception is almost invariably granted in relation to borrowing by states and state-controlled entities. It would be rather unusual for the lenders to concede this exception where the borrower is a private sector company. In essence, it enables the borrower to secure its local borrowings. These are defined as being all indebtedness other than 'external indebtedness'. External indebtedness is defined in Appendix B and in essence means any indebtedness denominated, payable or optionally payable in a currency other than the domestic currency of the borrower. The philosophy behind this exception is that the borrower should have a free right to arrange its domestic finance on whatever basis it considers in its best interests. There is a certain lack of logic in this approach because all the assets of the borrower would normally be available to satisfy all its holders of indebtedness, and to enable domestic indebtedness to be secured may prejudice the position of the lenders just as much as if foreign indebtedness was secured. However, the exception recognises the position in many countries that local financing from banks is effected on a secured basis, particularly where the facilities made available are on an overdraft or short-term basis. The borrower will argue that it cannot have access to domestic sources of finance closed to it but must be free to borrow on what is a customary basis in its own country. However, lenders could reply by seeking to put a control over the amount of local borrowing but in practice this is rarely sought, rather lenders recognise that they are not looking to recourse against the domestic assets of the borrower which may be, in practical terms, unavailable to meet external liabilities but rather to the foreign currency balances maintained by the borrower outside its domestic jurisdiction.

Thus lenders will generally accept that, in the public sector, restrictions on creating security are only to be imposed in relation to external indebtedness. It will be seen that the definition of 'external indebtedness' goes further than simply having regard to the currency of indebtedness as the person to whom such indebtedness is payable is also relevant. If it is payable to a person outside the jurisdiction of the borrower, it will be regarded as external indebtedness in whatever currency such indebtedness is denominated. This qualification (set out in the first optional paragraph 2) has more to do with ensuring that the borrower does not grant better terms to other foreign lenders than with ensuring that assets are encumbered to the prejudice of lenders. There is a trap contained in this optional language, notwithstanding that it is frequently to be found in loan agreements. It will be seen that the exception will not apply where indebtedness is payable to a person having its head office outside the domestic jurisdiction. In many cases local financing, which is generally provided on a secured basis, is made available not only by purely domestic banks but also branches of foreign banks. Thus, if a loan is made available by a branch of a foreign bank to a borrower in its own domestic currency this will be regarded as external indebtedness. It is generally argued by lenders that this is justified on the basis that such a bank is to be regarded as a foreign lender and should not be entitled to grab secured assets if the borrower has not extended the benefit of the creation of such security to the lenders. However, where the foreign banks with branches in the domestic jurisdiction of the borrower provide banking facilities on exactly the same basis as purely domestic banks, a borrower will almost invariably find that it is in breach of the negative pledge clause if it deals with branches of foreign banks. This would unduly restrict the borrower's freedom to seek finance from any bank it chooses that operates within its jurisdiction. In such circumstances the borrower should seek to have the language which is set out as the second option incorporated into the loan agreement. This will only constitute as external indebtedness, indebtedness which is booked to an account outside the domestic jurisdiction of the borrower. Foreign indebtedness would, therefore, be indebtedness which is repayable to an account outside the jurisdiction rather than to a person whose head office or principal place of business is outside the jurisdiction. This alternative has usually proved to be more satisfactory and acceptable to lenders when they realise that the more conventional language is likely to cause the borrower undue restriction in relation to access to local finance.

Where the borrower is a corporation and has subsidiaries in foreign countries, the concept of external indebtedness needs to be looked at carefully (assuming that the whole group is subject to the negative pledge clause). Thus, if a member of the group borrows in a currency other than the domestic currency of the parent company, this will not be regarded as external indebtedness and thus free of restriction unless such currency is also external to that particular member of the group which has entered into the borrowing arrangements. Lenders will seek to ensure that secured borrowings cannot be raised in one part of the group on a domestic basis which would fall outside the negative pledge clause, and then made available to another member of the group which, if it had borrowed direct, would have been regarded as borrowing external indebtedness. In other words the eventual utilisation of the funds will be looked at to see whether those funds would be regarded as external from the point of view of the eventual utiliser of the funds.

7. Project financing would have to be defined but the idea here is to exclude a certain venture from the agreement. If, for example, a government was developing a new gas field it may want to keep that project out of the deal altogether and arrange that financing separately.

8. This allows a security interest to arise against the borrower where, pursuant to legal action, a litigant is able to obtain an order of attachment of assets prior to the hearing of a dispute in the courts. It may be that this exception would already be covered by the first exception as such order of attachment would arise by operation of law (although not in the ordinary course of the borrower's operations). The clause optionally requires that the case be properly contested and provision be made in the event of the borrower losing, but it is thought that this concept is better dealt with in the 'Events of Default' section of the agreement, as the borrower could hardly extend the security to the lenders in the event of failure to discharge the order of attachment.

9. This exception allows a security interest already existing on assets acquired by the borrower to remain without having to be discharged, provided that the security was not granted in contemplation of the borrower's acquisition of that asset.

10. This exception enables the borrower to acquire new companies without having regard to whether such acquisition might breach the negative pledge clause provided that once the company becomes a subsidiary the amounts secured are not exceeded. This exception and the previous exception are both designed to ensure that the normal commercial policies

of the borrower with regard to acquisitions are not prejudiced by the negative pledge clause but that such clause will only govern any future creation of security. Without such exceptions the borrower might have to turn down opportunities simply because of the negative pledge clause, although from the lender's point of view there is a danger that the borrower may be exchanging unencumbered cash for assets which are encumbered by security interests. If the borrower has the intention of pursuing an active investment policy or regularly financing the purchase of assets by the creation of security then exceptions to the negative pledge clause will be needed.

11, 12 and 13. These exceptions follow a similar course to the exceptions set out in paragraphs 9 and 10. Exception 11 allows the borrower to finance its trading activities through or by reference to guarantees given by national credit institutions who often require, as counter security, charges over the documents of title relating to the goods sold. The exception contained in paragraph 13 assumes the borrower may be engaged in the forward financing of its trading activities and would need to secure to the lender its sales contracts and documents of title. Paragraph 12 restricts the exception (that relates to creating a security over assets to be purchased) to real property (which means land and buildings) and only up to a specified maximum amount.

It will be seen therefore that the negative pledge clause sets many traps within its language and that, on an examination of the activities of most borrowers, an inadvertent breach of the clause would be very likely without employing a number of these listed exceptions. Which exceptions are appropriate will depend on a close look at the overall business activities of the borrower, and any other companies or organisations which may be caught by the clause. Borrowers should ensure that all internal departments be alerted to the restrictions that they have accepted to ensure that, due to the development of new financing arrangements, an inadvertent breach of the clause does not arise. A problem to be watched is that it is common for the breach of the negative pledge clause to be an immediate default under the agreement with no time for the borrower to cure the default by discharging the security. Borrowers should seek to have written into their agreements a provision, allowing them to correct or cure an inadvertent breach, along the following lines (although many lenders will resist any provision designed to delay their remedies for such breach on the basis that delay might irretrievably damage their position and that the position is best dealt with by way of waiver. This, however, may pay insufficient regard to the effect of cross-default clauses whereby waivers may become necessary under other financial agreements):

A default occurs if the borrower does not comply with one or more of its obligations under [the negative pledge clause] and such default is not remedied or cured or the relevant security interest discharged or set aside within .. days of [its occurrence] [of its coming to the notice of the borrower] [after notice of that default has been given to it by the lender.]

APPENDIX A

The borrower shall not create, enter into or permit to exist, [and shall procure that its [principal subsidiaries] [subsidiaries] [agencies] do not create, enter into or permit to exist] any security interest on or with respect to any assets, revenues or rights to receive income, present or future, of the borrower to secure any indebtedness of the borrower [or others] nor will it create, enter into or permit to exist any indebtedness which is guaranteed by any [third party] [agency] unless the benefit of such security interest or guarantee is, at the same time or prior thereto, extended equally and rateably to secure the payment of principal and interest and other sums payable hereunder or some other security interest or guarantee, acceptable to the lender, is made available to the lender.

APPENDIX B

For the purposes of the negative pledge clause the following definitions shall apply:

Principal subsidiary	a subsidiary whose net worth comprises more than .. per cent of the net worth of the borrower and its subsidiaries;

Subsidiary	a person or company which is directly or indirectly controlled or more than 50 per cent of the equity share capital (or its equivalent) of which is beneficially owned by the borrower and/or one or more of its subsidiaries;
Security interest	any lien, pledge, charge, mortgage, hypothecation or any other encumbrance [and any deferred purchase, title retention, leasing, preferential arrangement, sale-and-repurchase or sale-and-leaseback arrangement] [but shall not include any arrangement under which the title in assets acquired by the borrower is retained by the supplier of such asset until payment of the purchase price therefor is received by the supplier];
Agencies	(1) an agency, authority, central bank, department, government, legislature, minister, ministry, official, or public or statutory person (whether autonomous or not) of, or of the government of, that state [or any political sub-division in or of that state]; and
	(2) any person who in any capacity whatsoever then owns, holds, administers or controls any of the reserves of that state; and
	(3) any other person which is then directly or indirectly controlled or more than 50 per cent of whose issued equity share capital (or equivalent) is then beneficially owned by, and/or by any one or more agencies of, that state [or any political sub-division in or of that state];
Indebtedness	includes any obligation (whether present or future, actual or contingent, secured or unsecured, as principal or surety or otherwise) for the payment or repayment of money;

External indebtedness

any indebtedness which is:
(1) denominated, payable or optionally payable otherwise than in the currency of .... or,
[(2) payable to a person incorporated,
domiciled, resident or having its head
office or principal place of business
outside .... [or is payable under an
instrument which could be negotiated
to such a person] or,]
[(2) payable to the account of any
person outside .... such person to
include the office outside .... of
a resident in .... but to exclude
the .... branch of a bank not resident in ....].

APPENDIX C

1. Liens arising solely by operation of law (or by an agreement to the same effect) and in the ordinary course of its operations [but any such lien must be discharged within . . days after it arises unless being contested in good faith (and by appropriate proceedings)].

2. Any security interest on commercial goods acquired for resale to secure indebtedness maturing not more than [one] year after the date on which it is originally incurred and to be paid out of the proceeds of sale of such commercial goods.

3. Any security interest arising in the ordinary course of banking transactions to secure indebtedness of the borrower maturing not more than [one] year after the date on which it is originally incurred.

4. Any security interest to secure indebtedness not exceeding £ .... or .. per cent of tangible net worth.

5. Any security interest granted by the borrower with the prior written consent of the lenders.

6. Any security interest to secure indebtedness not being external indebtedness.

7. Any security interest to secure indebtedness of the borrower incurred in connection with any project financing (as defined), provided that the assets or revenues of the borrower which are subject to such interest are (a) assets which are the subject of the applicable project or (b) claims or revenues which arise in the use or operation of, or the loss of or damage to, such assets.

8. Any security interest pursuant to any order of attachment, distraint or similar legal process arising in connection with court proceedings [provided that the execution or other enforcement thereof is effectively stayed and the claims served thereby are being contested at the time in good faith by appropriate proceedings and proper provision has been made for any adverse judgments].

9. Any security interest existing at the time of acquisition on any asset acquired by the borrower after the date of this agreement and not created in contemplation of that acquisition and any substitute security created on that asset in connection with the refinancing of the indebtedness secured on that asset.

10. Any security interest over revenues or assets of a company which becomes a subsidiary of the borrower after the date hereof, provided that the amount secured and outstanding at the date hereof is not later exceeded.

11. Any security interest arising under credit facilities obtained through or guaranteed by a national export credit institution and any guarantee of such credit facilities shall not be treated as indebtedness.

12. Any security interest over any real property acquired after the date hereof to secure the purchase price of that real property or the cost of building any structure on that real property but only if the security interest is created at the time of purchase and if the maximum amount secured does not exceed £ ....

13. Any pledges over and assignment of documents of title, insurance policies and sale contracts in relation to commercial goods created or made in the ordinary course of business to secure the purchase price of such goods or loans to finance such purchase price.

Events of Default

BY RICHARD G. A. YOUARD

General approach for negotiating default clauses

The usual principles of negotiation apply but borrowers should be particularly careful to be reasonable in dealing with default clauses. The clause covers the situation where payment by the borrower is threatened; if you try to reduce the lenders' protection too far they will begin to think that a default is a real possibility and that you know this.

Being 'reasonable' does not mean being weak. If you understand the lenders' objectives and identify your own carefully, you will usually find that a solution to every problem can be found which meets both needs without provoking a confrontation. Aggressiveness for its own sake, whether on the part of the lenders or the borrower, is usually counter-productive.

Make sure you understand the effect in your own situation. In most cases this will depend on the precise facts of your situation and on your policy for the future. Therefore you must apply the words of each paragraph of the default clause to your own situation, both at the time of negotiation and over the whole of the life of the loan.

The words of the default clause must be read particularly carefully but commercial common sense, assisted by the ordinary legal analytical approach, will almost always provide the answers. The fact that a borrower has not taken part in a Euromarket borrowing before should not inhibit the borrower from following the dictates of common sense. There is no special mystique about the default clause in Euromarket documents; indeed, a first-time borrower will often recognise points to which an experienced borrower (through over-familiarity with Euromarket documents) will not have given sufficiently careful attention.

The overall purpose of the clause is to enable the lenders to demand repayment of the loan in appropriate circumstances before the date for payment originally envisaged. This is reasonable if the position of the lenders is threatened. It is not reasonable if there is no real threat. The chief problem in default clauses lies in stating in advance what constitutes a real threat, i.e. what circumstances are appropriate for demanding repayment.

Borrowers sometimes fear that the lenders, while claiming to be making a term loan, are (through the drafting of the loan agreement) trying to change the arrangement into a demand loan. The inclusion of a large number of events of default does not in itself justify this fear. Normally, lenders have decided to make a term loan because their economic objective is to ensure a specific return on the use of their money for the stated term and, on this basis, repayment before the original maturity will be unwelcome. Furthermore, from the agent's point of view, the operation of the default clause (or, more likely, the threatened operation of that clause) is an extremely unwelcome event causing considerable expense and difficulty.

Nevertheless, the borrower's task is to confine the events of default to those which are justified in the particular case.

Note: Normal agreements only give a *power* to the lenders to call in the loan early (known as 'acceleration'); they do not provide for automatic acceleration, i.e. the lenders have to make a decision to demand early payment (scc pp. 179–180).

The borrower's initial task (in considering the lenders' draft loan agreement) is to decide which events should remain unaltered, which should be deleted entirely and which should be qualified to make them acceptable to the borrower. The first test should be: does the clause deal with an event which threatens the lenders' position? If it does, the paragraph may remain but may need qualification if it extends to events which do not really matter (i.e. do not indicate a threat to the lenders' position) or which unreasonably restrict the borrower's freedom of action. If the paragraph covers events which are not relevant to the lenders' position it should be deleted entirely.

Events of default fall into two basic categories:
1. Actual non-payment by the borrower.
2. Other events.

The purpose of including these other events (category 2) is to enable the lenders to take action before non-payment has actually occurred but when it is likely or possible. In other words, the other events give the lenders a time advantage so that, instead of having to wait until non-payment has occurred, they can take action in advance. To wait for non-payment may deprive the lenders of many alternative courses of action, some of which could benefit the borrower.

To explain the difference between the two categories in another way, non-payment indicates clearly to lenders that the borrower cannot or will not pay (disregarding administrative failures in the payment mechanism) while other events of default provide lenders with an 'early warning' system. The events which give early warning may not be very important in themselves but they alert lenders to the fact that something has happened which *may* indicate that the whole financial structure of the borrower is collapsing and the lenders may therefore wish to take quick action before the situation gets worse. Sometimes events of this second category are described as the 'tip of the iceberg', the iceberg (90 per cent of which is concealed) being the financial collapse of the borrower, only a small and apparently unimportant tip (the event of default) being visible.

The courses of action open to lenders (whether for non-payment or the other events of default) may be legal enforcement (usually the least likely) or requests for information followed by discussion followed by renegotiation. The renegotiation may well involve other lenders. Without the inclusion of the events of default other than non-payment the lenders may be unable to participate in renegotiations involving other lenders (particularly relevant to cross-default).

Note: Some borrowers feel that, since in the great majority of sovereign default situations renegotiation is by far the most likely course of events, the agreement should include specific clauses obliging lenders and borrower to renegotiate. This will almost certainly be unacceptable to lenders since (a) without their power to accelerate the loan they will have no bargaining position in a renegotiation and (b) the situation at the time of renegotiation cannot be foreseen accurately enough to enable the lenders to know (at the time of signing) what they are committing themselves to; in practical terms renegotiation always means concessions on the part of the lenders, coupled with advantages (extension of maturity etc.) for borrowers.

However, if the borrower can foresee certain likely situations then it may well be sensible to make specific provision in the loan agreement for what is to happen to the loan if those situations occur. The borrower may well get better terms by negotiating in this way before signing, when the lenders are still happy with the credit and keen to make the loan.

Some events of default (such as non-payment) are within the borrower's control, and some are outside that control. It is reasonable to include those within control; it may be unreasonable from the borrower's viewpoint to include those outside. However, the same test applies: does it significantly threaten the lenders' position?

Many events of default (but not non-payment) can be made reasonable by applying a materiality test. This can take many forms, including words to indicate that the event must matter in the context of the loan, or use of a 'threshold' figure (i.e. no default if the event involves less than $ .. million).

If there is a materiality test which does not depend on a single factual test (e.g. a threshold figure), someone must decide if the event is material—should it be the court or the lenders? (See pp. 181–182.)

When considering default clauses, remember to take into account the other provisions of the agreement, particularly representations and warranties and undertakings/covenants.

When considering the likelihood of actual acceleration, look carefully at the mechanism in the loan agreement for making the acceleration decision. This is usually at the end of the default clause. Normally the power is in the hands of the majority banks and often the agent also has the power to accelerate.

Note: 1. The bigger the syndicate, the more difficult and time-consuming for the agent to obtain an acceleration decision.

2. The different sizes and participations of the lending banks will probably give the power of acceleration to a small number of banks who can be identified in advance. Remember that in the last resort the lending banks have to look after their own interests, not those of the borrower.

3. The borrower may be able to take a more realistic view of events of default if the borrower can trust the agent and/or majority banks to act

reasonably. The identity of the banks concerned is most important. However, look also at the assigning clause to see if the identity of the majority banks is likely to change.

It is essential that borrowers ask themselves how competent the administrative machinery of government in their country really is—this is particularly relevant to cross-default and wherever references to governmental agencies are included. The question the borrower must ask itself is: do I have confidence that an efficient mechanism will exist, throughout the life of the loan, for monitoring whether the borrower is meeting its obligations and whether the governmental agencies are doing the same? A realistic answer to that question is absolutely essential. It is most unwise to accept a default clause which is likely to be triggered simply because the borrower cannot find out what is happening in its own governmental machine or cannot control what is happening. Optimism is not enough.

Some sovereign borrowers resist quite conventional protection for lenders on the argument that the clause in question is a limitation on the borrower's sovereign freedom of action or is an insult to the borrower's status as a sovereign body. While some extreme clauses should be resisted on these grounds, experience in the international financial markets indicates that those borrowers who use these arguments most freely give the impression of having insufficient self-confidence and therefore prejudice their own credit standing (and therefore the terms they can negotiate).

I suggest in this chapter that in various circumstances it may be acceptable to a borrower to rely on the lenders to some extent (for example, in allowing lenders to make certain decisions as to whether an event of default has occurred). I also suggest that certain provisions which at first sight might appear to be disadvantageous to borrowers, would in practice be acceptable because, for example, the lenders' overriding intention is that the loan should operate throughout its intended maturity exactly as envisaged during the first negotiations.

This approach is only appropriate if the borrower is dealing with an agent, a group of managers and, to a lesser extent, a syndicate which the borrower has confidence in. Just as borrowers vary in reliability, so banks vary in reliability and may change during the life of a medium-term loan.

As a general principle it is always risky to enter into a contractual arrangement with someone you do not trust, no matter how carefully you negotiate a contract. This is equally true in lending in the Euromarket.

There is no simple way for a borrower to find out which banks are the most reliable. This is a matter of experience and judgment. Borrowers— and in particular first-time borrowers—should use all the information available to them, particularly the experiences of other borrowers who have been in the market for some time, to identify the banks with whom they wish to deal. In a difficult situation, which may be the fault of neither borrower nor lender, a good working relationship matters far more than legal skills.

Application of principles to specific provisions

A specimen clause is attached by way of illustration. Notes have been included against certain paragraphs to indicate possible areas for negotiation and, in particular, qualification.

Materiality tests
The general idea behind most qualifications to events of default is to insert a materiality test. The difficulty with materiality tests which are not simple and factual (e.g. threshold figures), is the uncertainty they can produce at a time (possible default) when it is most important from the borrower's and lenders' point of view that the position should be crystal clear. An objective test (e.g. 'a material adverse effect on the interests of the lenders') can be decided by the court but that will probably be too late, since long before the matter gets to the court either the lenders or the borrower will have had to take a decision in the hope that their own interpretation is right.

The difficulty of deciding what is material is often solved by providing that the agent or the majority banks will decide. At first sight this appears to be very favourable to the lenders and in law that is correct. In practice, however, it will usually operate as a severe restriction on the freedom of the lenders, because no agent with a good reputation will want to be involved publicly in exercising a discretion (to enable acceleration to take place) if there can be any serious argument about the correctness of that discretion's use. This is less true of the exercise of a discretion by the majority banks since several of them would be involved and the effect of publicity would be less. Nevertheless, if the borrower can identify the banks who are likely to form majority banks and if those banks are reputable the mechanism may operate as a real restraint; in any case, it can take time to obtain an opinion from majority banks.

One advantage to the borrower of giving the decision to the agent or majority banks is that until the decision is made, there is no default (this may be helpful for its other loans which include cross-default clauses).

If the powers are given to majority banks, the borrower must be satisfied that, whether as a result of the relationship with the borrower or their standing in the financial markets generally, the majority banks are not likely to make an irresponsible decision.

Governmental agencies

If the loan is made to a sovereign borrower it is likely that the default clause will refer throughout to governmental agencies also. Thus in the cross-default provision (specimen clause (iv)) the wording could provide that an event of default would occur if any indebtedness of the borrower or of any governmental agency should not be paid when due. The inclusion of references to agencies is reasonable if the agencies are so closely linked or identified with the borrower that a significant event (such as default under a loan) occuring to the agency would justify the lenders in concluding that the whole of the borrower's structure was threatened. The exact situation in each country should be considered carefully. If certain governmental agencies are totally independent and it can reasonably be argued that a default on the part of that agency does not reflect on the general credit of the borrower, that agency should not be included.

Bearing these factors in mind, the definition in the loan agreement of 'governmental agencies' must be examined very closely. It is often very difficult to decide whether a default on the part of one of the state organisations can justifiably be said to reflect on the sovereign risk of the borrower. Borrowers should make sure that they do not restrict their freedom of operation too much in the years to come by allowing too wide a definition. On the other hand it is unrealistic to expect lenders to accept a very narrow definition if, say, the bulk of the nation's wealth is generated by one activity, through a state corporation wholly controlled by the government, and the definition does not include that corporation. The exact legal structure of the 'governmental agency' tends to be irrelevant if the performance of that 'agency', on a common sense basis, reflects on the sovereign risk aspect in the eyes of the financial market.

The events in the specimen clause attached fall into certain categories:

(i), (ii) and (iii): These paragraphs—non-payment, breach of undertakings under the loan agreement and breach of representations and warranties—relate specifically to the loan and are primarily matters within the control of the borrower. If the borrower does not meet its obligations the lenders are bound to be concerned.

(iv): cross-default. This is one of the most important provisions in the clause and in the whole agreement. It must be studied extremely carefully and its implications understood. Borrowers should consider what other loans they are likely to have in existence during the life of the loan being negotiated. Is it reasonable that acceleration under the other loans should trigger acceleration under the loan being negotiated? Should the other loans be *actually* accelerated or merely be *capable of* acceleration?

(v)−(xi) inclusive: These are events which are objective facts and tell the lenders that the borrower is in financial trouble. Each one indicates that the borrower is not meeting its obligations. However, it may well be possible to introduce a materiality test in some cases.

(xii)−(xiv) inclusive: These relate to the legal conditions upon which the lenders rightly insist before lending money. It is difficult to justify significant qualifications of these provisions.

(xv)−membership of the International Monetary Fund (IMF): It is usually impractical and, from a borrower's point of view, highly undesirable to include in sovereign loan agreements financial covenants which restrict the borrower's freedom of action in running its country in the way it thinks fit.

Lenders should recognise this and therefore, as a substitute, look to some kind of link with the IMF in the loan agreement since a healthy relationship between the borrower and the IMF is a comfort to lenders as to the way in which the borrower is dealing with its economy. Put in another way, lenders believe that if a sovereign borrower falls out with the IMF something serious is wrong.

Some borrowers believe that even this approach reflects on their political integrity, but while respecting their sensitivity I have never been convinced by this argument.

(xvi)−disposal or transfer of assets: This is only likely to be found in a loan to a government agency with a substantial commercial undertaking. It is reasonable for the lenders to expect the assets against which they have lent to remain within the borrowing agency.However, the borrower must consider carefully whether the wording allows sufficient flexibility for transactions (and possibly reorganisations) which are likely to occur within the life of the loan.

(xvii)−material adverse change: The specimen includes six different versions of what is usually referred to as a 'material adverse change' clause. One theme is common to all the alternatives—a change in the situation which, unlike the previous paragraphs, is not defined at all but which would threaten the position of the lenders. These clauses present considerable problems both to borrowers and to lenders. Borrowers are unable to identify reliably the sort of situation which could produce an acceleration; a situation which could be brought about by something totally outside the borrower's control. Lenders appear to have great flexibility but, for the very same reasons that a borrower cannot decide if the event has occurred, the lenders cannot decide either. Lenders know that an unjustified acceleration can cause real damage to the reputations of those lenders.

The wording of each alternative is different. Note particularly the difference between an extraordinary *situation* (which could be an accumulation of several small events over a long period) and an extraordinary *event,* which is not an accumulation but one single occurrence which produces the threat to the lenders' position. Note also the apparent discretion on the part of the lenders.

The uncertainty produced by any version of this clause makes it undesirable from the borrower's point of view, but a borrower in a weak bargaining position may be able to negotiate a tolerable version.

APPENDIX

*Specimen clause**

Events of default

Each of the following events shall be an Event of Default:

(i) if the Borrower shall fail to pay on the date upon which the same is due and payable pursuant to this Agreement any principal, interest, commitment commission or any other sum payable pursuant to this Agreement;

Note: Days of grace may be added allowing (say) five/seven/ten days for the payment of any sum or (more common) interest only. While Lenders recognise that administrative errors may happen, delaying the receipt of funds by the Agent, Lenders are in a difficult position if the time for payment has passed, nothing has been received and no explanation has been received from the Borrower. During that time (the grace period) Lenders ask themselves: 'Is this an administrative error or has the Borrower insufficient funds to meet its obligations?'. If Lenders allow too long a grace period and the Borrower is unable to pay, Lenders may have allowed other creditors to take some action which would give them an advantage. This is a topic on which many Lenders feel very strongly.

(ii) if the Borrower shall commit any breach of or omit to observe any other of its obligations or undertakings under this Agreement (other than failure to pay any sum due hereunder);

Note: (A) In considering this paragraph it is important to study the obligations/ undertakings in the Agreement. Are there any which would not threaten the Lenders' position if breached? If so, they could be excluded from this paragraph.

(B) This might be qualified by a materiality test, such as one of the following additional phrases:

(a) 'and, in respect of any such breach or omission which is capable of being remedied, such action as the agent may reasonably require has not been taken within 15 days of the Agent despatching notice to the Borrower advising it of such default and of such required action'; or

(b) 'and, in the case of a default which is capable of being remedied, such default continues unremedied for a period of more than 10/21/30 days.'

However, the Lenders can raise reasonable objections to these. During the 're-medy period' Lenders are at risk since if the default is not remedied and a real default situation is revealed, other creditors may have obtained an advantage during the period of, say, 30 days. Nevertheless, borrowers (particularly those who are not absolutely confident of their own governmental administrative competence) should try to obtain a remedy period.

---

*This is merely a collection of typical provisions, to illustrate the principles. It is essential in a real clause to look at the exact words very carefully.

(iii) if any representation or warranty made or deemed to be made by the borrower in or pursuant to this Agreement or in any notice, certificate, instrument or statement contemplated hereby or made or delivered pursuant hereto is incorrect;

Note: A materiality test could be included by adding (for example)
(A) 'in any material respect'; or
(B) 'provided that such event shall not be an Event of Default if in the reasonable opinion of the agent:
(a) such lack of truth or incorrectness has no adverse effect on the Borrower's ability to perform its obligations pursuant to this Agreement; and
(b) the matter which has made such representation or warranty untrue or incorrect is capable of remedy,
unless the Agent shall give notice to the Borrower requiring such matter to be remedied and such matter shall not have been remedied within 20 days of the date of receipt by the Borrower of such notice.'

Warning: If the paragraph includes the following: 'or if any event occurs as a result of which any of such representations or warranties, if deemed to be repeated at any time hereafter with reference to the facts subsisting at the time of such repetition would be untrue or incorrect', it means that the representations and warranties must be true on every day of, say, a ten-year loan. Is this practical? Most Lenders require at least some of the representations and warranties to be repeated during the life of the loan. To do so on a day by day basis is most unwise, since (particularly with a governmental administration which may not be completely efficient) some breach of the original representations and warranties is quite likely. Accordingly, if repetition is confined to, say, the beginning of each interest period, a satisfactory compromise may be achieved; this should be dealt with in the clause containing the representations and warranties.

(iv) any indebtedness of the Borrower shall not be paid when due for payment or shall be found not to have been so paid or becomes capable of being declared due prior to its stated date of payment or if payable on demand shall not be paid when demanded;
Note: (A) Extremely wide meaning of 'indebtedness' may be qualified by substituting 'External Indebtedness'. This must be defined: several alternatives are possible (e.g. currency of debt; residence of debtor). Alternatively (or in addition), the clause can be confined to 'Borrowed Money'.
(B) Note effect of '*capable of* being declared due'. Should Lender A be entitled to accelerate his loan if Lender B (in another loan) is entitled to accelerate that other loan but decides not to do so?
(C) A 'threshold' figure can be used to ensure materiality.
(D) Further qualification is possible by making the clause apply only to indebtedness owed to one or more of the Lenders. Is this reasonable?
The Borrower should try to avoid a cross-default clause which is so wide that it restricts the Borrower's freedom of action over the life of the loan. It is highly desirable to avoid a cross-default clause which extends to a default of the government or Governmental agencies which is not relevant to the sovereign risk aspect.

If the default does not cast doubt (on a common sense basis) on the Borrower's standing in the Euromarket (or, in other words, affect the ability of the Borrower to raise money in the Euromarket on reasonable terms) that default should not be caught by this cross-default clause.

(v) the Borrower declares any general moratorium on its indebtedness;

(vi) any Encumbrance upon the whole or any part of the undertaking or assets of the Borrower becomes enforceable and the person or persons entitled to the benefit thereof shall take steps to enforce the same;

(vii) there shall have occurred the liquidation of the Borrower or any order is made or resolution, law or regulation passed or other action taken for or with a view to such liquidation of the Borrower; *(Government Agency only)*.

(viii) the Borrower petitions or applies to any court, tribunal or other body or authority for the appointment of, or there shall otherwise be appointed, any administrator, receiver, liquidator, trustee or other similar officer of the Borrower or of all or any part of the Borrower's assets; *(Government Agency only)*.

(ix) the Borrower becomes, or is declared by any competent authority to be, insolvent or admits in writing its inability to pay its debts as they fall due or is or becomes subject to or applies for any bankruptcy proceedings; *(Government Agency only)*.

(x) all or any part of the assets of the Borrower are attached or distrained upon or become subject to any order of court or other process and such attachment, distraint, order or process remains in effect and not discharged for[15] days;

(xi) any other event occurs which, under the laws of [Borrowing country] or any other applicable jurisdiction or any political subdivision of either thereof, has an effect equivalent to any of the events referred to in paragraphs (vii) to (x) inclusive of this sub-clause;

(xii) any governmental authorisation, approval or consent necessary for the raising or repayment by the Borrower of the amount to be made available under the Facility on the terms and conditions described in this Agreement or for the payment of interest or other sums as stipulated herein or for any other matter or thing contemplated by this Agreement is withdrawn or modified or is revoked or terminated or expires and is not renewed or otherwise is not in full force and effect;

Note: A qualification can be added by inserting after 'withdrawn or modified' words such as 'in a manner which the agent shall reasonably find to be unacceptable'.

(xiii) this Agreement or any of the provisions hereof shall at any time for any reason cease to be in full force and effect, be declared to be void or shall be repudiated or the validity or enforceability hereof shall at any time be contested by the Borrower or the Borrower shall deny that it has any or any further liability or obligation hereunder;

(xiv) if at any time it is unlawful for the Borrower to perform its obligations hereunder;

(xv) if the Borrower ceases to be a member in good standing of the International Monetary Fund or of any successor (whether corporate or not) which performs the functions of, or functions similar to, those performed by the International Monetary Fund;

(xvi) the Borrower ceases or threatens to cease business as presently conducted or sells, transfers or otherwise disposes of the whole or any substantial part of its property or assets whether by one transaction or a series of transactions, related or not; *(Government Agency only)*.

Note: Flexibility of operation for the Borrower may be achieved by adding (for example) 'otherwise (in any such case) than in connection with the transfer of the whole of the Borrower's business to another agency of [government] acceptable to the Banks which expressly, irrevocably and unconditionally assumes in a manner acceptable to the Banks all of the Borrower's obligations under this agreement'.

(xvii) if an extraordinary situation shall occur which situation gives reasonable grounds to conclude, in the judgment of the Majority Banks, that a material adverse change in the financial condition of the Borrower has occurred;

or an extraordinary situation shall occur, or a change affecting the functions of the Borrower shall occur, which situation or change gives reasonable grounds to conclude, in the judgment of the Agent, that the Borrower will be unable or unwilling to perform or observe in the normal course its obligations under this Agreement;

or there shall occur any material adverse change in the business, assets or condition of the Borrower as of the date hereof as a result of which in the reasonable opinion of the Majority Banks the ability of the Borrower to pay its indebtedness hereunder would be adversely and substantially affected;

or an adverse event or change shall have occurred in the economic or financial situation of the Borrower (including, without limitation, its balance of payments and foreign exchange reserves), from which the Majority Banks shall conclude that the ability of the Borrower to fulfil its obligations under this Agreement has been materially impaired, provided that such an event or change shall not become an Event of Default until 15 days after notice thereof has been given to the Borrower by the Agent or the Majority Banks, during which period the agent shall make a good faith effort to consult with the Borrower concerning the effect of such event or change;

or an extraordinary event or change shall occur affecting the political or economic stability or capabilities of the Borrower which in the reasonable and good faith judgment of the Majority Banks jeopardises the ability of the Borrower to repay the loan when and as required by this Agreement;

or an extraordinary situation shall occur which situation gives reasonable grounds to conclude that a material adverse change in the financial condition of the Borrower has occurred.

The Borrower will notify the Agent forthwith in writing of any occurrence of an Event of Default or any event which, with the giving of notice and/or the lapse of time, may become an Event of Default. The agent may, and shall if it is so requested by the Majority Banks, at any time after the happening of an Event of Default (whether or not it shall have received any such notice), by notice in writing to the Borrower either declare that the undrawn portion of the facility has been cancelled or that the Loan has become forthwith due and repayable or both (either at the same or different times) and in any case that all interest and commitment commission and all other sums payable pursuant to this Agreement have become immediately due and payable whereupon: (a) the undrawn portion of the Facility shall be automatically cancelled and/or (as the case may be) the Loan shall become forthwith due and repayable; and (b) such interest, commitment commission and all other sums shall forthwith become due and payable.

Note: The power to declare the loan payable may be restricted to the Majority Banks (i.e. no power to the Agent generally). A possible (but rare) restriction is to require the agent or Majority Banks, as a first step, to give notice to the Borrower confirming that what has happened is an event falling within any of the above-mentioned events. Only when that confirmation had been given would the Agent or Majority Banks be entitled, as a next step, to declare the Loan payable.

Bond Issue Documentation

BY NICHOLAS WILSON

Historical background

The bond market in Europe commenced in the nineteenth century with issues designed to raise capital for developing countries, notably South American countries and, towards the end of the century, China and Russia. The terms of such issues were commendably short and bonds of this period are now collectors' items. Following World War Two the fairly general imposition of exchange controls rendered the growth of an international bond market impossible. However, in the early sixties the swift growth of US dollar deposits outside the United States resulted in a differential between US domestic and off-shore interest rates. Then, in 1963, the US imposed Interest Equalization Tax and this caused New York, which had been the principal centre for international finance since World War Two, to be no longer attractive to US investors in Yankee bonds or, in consequence, to foreign borrowers. The size of the Eurobond market has grown rapidly: since 1975 alone aggregate Eurocurrency credits have grown from US $28 billion in 1975 (of which Eurobonds were US $8 billion) to US $93 billion in 1980 (of which Eurobonds were responsible for US $13 billion).

Economic background

The essential difference between a Eurobond issue and a Eurocurrency bank credit is the fact that the lender or investor is typically either a retail or institutional investor who wishes to be able to realise the value of the securities quickly—which in effect involves a Stock Exchange listing for the securities—and, since many of the investors live in countries where the payment of tax is regarded as 'unnecessary', it is essential that payments on the bonds can be made in any of several financial centres free of any withholding tax imposed by the country of the borrower. Thus the two most distinguishing features of a bond issue are that the individual bonds are negotiable (and easily movable) and that interest is always paid gross.

Salient features of a Eurobond issue

The most important document in a Eurobond issue is, of course, the prospectus (the comparable document in a Eurocurrency bank credit being the 'information memorandum').

Prospectuses are, however, generally subjected to a higher degree of verification than information memoranda: partly because of the possibility of civil liability to a wide variety of investors; partly as a result of Stock Exchange regulation. The contents of a prospectus for a sovereign borrower are fairly standard although there is no set format: a description of the bonds is, of course, essential, and this is generally followed by a description of the borrower—the country's topography, demography, politics and economy. The latter section would typically consist of an outline of recent economic trends, five-year economic data, total and sectoral Gross Domestic Product (GDP), and details of production and employment with particular emphasis on significant export-oriented industries. Often, too, it would include details of the balance of trade and the terms of trade, balance of payments and other monetary statistics.

The Subscription Agreement—the 'underwriting agreement' in American terminology—is also a crucial document. It contains the 'nuts and bolts' of the issue: the method of issue, the details of the listing application and formalities, the mechanics of closing and settlement, the representations and warranties given by the borrower (and these do repay the time spent on them), the indemnities for liability resulting from inaccuracies or omissions in the prospectus, the responsibility for expenses, *force majeure* (see below) and governing law clauses.

The underwriting and selling group agreements are, at first sight, of little interest to the borrower but since (under English documentation) they may be sent out on behalf of the borrower, they should not be neglected. In particular, the restrictions on sales in various jurisdictions, which are set out in the Selling Group Agreement, ought to concern the borrower; partly (but not solely) because of the importance of the US Securities Act language.

It is not usual for a sovereign borrower to enter into a Trust Deed constituting its external debt. This is largely a matter of pride, although, given the breadth of discretions which UK trustees will accept—and will, in fact, exercise—I believe this may be an error of judgment: it is far better to have a trustee to whom one can turn for, say, a waiver of a technical breach than to risk the consequences of a disgruntled bond-holder seeking to accelerate his bond (and thereby perhaps accelerating other debt too). If there is no Trust Deed then either a Deed Poll (a unilateral declaration of the terms of issue) or a Fiscal Agency Agreement (a Paying Agency Agreement under another name) will be executed.

There are broadly speaking three methods of issue—a 'public' issue, a private placement and a 'bought deal' (the latter being a hybrid). By 'public' one really means 'not private', for there is rarely, if ever, an issue the prospectus for which can be freely distributed everywhere. Samurai, Yankee and Bulldog issues are about the closest one gets. There are varying degrees of private placement: those with a listing where the whole issue is (supposedly) placed 'firm' with a limited number of investors to those where there is no listing and the securities are in very large de-nominations (sometimes US $5 million) and are all taken by one pur-chaser. A 'bought deal' is generally a form of private placement where the principal terms are fixed before the documentation is settled. They are the invention of the devil—although certainly mothered by necessity.

Except in the case of very private placements, a Stock Exchange listing is nearly always essential. Many investors cannot purchase unlisted secur-ities and for sovereign borrowers the requirements are not onerous. London listing requirements for sovereign borrowers are less onerous than those of the Luxembourg Stock Exchange. Cost comparisons should always be made—not only on the initial listing fee but over the expected life of the issue.

One of the principal differences in documentation required between London and Luxembourg Stock Exchanges is the prevalence in London of the 'exchange telegraph card'. If there is a prospectus, an exchange telegraph card is needed as well, although there is now a tendency (in the case of AAA borrowers) to place securities on the basis of an exchange telegraph card alone, relying on the availability of statistical information in the Extel system to supplement the potential investors' knowledge. This is appropriate for borrowers such as Sweden, who have a large number of issues listed in London and who maintain an up to date 'service card', but it is not appropriate for a 'first-time borrower' in the London market. In the case of the Luxembourg Stock Exchange, frequent borrowers can avail themselves of the 'succinct' prospectus arrangements.

Special problems

Bearer documents

As mentioned, bearer documents are negotiable instruments and every precaution must be taken to ensure their safety from the moment of printing to the moment of delivery. Partly because of this security aspect and also partly because of the sheer volume of moving paper in such quantities, the emergence of clearing houses such as Euroclear and Cedel was inevitable. These enable the bonds to be held in depot and transactions to take place by the crediting and debiting of accounts rather than the physical movement of paper.

Not infrequently 'global bonds' are used. These are a temporary measure with one bond representing the whole issue and containing an undertaking to deliver definitive bonds in the appropriate denomination not later than a specified date. In this way printing problems can be alleviated.

Differences between US and UK styles of underwriting

A comparison of US and UK underwriting agreements might, at first sight, lead one to suppose that the transactions contemplated are entirely different. But, although for a variety of historical reasons the structure of these agreements is different, the effect is the same. Thus in London it is traditional for issuing houses which act as managers of an issue to accept joint and several liability for taking up the whole issue; in New York, because of the capital requirements of the New York Stock Exchange, it is traditional for each manager, and indeed each underwriter, to accept liability only for its underwriting obligation. Again, in London the primary obligation of the managers is to offer, on behalf of the borrower, the securities to a selling group; in New York the underwriters purchase the securities and the managers then re-sell them on behalf of the underwriters.

United States Securities Act of 1933

This Act dominates the terms on which Eurobonds—principally those denominated in United States dollars—can be sold.

Essentially the Securities Act prohibits the purchase by US nationals or residents, or purchases within the United States of 'unregistered' securities. Since the whole rationale for the Eurodollar market is to remain free from national regulation, it is crucial that issues are made in a manner which does not require registration. Thus virtually all Eurodollar selling group agreements contain elaborate restrictions designed to ensure that there is compliance with the Securities Act. There are circumstances in which bonds can be issued in the States without registration requirements: if offers are made to a limited number of individuals—say up to 40—in large lots, and such offers are limited to 'sophisticated institutional investors'. However, if a US private placement is contemplated it will almost certainly be necessary to have a 90-day 'lock-up', i.e. an arrangement pursuant to which no investor in the securities can receive definitive documents of title until 90 days after 'completion of the distribution' and then only against certification that he is not a US person (or that he has signed an investment letter).

It is perhaps worth mentioning that the World Bank is, in my view, undoubtedly a US person as that term is defined in virtually all selling group agreements. The World Bank itself takes the view that it is not a US person (i.e. not subject to US law) but this is not quite the same thing.

Stabilisation, over-allotment and price control

One of the more arcane provisions in Eurobond subscription agreements is that relating to stabilisation and over-allotment. In bald terms this is 'rigging the market', the purpose being to ensure that the initial secondary market prices of the bonds are truly reflective of the market forces and are not being distorted (generally downwards) as a result of sales by selling group members who have taken bonds merely in order to receive the selling group commission. It is important to establish that any stabilisation or over-allotment is done by the managers for their own account or for the account of the underwriters: it should never be paid for by the borrower.

Trustee or fiscal agent

'Trustee' and 'fiscal agent' are not different titles for the same creature: the trustee is a corporate representative of the *bondholders* who has a collateral but direct covenant from the borrower which he can enforce in his own name in addition to the direct covenant of the borrower on the face of the bonds. There is some debate as to whether the covenant on the bonds or in the trust deed is the primary covenant but the better view is that the trustee has a secondary covenant. By contrast, the fiscal agent is the agent of the *borrower* and as such is a wholly inappropriate person, however reputable, to exercise discretions or functions on behalf of the bondholders.

Here again there is a difference between English and American practice. An American trustee would almost invariably be a bank which actually received the principal and interest on the bonds and disbursed the funds through its own branches or other paying agents. Thus the payment to the trustee would fully discharge the borrower and any subsequent insolvency of the trustee or paying agents would be at the risk and for the account of the bondholders. Under English practice, by contrast, the trustee would only receive principal and interest from the borrower if there had been a default. Moreover, an English trust deed is so worded that a payment to the principal paying agent only discharges the borrower for so long as the funds remain available for collection by bondholders, with the effect that if the principal paying agent became insolvent the covenant would remain unsatisfied *pro tanto* and the borrower would have to pay the balance again.

Another difference worth mentioning is that in England, for historical reasons, the clearing banks have been reluctant to enter the corporate trustee business since one of their number was severely criticised (almost 50 years ago) for the conflict of interest which existed by virtue of it being both trustee and principal banker for a borrower. As a result, trustees in England tend to be insurance companies or, in one case, an independent trust corporation: the Law Debenture Corporation.

English trust law does have the merit of being extremely flexible and, as indicated above, English trustees are prepared to use their discretions sensibly—provided always, of course, that they have an adequate indemnity in the trust deed. In the United States trustees are always looking over their shoulders for fear of being attacked by their beneficiaries and thus are anxious not to have discretions or, if they have them, not to exercise them.

Force majeure clauses

So far as I know, *force majeure* clauses in their present form only became prevalent in Eurocurrency subscription agreements in the sixties. One's first reaction as a borrower is to bridle at the prospect of agreeing to pay underwriting commission in circumstances where the underwriters can be excused performance of their obligations for *force majeure,* but the reality is that, in the international context, underwriters are not underwriting exceptional risks but merely temporary aberrations within the market. It is to the credit of the Eurodollar market that I know of only one occasion —during the Six Days' War—where a *force majeure* clause has been exercised. The moral of this experience is that the damage which managers do to their reputation by invoking *force majeure* clauses far outweighs the incremental goodwill with other underwriters which accrues to them. Thus such clauses are not, in practice, as awesome and unilateral as they at first appear.

If a *force majeure* clause is to be included it is not unreasonable for a sovereign borrower (in contradistinction to an industrial borrower) to expect to be involved in the determination as to whether *force majeure* exists. Thus a reasonable *force majeure* clause might read as follows:

Notwithstanding anything herein contained, the Lead Manager on behalf of the Managers, (*after prior consultation with the Borrower if practicable*), may, by notice to the Borrower given at any time before the time on the Closing Date when payment of the subscription moneys would otherwise be due to the Borrower, terminate this Agreement if in the opinion of the Managers there shall have been such a change in national or international financial, political or economic conditions or currency exchange rates or exchange controls as would be likely to prejudice materially the success of the proposed issue of the Bonds. Upon such notice being given, the parties hereto shall (except as otherwise specifically provided) be released and discharged from their respective obligations under or pursuant to this Agreement.

The words in italics will be strongly resisted by most managers on the grounds that it is managers alone who should take the decision and that they should not be expected to risk delay in reaching a decision by being obliged to consult the borrower—indeed, the very circumstances may preclude such consultation. *A fortiori* they will resist any attempt to make the decision bilateral.

It is to be observed that US underwriting agreements often contain, in effect, not one, but two *force majeure* clauses. The traditional US provision is that if underwriters whose underwriting participations exceed 20 per cent of the issue, fail to pay at the closing, then all underwriters are excused. The corollary is that if underwriters whose participations amount to less than 10 per cent fail to pay, then the non-defaulting underwriters will 'step up' *pro tanto*. It will be appreciated that this clause gives, in effect, a unilateral right to terminate the underwriting agreement not to the managers but to any sizeable group of underwriters. Accordingly, any attempt to impose a traditional European *force majeure* clause in addition should be strongly resisted.

Negative pledges

It is in this field that one of the most marked differences occurs between syndicated loans and Eurobonds: banks, quite rightly, worry about the creation of *any* security interest which ranks ahead of their own unsecured lending. The managers of Eurobond issues, on the other hand, are more concerned about the comparative rating of other securities issued by the same borrower in the same market. There is a measure of reason in this approach but it inevitably leads to anomalies. As a result, both Eurobond issue managers and sovereign borrowers tend to settle for a negative pledge which only prohibits the creation of listed secured indebtedness denominated or payable in a currency other than the domestic currency of the borrower. Typical such negative pledge clauses read as follows:

The Borrower will undertake that it will not at any time while any of the Bonds are outstanding, secure or permit to be secured any External Indebtedness of the Borrower or any guarantee of any External Indebtedness of any other person by any mortgage, lien, pledge or other charge upon any of its present or future assets or revenues, without at the same time according to the Bonds the same security or such other security as may be approved by an Extraordinary Resolution of the holders of the Bonds. 'External Indebtedness' means all indebtedness which is expressed in, or capable of being discharged by payment of, a currency other than the national currency of the Borrower and which is payable to a non-resident of the Borrower.

The Borrower will not create any mortgage, pledge or other charge upon the whole or any part of its present or future revenues or assets to secure any External Indebtedness without securing the outstanding Bonds *pari passu* therewith and the instrument creating any such mortgage, pledge or other charge shall expressly provide therefor. 'External Indebtedness' means Indebtedness which is expressed or denominated in a currency or currencies other than the currency of the Borrower, or which is, at the option of the person entitled thereto, payable in a currency or currencies other than the currency of the Borrower.

The Borrower will not at any time while any of the Bonds are outstanding secure (i) any loan or other indebtedness which is in the form of, or represented by, bonds, debentures or other securities denominated in, or conferring an option on the holder for payment in, any currency other than the Borrower's currency and which is for the time being quoted, listed or dealt in on any Stock Exchange or other market on which such securities are ordinarily dealt in any part of the world, or (ii) any guarantee of any such loan or other indebtedness, by any mortgage, lien, pledge or other charge upon any of its present or future assets or revenues without at the same time according to the Bonds to the satisfaction of the Trustee the same security as is granted to such loan, indebtedness or guarantee or (at the option of the Borrower) providing other security reasonably equivalent thereto which is acceptable to the Trustee or approved by an Extraordinary Resolution.

Grossing up clauses

As mentioned above, a typical grossing up clause should ensure merely that the holders of the bonds are not subjected to a withholding tax imposed on payments of interest on the bonds simply by reason of the identity of the *borrower*. This simple statement does, however, become more lengthy when transposed into precise legal language which has universal applicability. One has to remember that because of the bearer nature of the bonds, reliance cannot be placed on double tax conventions. Moreover, one must also remember that there may be local withholding taxes, i.e. those imposed in the place of payment, for which the borrower should not assume responsibility. This can occur inadvertently as a result of loose wording of the tax clause.

Within the UK there is such a withholding tax which is levied on all payments of interest to UK residents. Thus, if a foreign resident presents a coupon in London he will only be paid gross upon production of an affidavit of non-residence. To ensure that this requirement can be enforced it is necessary to see that the 'payments' clause provides that payments will be made 'subject to applicable laws and regulations'.

Stamp duty

Stamp duty tends to be of decreasing importance in most jurisdictions but it is a consideration which should be on everyone's checklist.

Paying agency agreements

It is essential to remember that paying agents are invariably the agents of the borrower and not of the bondholders. Nevertheless, they are very much at arm's length with the borrower and the commissions payable for their services are becoming increasingly competitive. Possibly of greater importance is the point of time at which the principal paying agent requires to be put in funds. In my view there is no case for any paying agent asking for payment in New York earlier than the day before the due date for payment. It is worth pointing out that the cost of making a payment of interest on US $20 million 15 per cent bonds one day early is in excess of $8,000 (or over 40 cents a coupon), whereas the typical commission structure for payment of coupons would provide for payment of 2.5 per mille—$7,500 for the whole issue!

It is worth mentioning that Morgan Guaranty are now offering 'sealed bond arrangements', which are an ingenious attempt at surmounting the volume of paper problem referred to earlier. Pursuant to these arrangements Morgan Guaranty undertake to keep the bonds in sealed packages throughout the life of the issue and to disburse the interest received to their various account holders without cutting off the relevant coupons and against an indemnity in favour of the borrower for any loss occasioned by the misappropriation of uncut coupons. The purpose of such arrangement is to cut down the cost to borrowers of physical presentation when Morgan Guaranty knows from experience that approximately 60 per cent of each issue will remain in their vaults forever.

The paying agency agreement should also deal with cancellation and destruction of bonds—an important consideration because of the bearer nature of the securities. Such securities should never be transported 'live' if this can be avoided and certainly it can be avoided once the bonds and coupons have been paid.

Events of default

Events of default in bond issues are broadly similar to those contained in syndicated loan agreements. The one possible exception—to which I am strongly opposed—is that the cross-default clause only relates to defaults on listed external indebtedness. There is, in my view, no justification for this.

Legal Aspects of Project Finance: The Borrower's View

BY J. SPEED CARROLL

The first thing a borrower needs to know about project finance is that it is neither a miracle, a panacea nor a free lunch. The second key point, almost as important, is that project finance transactions are exceptionally complicated, time-consuming and difficult to put together. The benefits outweigh the frustrations only because the projects themselves are of such crucial importance to their sponsors that it is deemed essential that the new facilities be financed in one way or another.

There are many variations in the definition of 'project finance'. Sometimes it is used to mean only 'the financing of a project', regardless of the techniques employed. Most definitions, however, emphasise a difference in the types of credit looked to by the lenders. Project lenders will rely, at least in the first instance, on the assets and prospective cash flow of the project being financed, whereas lenders in conventional transactions apply different (and much more traditional) tests of creditworthiness. Make no mistake: the creditworthiness is still there, or at least it is supposed to be. The hard part is the analysis: finding each element of the credit and deciding whether, when everything is put together, the resulting structure is solid or full of holes.

Although the specific subject of this paper is the legal aspects of project finance, any overemphasis on the role that lawyers play in such transactions should be avoided. Working on project financing is very much a team effort, with each participating specialist—banker, businessman, engineer and lawyer—making a significant contribution to the overall financing package.

This said, what is the area of primary responsibility for the lawyers working on project finance transactions? First of all, the legal specialist performs background legal research (particularly on host country laws and optimum forms of investment and corporate organisation), the results of which affect the structure of the project. Subsequently, he or she works on the drafting and negotiation of the basic loan agreement and related financing documents. To put a somewhat finer point on it, the lawyer's principal task is the preparation of documentation that deals (as effectively as possible) with the commercial risks of a loan transaction that is inherently complicated because of the fact that, in a traditional sense, there is no fully creditworthy borrower in the picture. In consequence, the lawyer's role may be somewhat more crucial in project finance than in conventional loan transactions. The borrower must understand that, since 'project finance' lenders are, by definition, willing to trade established notions of balance-sheet and operating statement creditworthiness for a stack of contracts, economic studies and government approvals, some additional legal time and trouble must necessarily be required. This extra effort will establish the workability and coherence of the entire set of agreements and other documents affecting the project.

A few words should be said about the examination of this subject 'from the borrower's viewpoint'. This chapter attempts to do just that, but it would be misleading to suggest that there exists a substantial difference between the analyses undertaken by the borrower and the lenders. The preceding paragraph, for example, describes tasks that are initially allocated to the attorneys representing the lenders. The legal advisers of the borrower must, however, collaborate in the research, helping it along and ultimately confirming it; once the initial draft documents are prepared they will, of course, be negotiated with the borrower's lawyers as well as with the borrower itself. This process cannot be either effective or constructive unless there is a good understanding on each side, of what the lenders' requirements and objectives are, and of what characteristics must be possessed by the final project financing structure in order to be acceptable to the participating banks.

Problems of project documentation

A substantial portion of the time devoted to project finance is spent discussing risks and risk analysis—political risks, delays in completion, cost overruns, and so on. There are at least as many ways of grouping risks as there are project loan officers, but it is helpful in analysing problems of project documentation and project structure to use a simple, two-category breakdown in the first instance: that of commercial versus non-commercial risks.

By 'commercial' is meant risks associated with the out-of-pocket cash costs and the in-pocket cash sale prices experienced by the productive facility in the ordinary course of its business, both in connection with its construction and during the loan payout period.

'Non-commercial' means everything else. In other words, this category would subsume casualty loss, political risks such as expropriation or currency inconvertibility, the risk of incompetent management, and what may be called 'technical' or 'technological' (e.g. an inadequate natural resource base, in an extractive industry project; or a poor process design in a manufacturing project).

Risks in the 'non-commercial' category tend to encompass more or less catastrophic occurrences; they are not particularly susceptible of being dealt with by negotiated agreements and legal draftsmanship. (One may provide, for example, that it is an event of default if the LNG plant fails to liquefy the natural gas, or fails to do so at its rated capacity. It's not much comfort to anyone, however, since at that point both borrower and lender are in deep trouble.) In other words, warranting that a factory will work or that there are so many tons of ore in the ground does not make it so, and if it is not so, the appropriateness of the entire project finance concept, as applied to that particular project, may be called into question.

Since legal documentation does not deal very effectively with risks of this 'non-commercial' character, not a great deal will be said about them. Most risks of this nature are dealt with by some type of private or governmental insurance. Where insurance against these risks is unavailable or unduly expensive, it becomes necessary to revert from a 'pure' project finance approach and seek out some traditional form of security, sponsor guarantees being the most typical example. In the technical and technological area, the only real security comes from the engineers, geologists or other technical personnel who prepared the feasibility study, did the process design, and so on. More precisely, it might be said that the 'security' results from one's belief in the professional skills of the technical personnel; the checks and double checks of the outside consultants who reached the favourable conclusions that permitted the project to go forward in the first place.

In a few cases, the technical foundations may be supported by supplemental arrangements, such as 'make-up' agreements whereby a shortfall in production at the project site is compensated by make-up quantities furnished from another location operated by the owner or one of the project sponsors. On occasion, these 'make-up' agreements may involve problems of negotiation or draftsmanship that require innovative solutions, but the lawyer's role in the technical areas will, in most cases, consist primarily of seeing that: (i) the technical evaluations being relied upon are properly incorporated into the overall project loan documentation, and (ii) the consequences of erroneous or inadequate evaluations are fully spelled out.

Turning now to the commercial risk elements, it is helpful to look at the legal techniques available for use, and the current issues and problems being faced, under four distinct categories:

1. Construction and equipment cost.
2. Raw material and energy cost.
3. Operating cost over time.
4. Output sale price.

Construction and equipment cost

Most of the recent anguish in international project finance has arisen under this rubric. In the most brutal terms, how can lenders be expected to finance a project if no one knows what it will cost? The whole point of project finance is looking to the economics of the project itself—overruns of 100 per cent or more make a mockery of the original feasibility studies relied upon by the lenders; yet what is to be done? More often than not, the only rational course of action open to lenders is to 'throw good money after bad'. A project three-quarters complete may be essentially valueless. Better to come up with completion money and salvage something (or so the reasoning goes), than to write off the full amount of the currently outstanding loans.

However compelling this analysis may be once one is in the predicament, surely it is preferable to avoid it if possible. The large sums identified as 'contingency' in the typical feasibility study budget are hardly an adequate answer to the problem. Theoretically, it should be possible to eliminate risk entirely on construction and equipment costs by the simple expedient of entering into fixed-price contracts for procurement of the productive facilities. In the real world, however, it has become almost inconceivable that a reputable prime contractor would undertake the construction of a major automotive factory, natural gas liquefaction plant or aluminium smelter on a straight fixed-price basis. In many situations, it is questionable whether this kind of certainty, even if achievable, would be worth the price. Certainly any contractor quoting a delivered price on a major facility still in the feasibility study stage will take care to include contingencies upon contingencies, thus escalating, perhaps needlessly, overall project costs.

Worse yet, a contractor legally bound to an unrealistically low contract price may simply abandon the project rather than absorb the losses which its completion would entail. Although some sort of legal redress may be available in such situations, the real costs to the project's sponsors in terms of lost time and opportunity, plus the additional completion costs, may in the aggregate far exceed the defaulting prime contractor's ability to pay.

This said, it may nevertheless be possible to achieve much greater cost security to the borrower than has been the case with the traditional cost-plus approach, which provides little if any incentive to the contractor to stay within budgeted estimates. In some projects, for example, it may be possible to convert a cost-plus contract to a fixed-price basis after the contractor has had six months or a year to work on actual project procurement; the overall financing plan would not be finalised until that point. Perhaps even more important in controlling construction and equipment costs is the imposition on project procurement of appropriate legal structures and reporting requirements. A typical manufacturing project might, for example, include the following distinct operations, all of which are essential to the establishment of a properly functioning industrial complex: (i) transfer of technology by licence and/or technical assistance agreement; (ii) plant and process conception and design; (iii) site study, acquisition and preparation; (iv) construction of buildings; (v) procurement or supply of production machinery and equipment; (vi) installation of machines and equipment; (vii) plant organisation; (viii) initial (individual) equipment tests; (ix) overall plant performance tests; (x) preparation of operating and maintenance manuals; (xi) hiring of plant personnel; (xii) training of plant personnel; and (xiii) initial plant production management.

Each such operation consists in turn of countless sub-operations and the effective coordination of all aspects is an almost absolute precondition of success. The more these functions are divided up among varying contractors, consultants and project sponsors, the more difficult it will be to determine just who is responsible for doing what, how and when it will be done, and how it will be paid for. Indeed, the problems of coordination in complex projects probably explain the popularity of the 'turnkey' approach to project contracting. While it is hardly ever possible to include all facets of a major project in one contract, as the arrangement tends toward that ideal, the tasks of coordination are shifted from the project's sponsors to the prime contractor, and it becomes much easier to allocate responsibility for successful project completion and budgetary compliance.

This 'unity of responsibility' created by the turnkey concept also facilitates compliance with periodic progress reporting requirements that may be imposed both by lenders and the project sponsors. If the developments that may result in massive overruns are spotted soon enough, it may be possible to make design or scope changes which will minimise their impact. At the very least, the borrower, the lenders and the project sponsors should have sufficient data on hand to permit them to isolate the problem areas early and then to make rational decisions about the implications of specific overruns.

All too often, the unavailability of relevant information has allowed a project to drift until at some point it has become painfully obvious that, say, the project is half complete but two-thirds of the money has been spent. By that time it may be too late to do anything other than put up the additional funds required to complete the project. In consequence, it may never be fully known whether the excess costs resulted from: (i) higher than anticipated costs for raw materials, energy or transportation; (ii) excess labour costs; (iii) voluntary changes in project scope or definition by the owner; (iv) poor initial project design requiring subsequent modification; (v) accidental omission of important project elements in initial project definition and budgeting; (vi) intentional submission by contractors of unrealistically low figures as an inducement to sales; or (vii) some combination of these factors and variants thereof. Such a state of affairs is neither in the interest of the borrower nor the lenders.

In past years, not a great deal of attention has been paid in project loan documentation to procedures for periodic progress reporting, verification and control. The current situation, in which cost overruns abound and few participants seem to have any precise idea why, makes it likely that the area of project control will receive much more attention in the future.

The difficulties experienced in connection with construction costs—and they are many—explain the emphasis that is often placed on so-called 'completion guarantees' or covenants to provide overrun financing. Again, the borrower should understand that this is an effort by the lenders and the others responsible for structuring the transaction to back up the non-recourse project approach with something a bit more tangible: the guarantee or undertaking of an established, creditworthy party. Although the transaction may still be off balance sheet (more or less)—and thus the effort is still worthwhile—we are back in safe, familiar banking territory.

To summarise, then, this very long section on construction cost, it may be said that a quite significant part of the overall project evaluation has to do with how legally sound the buyer-seller contractual arrangements are. It is the borrower's job to get the best legal terms possible, as well as the best price and the best technology. Although the lenders and their counsel cannot usurp the borrower's function in negotiating appropriate turnkey, construction or equipment purchase contracts, neither can they entirely wash their hands of such matter.

If these basic contracts are well constructed there is a considerably greater possibility that the project itself will be well constructed.

Raw material and energy supply cost

In a manufacturing context, it is often the case that the cost of raw materials (including energy) will be an important factor in the financial viability of the overall project. Where that is so, it is sometimes thought advisable to lock in a guaranteed supply of the crucial materials at a known price, or at one which fluctuates only within tolerable limits. This may be easier said than done. The exceptionally wide price swings in ocean transportation and basic raw materials which have been encountered in recent years have made both sellers and buyers wary of predicting what a 'fair' price will be over a period of ten or 20 years. While market fluctuations remained within a relatively narrow band over substantial periods of time, it was perfectly reasonable to trade security of purchase and sale prices against the possibility that either buyer or seller at any particular time might have done somewhat better in the spot market. In many areas, it has now become all too apparent that a long-term price may turn out to be not simply disadvantageous, but ruinous in light of subsequent market considerations. In consequence, there is now a far greater acceptance than in the past of concepts such as periodic renegotiation, price indexing and automatic escalation.

While these devices obviously diminish price predictability from the standpoint of the lender and financial analyst, it is possible that without them there would be no long-term supply commitment whatsoever. In some cases, it may be that the existence of an assured supply of raw materials is even more crucial than the price at which they are acquired. More generally, it is to be hoped that a judicious combination of price floors, ceilings, maximum percentage deviations and formula escalation will ultimately produce a selling price that represents a reasonably fair long-term compromise of the conflicting interests of buyers and sellers in an erratic marketplace. Since complicated approaches of this sort are of relatively recent vintage, experience has not yet shown how well the theoretical models will work in practice.

In isolated circumstances, particularly where separate projects can, in effect, be vertically integrated, there may still exist some scope for more traditional long-term supply contracts. A mine may, for example, be financeable if it is assured an ore price of at least US $10 per ton during its first ten years of operation. Similarly, it may be possible to build and finance a smelter for the mine's ore if there are adequate guarantees that the ore price to the smelter will not exceed US $15 per ton during the first ten years of its operation. A mutually advantageous symbiotic relationship between mine and smelter may thus be established which can, at least in principle, be completely divorced from market realities during the loan payout period.

Operating cost

Not very many projects will succeed or fail on the basis of successful control of operating cost over time (assuming that raw material and energy cost is excluded from operating cost as in this analysis). Although some other factors enter in, the main item here is labour cost. Obviously the deleterious effect of a marked increase in local wage rates will be of much more consequence in labour intensive industries than in those which tend to be capital intensive. Local labour cost may be absolutely determinative, for example, in the case of a large, non-mechanised agricultural or 'agribusiness' project, whereas a high-technology refinery employing relatively few persons, many of whom are highly skilled, may be able to withstand multiple wage increases without difficulty simply because its total payroll cost is in any event very small in proportion to the value of its production.

Where labour cost is found to be a significant factor, it is likely that an agency of the local government will be among the sponsors for just that reason: the project will provide more jobs. Thus it may be possible to contemplate entering into side agreements for government wage subsidies, for example, to take effect if generalised extraordinary wage increases were to jeopardise the delicate balance of the project's economics. In an appropriate case, the existence of some such standby arrangement for wage stability might be the final element necessary to convince lenders that the project is appropriate for project finance treatment, since it would indeed be able to stand on its own two feet in the face of any reasonably foreseeable contingency.

Sale of project output

The first three sections of this analysis of commercial risks deal with threats to the project in its early life. Like the young of most species, a project is particularly vulnerable before it has entered into its productive phase: lots of debt is outstanding, time is running out and no cash flow stream is yet available to offset the twin problems of added costs and missed deadlines.

It is, however, only after a project reaches its operational stage that most of the familiar 'project finance' security features come into play. A key aspect of many such financings is, for example, an offtake agreement or long-term sale agreement relating to the project's output. One or more of the project's sponsors may be among the purchasers, but whether or not this is the case, the purchasers will certainly be well established and creditworthy, and preferably multinational so as to insulate the project's financial standing from the vagaries of a single national economy.

Indeed, the principal 'security' that the lenders have in many project loans is an assignment of, or beneficial interest in, the cash flow generated by the project's sale of its output to its long-term purchasers. Often the purchaser's obligation is of the 'take-or-pay' variety, particularly where it is the existence of the long-term purchase commitments that makes possible the financing of the project. Reduced to its simplest terms, take-or-pay means that the purchaser is subject to an absolute and unqualified obligation to make periodic payments in a minimum amount (usually enough to cover debt service including scheduled amortisation), whether or not the purchaser actually accepts delivery of the project's output.

In practice, however, there may be some exceptions to the hell-or-high-water type of absolute purchase obligation. The question of *force majeure* is, for example, treated in a variety of ways. But whatever may be the specific parameters of a particular transaction, the purpose is always the same: to guarantee, insofar as possible, to the project lenders a level of project sales that will be adequate to retire the debt on schedule. Long-term and (relatively) absolute purchase obligations of this sort are said to be 'financeable', and it is probable that many existing projects would still be looking for financing were it not for the techniques of assignment of sales proceeds to a trustee that have been developed, which can be coupled with a lender's belief in the purchaser's ability and willingness to make the required payments on schedule. The borrower's initial reaction may be to resist imposing such heavy legal obligations on the purchasers of its product. Some flexibility is possible, but it would be unwise to go too far in that direction, lest the banks deem the obligation no longer financeable.

Much of the attention in the negotiation of project finance transactions is focused on the take-or-pay obligations, which is only natural, since the assignment of benefits under such agreements will provide the principal security available to lenders in most cases. The fact that such obligations may stretch out over substantial debt amortisation periods also empha-sises their importance. It should be pointed out, however, that the sale on a take-or-pay basis is the converse of the fixed-price raw material purchase situation, so that all the previously discussed problems of price definition over long periods of time are equally present.

The serious question to be answered here is whether a fixed price purchase obligation can really be relied upon over the long term if the contract price ceases to be realistic in the light of subsequent develop-ments. However legally airtight the documentation may be, an agreement which obliges one party to sell or purchase a commodity over long periods at a price which is at marked variance with that established by the marketplace is subject to very great strains indeed. It could be that one dark day the whole arrangement will begin to come apart at the seams. In consequence, the major challenge facing practitioners in this field is that of devising price formulae which will retain sufficient 'certainty' to satisfy project lenders while incorporating enough flexibility to meet the needs of both buyers and sellers in an increasingly volatile international market-place.

Problems of financial documentation

The techniques and documents discussed thus far relate to the financial health and soundness of a project, and so they may properly be categorised as 'project finance' materials. There exists, however, a further group of documents which have an even closer connection to the financial aspects of the project as such. The following items constitute a representative, if not necessarily exhaustive, listing of what must be dealt with in a particular situation.

Types of documents

Loan and credit agreements—sources. Here the most remarkable factor is the quite surprising variety of fund sources that may be tapped in connection with the realisation of a single project. It is well to bear in mind that project construction and operating funds in a single project may be provided in the form of borrowings or finance of any or all of the following types: (i) loans from international agencies, the World Bank and regional development banks; (ii) commercial bank loans; (iii) loans from project sponsors; (iv) purchaser credits; (v) supplier credits; (vi) governmental export credits; (vii) host country local currency credits.

One very important recent development in this area is that variously referred to as co-financing, cooperative financing or complementary financing. This cooperative approach to international project lending was originally worked out between the public international development banks and representatives of the lead managers of the private bank syndicates that are from time to time called upon to make loans in support of the public banks' projects. The basic idea is to tie the syndicate loan (which is made on ordinary commercial terms) very closely to the development bank loan, with the expectation of bringing it under the protective 'umbrella' that has always been thought to be possessed by the World Bank and similar institutions.

These co-financing transactions take one of two forms; the simpler being that worked out with the World Bank and Asian Development Bank. In these cases, the development bank makes available to the private bank syndicate all or most of its internally-generated project evaluation reports and materials. This type of information (and the continuing follow-up supervision that goes with it) has not previously been available to private banks, and its preparation by, or on behalf of, a typical Eurodollar loan syndicate would be both impractical and prohibitively expensive. Moreover, the development bank includes default on the syndicate loan as one of the events of default under its own loan, and the two transactions are closely linked in other ways, such as by having the development bank serve as collection agent for principal and interest payments made by the borrower with respect to the syndicated Eurodollar loan. Although the development bank would, of course, have the option of not declaring a default on its loan even though payments ceased to be made on the private loan, it is nevertheless felt that the two loans are intertwined closely enough to permit a significant reduction in the rate that would otherwise be quoted to the borrower, simply because of the greater security achieved.

The approach worked out with the Inter-American Development Bank (IADB), called complementary financing, is even more innovative. Many of the features are the same, but instead of a syndicate loan made in conjunction with a development bank loan, the IADB makes two loans: one on its own usual form, at a fixed rate; and the other on a form prepared by the IADB for use by a syndicate of commercial banks, containing the usual commercial Eurodollar floating rate provisions. Immediately after the loans are made, the IADB sells a 100 per cent participation, on a non-recourse basis, to the commercial bank syndicate which actually negotiated the loan in the first place. Thus the IADB is the *named* lender, but the full economic impact of the loan is on the syndicate. Under this system, it seems that the 'umbrella' is virtually leakproof, in that any default on the Eurodollar loan must be viewed as a default vis-a-vis the IADB, since it is not only collection agent but also the lender of record named in the Eurodollar loan agreement. As these approaches become better known, their popularity will probably soar, and we will see a great deal more capital for projects in developing countries being mobilised on this basis. Co-financing has the singular advantage of providing something to each participant that it cannot achieve in any other manner.

Turning now to the loan agreement, the obvious point is that it is the basic document around which everything else is hinged. A brief discussion of its contents appears as the final portion of this chapter. There are, however, several other project finance documents with which the novice borrower and its lawyers may be somewhat less familiar. It is useful to consider these collateral agreements first, so that the way they fit into the overall structure can be understood when the terms and conditions of the loan agreement are analysed. These include:

Inter-creditor agreements. These are of no direct consequence to the borrower, since it will not be a party. The borrower should, however, be aware that such agreements are often required because there are so many lenders from so many countries supporting the project on so many different sets of terms and conditions. The inter-creditor agreement is essentially a procedural document, spelling out such matters as: (i) how future consents, waivers or amendments are to be obtained or ratified, as among the members of the lending group; (ii) what percentage in interest of the total amount of loans is required to authorise an action which will affect all lenders (e.g. declaration of default); (iii) the extent, if any, to which all lenders will participate in the security of an asset seized by one of them, and so on. In brief, this document represents an attempt to deal with trouble before it has arisen. Although the borrower does not sign it, it is the borrower's need for funds from diverse sources that gives rise to its existence.

The next two items may conveniently be considered together. They are: *Investment Agreement*, and *Joint Venture Agreement.* These are similar in nature and purpose to the loan and inter-creditor agreements, but with reference to equity investment. In other words, an investment agreement would be entered into between the project's sponsors and a group of equity investors in order to evidence the obligation of the investors to furnish specified quantities of capital to the project according to a predetermined schedule. As with a loan agreement, the obligation to advance equity capital will normally be conditional upon satisfactory fulfilment by the sponsors of a series of conditions precedent.

The equity counterpart of an inter-creditor agreement could be called an inter-investor agreement or an agreement among investors, but the most probable appelation is the familiar catch-all of joint venture agreement. Whatever its name, such an agreement would regulate procedural matters such as voting rights within the equity investors' group, assertion of claims or defences vis-à-vis the host government, and similar matters. Where it is contemplated that the equity participants will play an active part in the business of the project, there may be an allocation of operational responsibilities set out in the joint venture agreement, and subjects such as the investors' obligations to second personnel to the project staff may also be dealt with.

Obviously neither category of equity agreement will exist where the project is wholly owned by the host government, but some projects are so large these days that a certain amount of foreign equity may be deemed desirable, and in that case it may be necessary to face up to the rather delicate problems sometimes posed by these agreements.

Security agreements. These can be of many different varieties. The various sponsor guarantees already referred to would be included, as would mortgages, pledge agreements or other documents creating a lien on the project's fixed or movable assets. Trust agreements make up a quite important sub-division of this category, since the lender's rights in the project's cash flow stream will inevitably be exercised through a bank which acts as trustee on behalf of all parties having an immediate or ultimate interest in the cash flow.

Normally raw material and energy costs, current operating expenses (including wages) and debt service are among the first items the trustee is obliged to pay out, with any remainder being divided up among process licensers, equity investors and other claimants. Where there are different groups or classes of lenders, it is possible to provide either that they will all share in distributions of available funds on a *pro rata* basis, or that a particular order of payment be followed as among lenders. If the same subject is also dealt with by an inter-creditor agreement, the two documents should, of course, be consistent in all respects. In the event of any disparity between the two, the trustee will, in making distributions, be guided exclusively by the provisions of the trust agreement, and any instructions that may be properly given pursuant thereto. Quite correctly, the trustee will refuse to take notice of any inconsistent provisions contained in extraneous materials.

The final category of documentation that requires consideration is that of: *Legal opinions.* In a complicated transaction involving lenders or investors from a number of countries, the structuring of the legal opinions may be almost as difficult as structuring the transaction itself. Deciding who will give opinions, when, and on what subjects can be a trying endeavour when lawyers from six or eight countries are involved, each with their own customary pattern of doing things. Moreover, it is necessary to make certain that there are no inadvertent gaps between the opinions of the various counsel. Some subjects may, with the full knowledge and consent of the lenders, be intentionally excluded from the scope of all the opinions—the effect of usury statutes, for example. Certain types of exclusions are, in fact, quite normal. Much to be feared, however, is the situation in which everyone believes that a subject excluded from one opinion is covered somewhere else, but no one has taken care to see that this be done. Because of the complexity, double and triple checking is required each time new draft documents are prepared—it is simply too easy to let something important slip by, and often it is the most obvious points that are the hardest to spot.

Content of loan and credit agreements

Returning now to the subject of loan agreements it may be said that, in general, loan agreements in project finance transactions look much the same as other loan agreements, supplemented by a certain number of additional provisions specifically addressed to the 'project' nature of the transaction. Other contributions in this volume deal in detail with the content of typical Eurodollar loan agreements, so for present purposes it may be adequate to note that the heart of any loan agreement is contained in four sections: (i) borrower's representations; (ii) conditions of closing; (iii) covenants; and (iv) events of default.

The following paragraphs will indicate some of the ways in which the 'boilerplate' items in these loan agreement sections might be supplemented or modified by provisions specifically addressed either to the project itself or to project financing concepts generally.

Borrower's representations. There will probably be little, if any variation in the standard representations (or warranties) concerning due organisation of the borrower, its corporate authority to engage in its business, the fact that it is not operated in violation of law, and so on. You may anticipate finding specific representations concerning the agreements which form a key part of the project structure. If, for example, the government of the host country has agreed to provide land, to create port facilities or other infrastructure, or to apply a particular tax regime, lenders will normally require that the borrower warrant the validity of such arrangements.

It may be reasonable for the lenders to require that similar representations be made with regard to process licences, investment agreements, construction contracts, third party and sponsor guarantees, or any other documents forming significant aspects of the total structure. The borrower will, in addition, probably be required either to represent that any governmental approvals required for the validity of these arrangements have been obtained prior to signature of the loan agreement or to agree to a condition stipulating that they will be obtained prior to drawdown of the funds.

More difficult questions may arise as to the extent (if any) that the borrower can or should warrant the accuracy of feasibility studies, geologists' reports and other technical documentation. As already noted, it is, as a practical matter, necessary for *all* parties involved to place great reliance on technical studies of this sort since significant errors in the basic data may mean that the cash flow required to retire the debt will not be forthcoming. Reliance is one thing, however, and warranting accuracy quite another; it may well be that requests that the borrower stand foursquare behind the engineering studies will be deemed unacceptable, particularly if the borrower is a substantial corporation or there are sponsor guarantees running to the borrower's obligation.

Conditions of closing. In the usual case, conditions of closing have to do with: (i) the continued truth and accuracy of any representations that may have been made concerning good standing, financial condition, and the like; (ii) obtaining, during the period between signature of the loan agreement and closing, any required approvals; and (iii) the due execution of collateral agreements, and generally the completion of any pending matters necessary to demonstrate that the entire financing structure is in place.

The project finance loan agreement is perfectly consistent with this approach, the only probable difference being a longer shopping list of items to be accomplished by the sponsors and/or borrower prior to drawdown of funds. It may, for example, be appropriate to require that liens or mortgages on tangible assets be perfected prior to closing; that insurance cover be obtained; that all equity capital payable under an investment agreement be received; that any required technical evaluations be satisfactorily performed, that the construction of complementary infrastructure be commenced or accomplished and, in general, that a demonstration be made that circumstances are opportune for undertaking the major work at hand: construction and equipment of the project itself.

In almost every case, one of the more significant conditions of closing will have to do with the receipt, in satisfactory form, of all required legal opinions. This is the point in time at which the project's legal structure is tested and, if appropriately drafted opinions are forthcoming from reliable counsel, the lenders are either: (i) assured that the plans originally envisaged have been put into effect, or (ii) informed of the exact nature and scope of any deviations from the legal structure envisaged in the loan agreement. Any risks inherent in the loan agreement have been consciously assumed by the lenders. Receipt of opinions from all participating counsel is the process by which the lenders check to see whether there are other unanticipated risks lurking in the back-up documentation, approvals, contracts, guarantees and so on.

Covenants. In general, loan agreement covenants deal with the post-closing conduct and financial situation of the borrower. In a project finance transaction, it would be logical for the covenants to relate only to the business and assets of the project, since they are intended to be quite distinct from other assets of the borrower, but in fact a hybrid approach is often followed, since lenders frequently believe that some actions of the borrower could jeopardise the project despite its theoretical severability and self-financing character.

In project finance loan documentation, one would expect to see first of all a covenant that the loan proceeds will be applied only to the construction, equipment, working capital, etc. of the project and not to any other business of the borrower. This has been an area in which some difficulties have arisen in the past, and it seems not unlikely that some further refinement of existing project control techniques may be developed so as to permit lenders greater scope for verifying compliance with this type of covenant.

Quite a few additional covenants may be called for. Usually the 'affirmative' covenants will require that the borrower's (or project's) business be properly conducted in accordance with law and applicable regulations; that all applicable governmental approvals and licences be maintained in force; that the insurance cover (already shown to exist as a condition of closing) be maintained in force throughout the loan payout period, although perhaps in descending amounts as principal is repaid; that taxes be paid; that proper books and records be maintained and financial statements furnished to the lenders on a periodic basis (with, not infrequently, the lenders having the right to send their own auditors or personnel to inspect the project's books of account and verify its financial statements); and that other matters of a similar character be duly and properly accomplished.

There may well be a covenant requiring the borrower to execute supplemental documentation, particularly trust agreements or other sorts of security agreements that may, as a practical matter, not be able to be fully negotiated and signed prior to the time funds are needed for construction of the project.

Another important affirmative covenant will deal with the circumstances in which the borrower is obliged to provide formal notices to the lenders. Some situations are obvious: serious litigation or tax problems, for example, or impending insolvency. Other points may be rather more troublesome. When should the lenders be notified of delays in realisation of the project's construction schedule? When a substantial delay has occurred, presumably, but what is that—a week? A month? The technical characteristics of different projects may dictate considerably different approaches to questions of this nature.

The typical affirmative covenants will, in all probability, be supplemented by a series of 'negative' covenants, of which, again, some are obvious and some less so. It is, for example, reasonable in most cases for the lenders to extract a promise that the borrower will not, without the prior permission of the lenders, merge with another entity or sell any substantial part of its assets otherwise than in the ordinary course of its business. Moreover, it may not be inappropriate to place similar restrictions on: (i) transactions with affiliated companies and (ii) the creation of liens on project assets in favour of parties other than project lenders (the so-called 'negative pledge' clause). In cash flow financing, the borrower can anticipate that it will be subject to severe restraints on its ability to contract additional debt (except on a fully subordinated basis) without the permission of the project lenders. Increasing the debt portion of a project's debt/equity ratio could obviously jeopardise the project's financial viability, and usually this will be evident to borrowers as well as lenders.

On the other hand, the lenders' request that the project's scope or nature not be materially altered without their prior consent may meet with some resistance, not necessarily through an objection in principle on the part of the borrower, but because many technical modifications may be required during the course of construction of a complex facility, and it may be exceedingly difficult to arrive at an objective standard for determining which of such modifications should be deemed 'material'. The same type of resistance may be met if the lenders wish to have a right of prior approval of any amendments of the set of agreements that make up the total project package. The borrower may feel unduly hamstrung in its efforts to get on with the job if it is required to wait for the lenders' approval before changing equipment suppliers, for example, or expanding the terms of reference of a plant construction contract. The lenders, however, may feel that these agreements constitute an important part of their initial credit evaluation, and they may be concerned that, without such protective covenants, the value or stability of the credit could be adversely affected without their knowledge or participation. These conflicting positions can usually be compromised, if not necessarily reconciled, but a fair amount of effort may be expended in the process. Understanding on both sides is required.

Finally, the question of financial covenants must be considered. These come in a wide assortment of both affirmative and negative varieties, each of which applies some sort of test of the financial health of the borrower: asset or liability ratios, maintenance of specified amounts of working capital or a stipulated net worth, and limitations on incurring certain types of obligations are all well known approaches. In some types of financings (insurance company private placements for typical corporate borrowers, for example), these may be the most difficult parts of the entire negotiation. Sophisticated financial covenants of this nature play a more limited role in project finance transactions, however. Perhaps this is simply because the focus is on the cash flow and the security devices which apply to it; and it may also be that many of the entities which borrow on a project finance basis would come off rather poorly on the more traditional financial measures. A simple restriction on payment of dividends may, for example, be more appropriate than a net worth test. It is not really the lawyer's job to speculate about such matters, however, since in any event it will be the bankers and business people on the borrower's side who decide what financial boundaries are appropriate for a particular transaction, and the lawyers only have to work out the details and write it all down once the decisions are made.

Events of default. Of course no one likes to talk about these, even lawyers, since they have such a decidedly negative aspect. Still, it seems not unreasonable to permit the lenders to declare the entire debt due and payable if: (i) the borrower has failed to pay principal or interest when due to the lenders, (ii) the borrower's representations or warranties turn out to have been false, (iii) the borrower fails to live up to one of its covenants after receipt of formal notice that it is expected to do so, or (iv) the borrower loses an essential government approval, is nationalised or ex-propriated, or otherwise becomes unable to conduct its business (as, for example, through bankruptcy or insolvency).

Beyond these fundamental guideposts the terrain is uncertain, although far from unexplored. Cross-default provisions relating to other outstanding debt of the borrower (or, sometimes, of the guarantors) are not uncommon, even though a respectable argument can be made that the lenders' security is not really imperilled by a default on other debt if the project's cash flow has really been segregated from the borrower's other business and assets. Perhaps it is just a bit difficult for the lenders to believe that all these fancy project finance mechanisms will work as planned when the seas get really rough; after all, bankers have always liked to have an anchor to windward.

In the realm of provisions addressed specifically to the project, there is even less unanimity of view. In most cases, it is probably reasonable to permit acceleration of the debt if either borrower or host government fails to comply with the terms of a basic law or agreement regulating the relationship between them or the status of the project. In some cases, however, an *ad hoc* (and tolerated) noncompliance may be in the best interest of the project. Should the bankers really have the right to step in and upset such an arrangement? The short answer is that they wouldn't do so if the arrangement in fact made sense, but such informal assurances may provide little comfort to a borrower concerned about losing flexibility of operations and control over its own destiny.

To what extent is it appropriate to provide an event of default if there is a material delay in accomplishing the construction of the project, or a material alteration of the project's scope or character (assuming there are no covenants on these points)? Suppose in a few years the borrower fails to honour the take-or-pay sales contract. Should the lenders have an unqualified right to call the remainder of the loan outstanding at that time? Sometimes the loan agreement will contain a vaguely worded provision making it an event of default if there are political or other events which 'render unlikely the successful completion of the project or the repayment of the loans'. Is it really fair to provide the lenders with such a sword of Damocles? The answers to these questions may seem clear to some persons in some specific situations, but it is still too early in the history of complex project finance transactions to adopt a categorical approach.

Indeed, the scope of most of these loan agreement provisions is (and should remain) negotiable. Projects, borrowers and circumstances do differ, and the project loan documentation should take account of it. Although many of the points may seem very fine indeed when the lawyers are haggling about them, they do so with a purpose. They know from experience that when a loan or a project gets into trouble, everyone starts to read the fine print.

* * *

Recent developments in co-financing

Since 1981 increased attention has been focused on ways to expand co-financing in an attempt to stimulate the flow of private capital to Third World nations. Changes in the basic structure of co-financing schemes have been proposed to make the vehicle more attractive to commercial banks and more advantageous to borrowers. The most significant innovations have been adopted by the World Bank, which recently completed a major review of its procedures. In January, 1983, the World Bank introduced a trial programme of new co-financing techniques designed to increase commercial bank participation in international project lending.

The new instruments, to be tested over the next 12 to 24 months, are intended to supplement, but not to replace, the World Bank's present modes of co-financing with the private sector. Under the original approach, the World Bank and the commercial banks enter into parallel but wholly separate loan agreements with the borrowing countries which are linked by non-mandatory cross-default provisions, a memorandum of agreement between the World Bank and the private sector lender and other features mentioned above. To provide co-lenders with a closer association with the International Development Bank, the new arrangements contemplate participation by the World Bank in the financing from commercial sources as well as, of course, making its own direct loan to the project borrower.

Three new approaches to co-financing have been devised by the World Bank, each intended to provide enhanced security for commercial lenders while at the same time improving the terms available to borrowers, principally by a lengthening of maturities.

1. *Direct financial participation in later maturities.* Under this approach, the World Bank would participate in a commercial bank loan to the extent of 15–20 per cent of the total loan. Repayments of principal would be made first to commercial lenders until they had been fully repaid; only then would payments be applied to the World Bank's share. The resulting average maturities would be extended significantly beyond those available in the commercial lending market. As the loan is amortised and the final maturities come within a more usual commercial banking range, the World Bank's share would be available for sale to the commercial lenders.

2. *Contingent participation in later maturities.* The second possible approach would provide for fixed annual debt service payments by the borrower on the commercial bank loan, despite the fact that the interest rate would remain variable. If the average interest rates during the term of the loan are higher than anticipated and amortisation is therefore not completed on the original schedule, the World Bank would have a contingent commitment to finance the balance of principal outstanding at final maturity.

3. *Guarantees of later maturities.* In the third approach, the World Bank would not participate in the commercial bank loan directly but would guarantee repayment of the later maturities of the loan. This approach is designed to provide greater incentive for the co-lenders to extend maturities beyond those normally available in the commercial market.

A total of US $ 500 million has been designated for some 15 to 20 trial projects utilising these approaches. Since the average World Bank share of each commercial transaction is estimated to be approximately 20 per cent, a fully implemented pilot programme would generate total co-financings of about US $ 2.5 billion.

Although I understand that some studies as to how co-financing could be made more effective are under way at the other international development banks, no specifically comparable evolution has occurred with regard to Asian Development Bank co-financing or in the 'complementary financing' programme offered by the Inter-American Development Bank. As previously stated, the contractual relationship under the complementary loan agreement is directly between the IADB and the borrower, even though the economic risk has been transferred to the commercial lenders. Thus a default under the commercial loan is a direct default against the IADB. If such a default occurs before the full disbursement of a loan, the IADB can terminate its obligation to make further disbursements and declare the amounts already dispensed immediately due and payable. Naturally, acceleration may also occur where a default has occurred after full disbursement. An additional remedy available to the IADB in a default situation, through the operation of cross-default clauses, is its power to suspend disbursements under other loans granted by the IADB to the defaulting borrower.

Although it is still too soon to tell whether the new World Bank initiatives will be attractive to the financial community, it seems safe to say that interest in this area will continue and that new approaches will continue to be tried until a formula has been found that is satisfactory to all concerned. In this way, an additional increment of the vast sums necessary for economic development can be mobilised from the private sector.

* * *

A chapter of this length can only scratch the surface of a fascinating and rapidly evolving subject. Little or nothing has been said about a number of legal and quasi-legal subjects, such as how to deal with currency fluctuation problems, the corporate structure of projects, anti-trust law considerations, creation and utilisation of host government incentives, sovereign immunity and the Act of State Doctrine, choice of applicable law, or mechanisms for dispute resolution, nor indeed is there any analysis of the tax consequences of any of the choices made in structuring projects of the scale now required to function effectively in a competitive world. Suffice it to say that such matters must and can be dealt with—although usually on an *ad hoc* and project by project basis. Certainly the obstacles are great, but the need to overcome them is even greater.

Project finance: a selective bibliography

Books:
Nevitt, Peter K., *Project financing,* 2nd edition, New York, AMR International, 1978.
Sweeney, Joseph C., (ed.), 'International project finance', Annual proceedings of the Fordham Corporate Law Institute, Matthew Bender, New York, 1975.

Articles:
Alter, G.M., 'World Bank goals in project financing', 15 *Finance and Development,* June 1978, pp. 23–25.
Benson, R. Neil, 'Project financing—banking's response to a new environment', 87 *Canadian Banker and ICB Review,* December 1978, pp. 22–29.

Burke, R.A. and Schoch, S.J., 'Project financing: pipeline to growth', 96 *Finance,* July 1978, pp. 10−16 and 68.

Clarke, Pamela and Martin, Sara, 'The big swing to project finance', *Euromoney,* October 1980, pp. 233−243.

Freeman, Harry L, 'Project development and structuring: the metamorphoses of the financing facilities of the Overseas Private Investment Corporation', 7 *Law and Policy in International Business,* Summer 1975, pp. 739−764.

Hubert Jr., F.W.R., 'Some current methods of financing oil and gas exploration and development', 25 *Oil and Gas Tax Quarterly,* March 1978, pp. 320−339.

Hull, C.W., 'Project structure and financing', 12 *Journal of International Law and Economics,* 1978, pp. 199−207.

Hunt, J.F. and Camp, H.L., 'Project financing—oil and gas ventures', 27 *Oil and Gas Institute,* 1976, pp. 215−258.

Leeper, Rosamund, 'Perspective on project financing', 129 *The Banker,* September 1979, pp. 77−83.

Leeper, Rosamund, 'Project finance—a term to conjure with', 128 *The Banker,* August 1978, pp. 67−73.

Martin, M.P., 'Project financing for offshore and onshore gas facilities; alternative methods of financing from a legal viewpoint', 28 *Oil and Gas Institute,* 1977, pp. 273−291.

McDougall, D.A., 'The role of project financing in developing Australia's natural resources', 94 *Banker's Magazine of Australasia,* October 1980, pp. 169−176.

Sarmet, Marcel, 'International project financing—the European approach', 130 *The Banker,* August 1980, pp. 89−90 ff.

Radez, Richard E., 'Opportunities in project financing', 128 *The Banker,* August 1978, pp. 53 ff.

Stansbury, Philip R., 'Trends in international project contracting and financing', 20 *Private Investors Abroad—Problems and Solutions in International Business,* Southwestern Legal Foundation, Matthew Bender, New York, 1977, pp. 127−146.

Stebbins, R.B., 'Perspective on project financing', 161 *The Bankers Magazine,* May/June 1981, pp. 53−56.

Stebbins, R.B., 'Project financing: a banker's perspective', 62 *Journal of Commercial Bank Lending,* October 1979, pp. 36−43.

Wynant, Larry, 'Essential elements of project financing', 58 *Harvard Business Review,* May/June 1980, pp. 165−173.

Wynant, Larry, 'Project financing: Coping with the capital demands for resource projects', 45 *Business Quarterly,* Summer 1980, pp. 59−69.

Selected Specimen Clauses for Syndicated Loans

By FRANCIS CHRONNELL AND PATRICIA WATSON

The purpose of this chapter is to give a borrower some practical illustrations of how specific clauses in a syndicated Eurodollar loan agreement can be modified in its favour. In order that the borrower can make proper use of the illustrations given, however, some important comments must be made about the format of the chapter, certain basic assumptions which have been made in the drafting of the clauses, and the chapter's limitations. Indeed, without an understanding of these matters, the chapter could be misleading, rather than helpful.

The structure of the chapter is that a number of clauses dealing with certain aspects of a syndicated Eurodollar loan transaction are set out in the form in which lenders could propose that they be included in the loan agreement, and underneath each clause is shown how a clause in that specific form could be amended in the borrower's interests. The version of each clause which could be proposed by the lenders is referred to as the 'Initial Version'. In each case, the wording of the Initial Version is taken as the basis for the version which is referred to as the 'Modified Version'. The Modified Version will sometimes only involve an addition to the Initial Version so that the Initial Version will simply be made to form part of a longer clause without the wording itself being amended. In most cases, however, the wording of the Initial Version will be amended (and sometimes also added to).

The modifications are shown in *italics* (in the case of proposed alternative wording and additions) or indicated by asterisks** (in the case of deletions where no proposed alternative wording takes the place of the wording deleted).

In this way the reader can see, by comparing the two versions, exactly how the wording of the Initial Version has been modified. The Modified

Version of each clause is then followed by a commentary (referred to as the 'Comment') which explains some of the amendments made and/or the clause itself where such an explanation is thought to be helpful. Some of the amendments are, however, self-explanatory or are discussed sufficiently elsewhere in these Guidelines and so are not the subject of further comment in this chapter.

The reason for selecting the clauses set out below is not that they are thought to be the most important clauses in the loan agreement from the borrower's point of view. Some of them are clearly extremely important, but others are less so and a number of important clauses have been omitted. The clauses selected are only those in respect of which it is thought that it would be helpful to the borrower if the kind of advice given in these Guidelines were illustrated by some specific wording for the borrower to look at. Some clauses lend themselves well to this treatment but others do not and those which do not have been avoided for that reason. To illustrate the point, examples of the latter type of clause are those often referred to as the 'substitute basis clause' and the 'increased costs clause'. Both of these can be modified in many ways from the borrower's point of view but they tend to be lengthy and complex (particularly the substitute basis clause) and it is thought, in these cases, that looking at detailed hypothetical wording might be confusing, rather than assist the borrower's understanding of the clear and straightforward suggestions made elsewhere in these Guidelines (see Wood, pp. 131–132 and 133–134). Another clause which has been omitted although it is one of the most important clauses in a loan agreement is the clause known as the 'negative pledge'. This is omitted because the approach adopted by Harris in the chapter 'Negative Pledge' is to look at detailed wording of a negative pledge and how it may be modified in the borrower's favour and it is thought that to repeat the exercise here would be superfluous and possibly confusing. There are, in addition, numerous other amendments in the borrower's favour which could be made to a loan agreement but which are not illustrated here. Suggestions (though not necessarily wording) for these are given elsewhere in these Guidelines and it probably would not assist the borrower further to duplicate those suggestions here.

To say that to look at specific wording can help convey a particular point is not to say that the wording given in the clauses in this chapter is sacrosanct. There is more than one way to draft any provision in a loan agreement and the reader should not be too concerned with the precise form of words used to modify the Initial Version: it is the principle behind each modification which is important and while it is essential to draft in a way which conveys that principle clearly, the particular words chosen are usually not the only words which would serve the purpose. A related point is, of course, that it is unlikely that a borrower will be presented with a clause drafted on behalf of the lenders in a live transaction using precisely the same words as are used in the equivalent clause set out here. That does not necessarily mean that those lenders are attempting to provide something unusual (although it may mean that) and it would not usually be appropriate for the borrower to attempt to delete a clause in its entirety and substitute another clause (for example, one given here) which provides a similar thing in different words. (Where it would, however, be appropriate to try to substitute complete clauses in such circumstances would be where the borrower is trying to standardise, say, the events of default clauses throughout all its loans.) The borrower in a live transaction should, therefore, normally concern itself with the form of clause actually presented to it and see how that form could be amended. It is especially when faced with a draft loan agreement that the borrower must look behind the precise wording used in the Modified Version of the clauses in this chapter. While such wording is appropriate to modify the Initial Version of the relevant clause as set out here in order to reflect the principle behind the modification, a different version proposed by actual lenders will often require different wording to modify it.

The modifications incorporated into the Modified Version of the clauses set out below do not purport to be in any particular case either the best a borrower could ever hope to achieve or the least it should be expected to achieve. Much depends on the circumstances of each set of negotiations, including the relative bargaining strengths of the borrower and the lenders, the political, economic and commercial environment, the state of the relevant market and the particular requirements of the borrower; but it would be neither practicable nor helpful to try to indicate which borrower or type of borrower should expect to obtain the modifications suggested below, or something better, or be prepared to accept some less favourable wording. The borrower should not, therefore, be afraid of pressing for a better position than is illustrated below if the circumstances seem to permit. On the other hand, the borrower should not feel that its best position in the circumstances has not been achieved if it fails to obtain the modifications suggested.

For the purposes of this chapter, it is assumed for convenience that the borrower is the state itself and not a state entity such as a government department or a state-owned corporation. Many of the same considerations will apply where a borrower is a state entity but there will be some differences, and some consideration has been given to such matters elsewhere in these Guidelines.

Words which have capital initial letters in the clauses set out below would be defined in the loan agreement in question but such definitions are only given below when that is felt to be necessary to the understanding of a clause.

Severality of Banks' Obligations

Initial Version

'(a) The obligations of each Bank under this Agreement are several: the failure of any Bank to perform such obligations shall not relieve any other Bank, the Agent or the Borrower of any of their respective obligations or liabilities under this Agreement nor shall the Agent be responsible for the obligations of any Bank (except for its own obligations, if any, as a Bank) nor shall any Bank be responsible for the obligations of any other Bank under this Agreement.'

Modified Version

Add: '*(b) If any Bank shall fail to contribute to an Advance for a period of 5 Banking Days after the date of that Advance, the Borrower may, without prejudice to any other rights it may have against such Bank, within 10 Banking Days of the end of such period (but only if such failure is then continuing) by notice to the Agent cancel forthwith the undrawn amount of such Bank's Commitment whereupon the undrawn amount of the total of the Commitments of all the Banks shall be reduced by the undrawn amount of that Bank's Commitment and the Agent shall, if so requested by the Borrower, use all reasonable endeavours during a period not exceeding 30 days after receipt of such notice to find another bank or financial institution acceptable to the Borrower (the 'New Bank') to assume the cancelled obligations of such Bank (the 'Old Bank') under this Agreement. If the New Bank agrees in writing with the Borrower and the Agent to assume the cancelled obligations (or any part thereof) of the Old Bank under this Agreement, then the total of the Commitments of all the Banks under this Agreement shall be increased accordingly.*'

Comment

Because the obligations of the Banks in a syndicated Eurodollar loan agreement are several, as is provided in paragraph (a), Borrowers sometimes ask for a provision such as paragraph (b) to be inserted into the loan agreement to give the Borrower the right to call upon the Agent to assist in making good the full complement of Banks if any Bank should fail to perform its obligations under the Agreement.

The wording of paragraph (b) can be adapted for use also in cases where a Bank is prepaid or its Commitment is cancelled for taxation, illegality or increased costs' reasons and the Borrower wishes to be able to request that the amount of the loan be restored.

Payments

Initial Version

'(a) All payments to be made by the Borrower under this Agreement shall be made in full, without any set-off or counterclaim and, subject as provided in [tax grossing-up clause], free and clear of any deductions or withholdings whatsoever, in Dollars on the due date to the account of the Agent at .... or at such other bank in such other place as the Agent may have notified to the Borrower.'

Modified Version

'(a) All payments to be made by the Borrower under this Agreement shall be made in full, without any set-off or counterclaim and, subject as provided in [tax grossing-up clause], free and clear of any deductions or withholdings *for or on account of any present or future taxes, levies, imposts, duties, fees or charges of whatever nature levied or imposed in [country of Borrower] or by any authority therein or thereof having power to tax (hereinafter referred to as 'Taxes') (other than Taxes payable in respect of a sum payable under this Agreement to a person who is subject to Taxes otherwise than by reason merely of being a Bank or the Agent)*, in Dollars on the due date to the account of the Agent at .... or at such other bank in such other place as the Agent may have notified to the Borrower.

(b) If at any time it shall become unlawful or impracticable for the Borrower to make payment under this Agreement to the relevant account or bank referred to in (a) above or in Dollars, the Borrower may agree with each or

any of the Banks alternative arrangements for the payment by the Borrower direct to such Bank of amounts due to such Bank under this Agreement and upon reaching such agreement such Bank shall immediately notify the Agent.'

Comment

It is standard in syndicated loan transactions that all payments by the Borrower are to be made to a specified account of the Agent with a bank in New York City (if payments are to be made in US Dollars) or in the principal financial centre for the currency concerned (if payments are to be made in a currency other than US Dollars) so as to enable the Agent to monitor payments received from the Borrower. In certain circumstances (the US 'freeze' order on Iranian assets being a good example) the Borrower may be prevented from making payment to the specified account of the Agent. In those circumstances paragraph (b) provides an alternative procedure to enable the Borrower to discharge its obligations in another way. It should be noted that the alternative procedure is subject to the specific agreement of particular Banks at the time the problem arises and does not bind the Banks in advance to implement alternative payment arrangements.

For a commentary on the additional wording in paragraph (a), see the Comment in 'Tax Grossing-Up' below.

Tax Grossing-Up

Initial Version

'(a) If at any time any applicable law, regulation or regulatory requirement or any governmental authority, monetary agency or central bank requires the Borrower to make any deduction or withholding in respect of Taxes from any payment due under this Agreement for the account of any Bank or the Agent, the sum due from the Borrower in respect of such payment shall be increased to the extent necessary to ensure that, after the making of such deduction or withholding, each Bank and the Agent receives on the due date for such payment a net sum equal to the sum which it would have received had no such deduction or withholding been required to be made and the Borrower shall indemnify each Bank and the Agent against any losses or costs incurred by any of them by reason of any failure of the Borrower to make any such deduction or withholding.'

Modified Version

Add: '*... Provided that the Borrower shall not be obliged to make any such increased payment as is referred to in this paragraph (a) to any person who is subject to Taxes otherwise than by reason merely of being a Bank or the Agent. At any time after it shall have been required to make any such increased payment to any Bank the Borrower may, on giving not less than 15 days' notice to the Agent, prepay to the Agent for account of such Bank on expiry of such notice the whole (but not part only) of such Bank's Contribution.*

(b) If, following any such deduction or withholding as is referred to in (a) above, the Agent or any Bank shall receive or be granted a credit against or remission for any Taxes payable by it, the Agent or such Bank shall, subject to the Borrower having made any increased payment in accordance with (a) above and to the extent that the Agent or such Bank can do so without prejudicing the retention of the amount of such credit or remission and without prejudice to the right of the Agent or such Bank to obtain any other relief or allowance which may be available to it, reimburse the Borrower such amount as the Agent or such Bank shall certify to be the proportion of such credit or remission as will leave the Agent or such Bank (after such reimbursement) in no worse position than that in which it would have been had there been no such deduction or withholding. Such reimbursement shall be made forthwith upon the Agent or such Bank certifying that the amount of such credit or remission has been received by it.'

Comment

Paragraph (a) of this clause provides, in essence, that if any payment by the Borrower becomes subject to a deduction or withholding for 'Taxes' (as defined in 'Payments' above) then the Borrower will 'gross up' the payment so that the Agent and the Banks receive the same net amount which they would otherwise have received had there been no such deduction or withholding.

The first part of the modification to paragraph (a) of 'Payments' above (i.e. up to the definition of 'Taxes') and the carrying-over into this tax grossing-up clause of the defined term 'Taxes' are intended to provide, in effect, that taxes etc. in jurisdictions other than the Borrower's own country (e.g. in the place of payment) may be deducted or withheld from payments without the Borrower being obliged to gross up. The Borrower should be very wary of the drafting of the payments clause and the tax grossing-up clause and the way they link together as it may not be easy to see at first glance whether it is, in effect, only withholding taxes etc. imposed by the taxing authorities of its own country on payments made under the loan agreement or also other taxes which it is being asked to bear.

The first additional sentence in the Modified Version of this tax grossing-up clause (taken together with the similar wording which appears in parentheses in the modification to paragraph (a) of 'Payments' above) ensures that the Borrower may make a deduction or withholding for Taxes and is not obliged to gross up in favour of the Agent or any Bank if the Agent or that Bank, as the case may be, is subject to Taxes because it is, for example, resident or has a permanent establishment in the Borrower's country. The second additional sentence gives the Borrower a right of prepayment if it is obliged to gross up in favour of a Bank.

Banks may obtain a double benefit by virtue of a grossing-up provision since they may be able to claim some form of tax credit in relation to the withholding tax which has been deducted even though a grossing-up payment has been made. The intention behind paragraph (b) of this clause (usually referred to as a 'tax clawback') is to neutralise this benefit, although it should be noted that Banks are unlikely to make a very firm commitment in respect of tax credits received, as can be seen from this example, due to the difficulty often in knowing whether a tax credit has been received or not and also the problem in how to allocate tax credits among different transactions where the relevant Bank does not have enough taxable income available to absorb all its tax credits.

Events of Default

Initial Version

'(a) There shall be an Event of Default if:

(i) the Borrower fails to pay any sum payable by it under this Agreement when due; or

(ii) the Borrower commits any breach of or omits to observe any of its obligations or undertakings under this Agreement (other than failure to pay any sum when due); or

(iii) any representation or warranty made by or in respect of the Borrower in or pursuant to this Agreement or in any notice, certificate or statement referred to in or delivered under this Agreement proves to have been incorrect in any material respect when made or would have been incorrect in any material respect if repeated at any time when any moneys are owing under this Agreement with reference to the facts and circumstances existing at such time; or

(iv) any Indebtedness of the Borrower or any Government Agency is not paid on due date or becomes due or capable of being declared due prior to the date when it would otherwise have become due or any guarantee or indemnity given by the Borrower or any Government Agency in respect of Indebtedness is not honoured when due and called upon; or

(v) any consent, authorisation, licence or approval of, or registration with or declaration to, governmental or public bodies or authorities or courts required by the Borrower to authorise, or required by the Borrower in connection with, the execution, delivery, validity, enforceability or admissibility in evidence of this Agreement or the performance by the Borrower of its obligations under this Agreement is modified or is not granted or is revoked or terminated or expires and is not renewed or otherwise ceases to be in full force and effect; or

(vi) an encumbrancer takes possession or a receiver or similar officer is appointed of the whole or any part of the assets, rights or revenues of the Borrower or any Government Agency or a distress, execution, sequestration or other process is levied or enforced upon or sued out against any of the assets, rights or revenues of the Borrower or any Government Agency and is not discharged within seven days; or

(vii) the Borrower or any Government Agency suspends payment of its debts or is unable or admits inability to pay its debts as they fall due or proposes or enters into any composition or other arrangement for the benefit of its creditors generally or proceedings are commenced in relation to the Borrower or any Government Agency under any law, regulation or procedure relating to reconstruction or readjustment of debts or the Borrower declares a moratorium on the payment of any part of its Indebtedness; or

(viii) any event occurs or proceeding is taken with respect to the Borrower or any Government Agency in any jurisdiction to which it is subject which has an effect equivalent or similar to any of the events mentioned in (vi) or (vii) above; or

(ix) any Government Agency suspends or ceases or threatens to suspend or cease to carry on its business; or

(x) the Borrower ceases to be a member in good standing of the International Monetary Fund or ceases to be eligible to utilise the resources of the International Monetary Fund or the International Bank for Reconstruction and Development (or any successors thereof); or

(xi) it becomes unlawful for the Borrower duly and promptly to perform any of the obligations expressed to be assumed by it under this Agreement or for the Central Bank duly and promptly to perform the obligations expressed to be assumed by it under the Central Bank's Transfer Guarantee, or this Agreement or the Central Bank's Transfer Guarantee for any reason ceases to be in full force and effect; or

(xii) any other event occurs or circumstance arises which, in the opinion of the Majority Banks, is likely materially and adversely to affect the ability of the Borrower to perform all or any of its obligations under or otherwise to comply with the terms of this Agreement.

(b) The Agent may and if so requested by the Majority Banks shall, without prejudice to any other rights of the Banks, at any time after the happening of an Event of Default by notice to the Borrower declare that:

(i) the obligation of each Bank to make its Commitment available shall be terminated, whereupon the Commitments shall be cancelled forthwith; and/or

(ii) the Loan and all interest and commitment commission accrued and all other sums payable under this Agreement have become due and payable, whereupon the same shall, immediately or in accordance with the terms of such notice, become due and payable.'

Modified Version

'(a) *Subject to the provisions of (b) below,* there shall be an Event of Default if:

(i) the Borrower fails to pay any sum payable by it under this Agreement when due *and, in the case of payments other than principal, such sum remains unpaid for five days after due date*; or

(ii) the Borrower commits any breach of or omits to observe any of its obligations or undertakings under this Agreement (other than failure to pay any sum when due) *and, in respect of any such breach or omission which is capable of remedy, such action as the Agent may reasonably require shall not have been taken within 30 days of the Agent notifying the Borrower of such default and of such required action*; or

(iii) any representation or warranty made *or repeated* by** the Borrower in** this Agreement or in any notice, certificate or statement referred to in or delivered under this Agreement proves to have been incorrect in any material respect when made *or repeated***; or

(iv) any [*Borrowed Money*] [*External Debt*] of the Borrower [or any Government Agency] is not paid on due date *(as extended by any applicable days of grace)* or becomes due** prior to the date when it would otherwise have become due *following a default and payment is validly demanded* or any guarantee or indemnity given by the Borrower [or any Government Agency] in respect of [*Borrowed Money*] [*External Debt*] is not honoured when due and called upon; or

(v) any consent, authorisation, licence or approval of, or registration with or declaration to, governmental or public bodies or authorities or courts required by the Borrower to authorise, or required by the Borrower in connection with, the execution, delivery, validity, enforceability or admissibility in evidence *in the courts of* [*country of Borrower*] of this Agreement or the performance by the Borrower of its obligations under this Agreement is modified *in a manner which the Majority Banks reasonably consider is unacceptable* or is not granted or is revoked or terminated or expires and is not renewed or otherwise ceases to be in full force and effect; or

(vi) an encumbrancer takes possession or a receiver or similar officer is appointed of the whole or *a substantial* part of the assets, rights or revenues of the Borrower [or any Government Agency] or a distress, execution, sequestration or other process is levied or enforced upon or sued out against *the whole or a substantial part* of the assets, rights or revenues of the Borrower [or any Government Agency] and is not discharged within *fifteen* days; or

(vii) **[any Government Agency suspends payment of its debts or is unable or admits inability to pay its debts as they fall due or proposes or enters into any composition or other arrangement for the benefit of its creditors generally or proceedings are commenced in relation to **any Government Agency under any law, regulation or procedure relating to reconstruction or readjustment of debts or] the Borrower declares a *general* moratorium on the payment of **its [*Borrowed Money*] [*External Debt*]; or

(viii) any event occurs or proceeding is taken with respect to the Borrower [or any Government Agency] in any jurisdiction to which it is subject which has an effect equivalent or similar to any of the events mentioned in (vi) or (vii) above; or

[(ix) any Government Agency suspends or ceases or threatens to suspend or cease to carry on its business; or]

(x) the Borrower ceases to be a member in good standing of the International Monetary Fund or ceases to be eligible to utilise the resources of the International Monetary Fund or the International Bank for Reconstruction and Development (or any successors thereof); or

(xi) it becomes unlawful for the Borrower duly and promptly to perform any of the obligations expressed to be assumed by it under this Agreement or for the Central Bank duly and promptly to perform the obligations expressed to be assumed by it under the Central Bank's Transfer Guarantee, or this Agreement or the Central Bank's Transfer Guarantee for any reason ceases to be in full force and effect or**

[*Provided that there shall not be an Event of Default solely by reason of any of the events or circumstances described in (iv), (vi), (vii), (viii) or (ix) above taking place with respect to any Government Agency unless, in the reasonable opinion of the Majority Banks, the ability of the Borrower to perform all or any of its obligations under, or otherwise to comply with the terms of, this Agreement shall be materially and adversely affected.*]

(b)   None of the events or circumstances described in paragraphs (a)(ii) to (a)(xi) above shall constitute an Event of Default unless and until the Agent after consultation with all the Banks shall have certified to the Borrower that in the reasonable opinion of the Majority Banks the event or circumstance concerned is materially prejudicial to the Banks as lenders in respect of the Facility.

(c)   The Agent** if so requested by the Majority Banks shall, without prejudice to any other rights of the Banks, at any time after the happening of an Event of Default *so long as the same is continuing* by notice to the Borrower declare that:

(i) the obligation of each Bank to make its Commitment available shall be terminated, whereupon the Commitments shall be cancelled forthwith; and/or

(ii) the Loan and all interest and commitment commission accrued and all other sums payable under this Agreement have become due and payable, whereupon the same shall, immediately or in accordance with the terms of such notice, become due and payable.'

Comment

The events of default clause is one which should be scrutinised extremely closely by the Borrower and its lawyers. Events of default clauses vary greatly in their length and stringency and there are a number of ways in which their scope can be cut down in the Borrower's favour. Some ideas are illustrated here and more detailed advice and a number of further or alternative suggestions are given elsewhere in these Guidelines. It may not be possible for the Borrower to obtain all the types of relaxation suggested here and elsewhere and the Borrower should focus on those which are particularly important to it at the relevant time.

The expressions 'Borrowed Money' and 'External Debt' are given as alternatives in the Modified Version and both expressions are narrower than 'Indebtedness' in the Initial Version. 'Indebtedness' is usually very widely defined to mean any obligation for the payment or repayment of money, including contingent obligations. 'Borrowed Money' will usually mean 'Indebtedness' which is incurred through any method of raising finance including loans, bonds, guarantees, acceptance or documentary credit facilities, deferred payments for assets acquired and rental payments under leases which are entered into primarily as a way of raising finance or of financing the acquisition of the asset leased, and so will not usually cover, for example, ordinary trade credit where 'technical' defaults could arise frequently. 'External Debt' will usually mean only that 'Borrowed Money' which is denominated or payable in currencies other than that of the Borrower's country or which is owed to non-residents of the Borrower's country. These definitions themselves can be modified but clearly the narrowest concept (and therefore the most beneficial to the Borrower) will be that of 'External Debt'.

References to Government Agencies have been placed within square brackets to suggest that they be excluded as far as possible. Where it would not be commercially acceptable to the lenders to exclude Government Agencies altogether, the definition of 'Government Agencies' should not be wider than is absolutely necessary to protect the lenders' position.

Paragraph (xii) dealing with material adverse changes is better deleted wherever possible and the lenders left to rely on the specific events of default set out in the other paragraphs. If the lenders intend to sweep up in the material adverse change paragraph problems which they may have failed to cover in the other paragraphs they could be asked to specify the kind of event they have in mind so that the Borrower is given the opportunity to accept or reject its inclusion as a particular event of default. If, however, it is necessary for the Borrower to accept such a paragraph, various versions of it are given by Youard in the chapter 'Events of Default' and the Borrower will be able to see from those how the scope of the paragraph can be lessened.

The Borrower could, in addition, try to ensure that, at least for the purposes of this clause, the expression 'Majority Banks' means, say, Banks the aggregate of whose participations in the loan at any relevant time exceeds two thirds (rather than one half, which is likely to be the proportion proposed by the lenders) of the participations of all the Banks.

Illegality

Initial Version

'If any law, regulation or regulatory requirement or any judgment, order or direction of any court, tribunal or authority binding upon a Bank in the jurisdiction in which it is formed or has its principal or lending office or in which any action is required to be performed by it for the purposes of this Agreement (whether or not in force before the date of this Agreement) renders it unlawful for that Bank to contribute to Advances or to maintain or fund its Contribution, that Bank shall promptly inform the Agent whereupon the Agent shall forthwith notify the Borrower. If it shall so be unlawful for that Bank to contribute to Advances its Commitment shall be cancelled. If it shall so be unlawful for that Bank to maintain or fund its Contribution the Agent shall, at the request and on behalf of that Bank, give notice to the Borrower requiring the Borrower to prepay the Contribution of that Bank either (i) forthwith or (ii) on a future specified date and the Borrower shall prepay such Bank's Contribution in accordance with such notice.'

Modified Version

'If any law, regulation or regulatory requirement or any judgment, order or direction of any court, tribunal or authority binding upon a Bank in the jurisdiction in which it is formed or has its principal or lending office or in which any action is required to be performed by it for the purposes of this Agreement (*coming into force after* the date of this Agreement) renders it unlawful for that Bank to contribute to Advances or to maintain or fund its Contribution, that Bank shall promptly inform the Agent whereupon the Agent shall forthwith notify the Borrower. If it shall so be unlawful for that Bank to contribute to Advances its Commitment shall be cancelled. If it shall so be unlawful for that Bank to maintain or fund its Contribution the Agent shall, at the request and on behalf of that Bank, give notice to the Borrower requiring the Borrower to prepay the Contribution of that Bank *within a specified period ending on the latest date permitted by such law, regulation, regulatory requirement, judgment, order or direction* and the Borrower shall prepay such Bank's Contribution in accordance with such notice. *Without prejudice to the cancellation of such Bank's Commitment or the obligation of the Borrower to make such prepayment, the Borrower, the Agent and such Bank shall negotiate for a period not exceeding 30 days, during which such Bank shall use its best endeavours to make available its Commitment and/or maintain its Contribution in whole or in part from another jurisdiction or in a manner which is not unlawful.'*

Comment
The wording set out in paragraph (b) of 'Severality of Banks' Obligations' above (p. 227) can be adapted as a further modification to this clause to allow the Borrower to request a restoration of the amount of the loan in the case of a prepayment or cancellation for illegality reasons.

Set-Off

Initial Version
'The Borrower authorises each Bank to apply any credit balance to which the Borrower is then entitled on any account of the Borrower with that Bank in satisfaction of any sum due and payable from the Borrower under this Agreement. For this purpose each Bank is authorised to purchase with the moneys standing to the credit of such account such other currencies as may be necessary to effect such application. Each Bank shall notify the Agent and the Borrower forthwith upon the exercise or purported exercise of any right of set-off giving full details in relation thereto.'

Modified Version
'*Subject as provided below,* the Borrower authorises each Bank to apply any credit balance to which the Borrower is then *solely and beneficially* entitled on any account of the Borrower with that Bank in satisfaction of

any sum due and payable from the Borrower *to that Bank* under this Agreement *Provided that each Bank agrees that it shall not exercise any right of set-off available to it (whether arising pursuant to this paragraph or otherwise) in respect of amounts exceeding in aggregate such Bank's maximum participation in the Loan.*** *No Bank shall be obliged to exercise any right of set-off available to it.* Each Bank shall notify the Agent and the Borrower forthwith upon the exercise or purported exercise of any right of set-off giving full details in relation thereto.'

Comment
In many jurisdictions, including England, banks have a right of set-off in certain circumstances (which are not always clear-cut) as a matter of law and attempts in the loan agreement to extend, as a matter of contract, the rights which may be available to the Banks at law are in danger of being construed as creating a charge on any deposits the Borrower may have with the Banks. It is particularly important from this point of view that the Borrower's credit balances with any particular Bank may only be set off against sums due and payable to that Bank. However, it should be noted that under the sharing of payments clause (see next clause) a Bank may be obliged to share with the other Banks disproportionate payments which it receives or recovers, so that a Bank could set off from the Borrower's credit balance with that Bank an amount which was equal to the sum then due and payable to it, share that amount with the other Banks and, because of the effect of the sharing of payments clause, the amount which it gave away to the other Banks would remain 'due and payable' to it. If there was still a credit balance of the Borrower remaining with that Bank, that Bank would, therefore, be able to keep setting off parts of it and sharing them with the other Banks until either all the Banks including itself were paid in full or the credit balance ran out. The proviso at the end of the first sentence of the Modified Version of this set-off clause limits the total amount which a Bank can set off to the amount of that Bank's participation in the loan.

Sharing of Payments

Initial Version
'If at any time the proportion which any Bank has received or recovered in respect of its portion of any payment to be made by the Borrower for the

account of such Bank and one or more other Banks under this Agreement is greater (the amount of the excess being referred to in this paragraph as the 'excess amount') than the proportion thereof received or recovered by the Bank receiving or recovering the smallest proportion of its portion thereof, such Bank shall pay an amount equal to the excess amount to the Agent, which shall treat such payment as if it were part of the payment to be made by the Borrower and as between the Borrower and such Bank the excess amount shall be treated as not having been paid.'

Modified Version
Add: '... *while as between the Borrower and each Bank it shall be treated as having been paid to the extent receivable by that Bank Provided that if the Loan shall have become due and payable pursuant to [events of default clause], such Bank shall not be entitled to exercise on more than one occasion the rights which have given rise to such Bank receiving the excess amount.*'

Comment
The Initial Version given here is a shortened form of the sharing of payments clause, which clause is becoming more sophisticated (as well as longer and more detailed) in the aftermath of the difficulties encountered by banks in connection with the sharing of disproportionate receipts which resulted from the restrictions on financial transfers between Argentina and the UK during 1982 and 1983. However, whatever the version adopted by the lenders, a sharing of payments clause combined with a right of set-off is likely, as pointed out in the Comment in 'Set-Off' above, effectively to enable one Bank with a deposit larger than its participation to siphon that deposit off for the benefit of the other Banks. A limit on this ability was suggested by way of a proviso to the set-off clause above. If such a proviso was not acceptable to the lenders, another approach is the wording set out in the Modified Version of this sharing of payments clause which restricts the siphoning-off process at least where the loan is accelerated after an event of default.

Assignment

Initial Version
'(a)   Each Bank may assign all or any part of its rights or benefits or

transfer all or any part of its obligations under this Agreement to any one or more banks or other financial institutions (an 'Assignee'). Written notice of any assignment of all or part of any Bank's rights or benefits under this Agreement shall be given to the Borrower and the Agent as soon as practicable after the same has been effected. Any transfer of all or part of any Bank's obligations under this Agreement may only be effected:

(i) with the prior written consent of the Borrower and the Agent (such consents not to be unreasonably withheld), unless the Assignee shall be a subsidiary or the holding company of the transferor Bank or a subsidiary of such holding company (in which case no such consents shall be required); and

(ii) if the Assignee, by delivery of such undertaking as the Borrower and the Agent may approve, becomes bound by the terms of this Agreement and agrees to perform all or, as the case may be, part of the transferor Bank's obligations under this Agreement.'

Modified Version
'(a) Each Bank may assign all or any part of its rights or benefits or transfer all or any part of its obligations under this Agreement to any one or more banks or other financial institutions (an 'Assignee'). *Any assignment of all or part of any Bank's rights or benefits under this Agreement may only be effected with the prior written consent of the Borrower (such consent not to be unreasonably withheld).* Written notice of any assignment of all or part of any Bank's rights or benefits under this Agreement shall be given to the Borrower and the Agent as soon as practicable after the same has been effected. Any transfer of all or part of any Bank's obligations under this Agreement may only be effected:

(i) with the prior written consent of the Borrower and the Agent**; and

(ii) if the Assignee, by delivery of such undertaking as the Borrower and the Agent may approve, becomes bound by the terms of this Agreement and agrees to perform all or, as the case may be, part of the transferor Bank's obligations under this Agreement.

Any consent required to be given by the Borrower under this paragraph (a) shall not be regarded as unreasonably withheld by the Borrower if the Borrower certifies to the assigning Bank concerned that the grant of such consent would be contrary to the interests of [country of Borrower].

(b) If any Bank acts through any branch other than that specified in the

execution pages of this Agreement or if any Bank assigns all or any part of its rights or benefits or transfers all or any part of its obligations under this Agreement then the liability of the Borrower (including, without limitation, under [tax grossing-up and increased costs clauses]) to that Bank acting through its other branch or to the Assignee, as the case may be, shall in no case (unless the Borrower has agreed otherwise) exceed the amount of the liability of the Borrower had no such change of branch, assignment or transfer taken place.'

Comment

The modifications to this clause are intended to give the Borrower more control over changes in the identity of syndicate members (including changes within the same corporate group as the assigning or transferor Bank, since, for example, the assignee or transferee member of the group might be resident in a hostile jurisdiction) and to avoid the Borrower sustaining any increased liability as a result of a change in lending branch or an assignment of rights or benefits or a transfer of obligations.

Sometimes a sovereign Borrower may wish to withhold its consent to an assignment for political reasons and the final sentence in paragraph (a) is intended to ensure that if the Borrower decides that an assignment would be contrary to its national interests it may withhold its consent, without divulging to the relevant Bank the reasons for its decision, and the withholding of its consent will not be deemed to be unreasonable (and therefore invalid).

Paragraph (b) protects the Borrower from all increased liabilities at any time resulting from a change in lending branch, assignment or transfer. Some versions of this paragraph protect the Borrower only from certain specified increased liabilities (usually under the tax grossing-up and increased costs clauses, which are perhaps the major areas with which the Borrower will be concerned in any event) and which arise only at the time of the change in lending branch, assignment or transfer and not afterwards. The Borrower should therefore be wary of the drafting of this clause.

Law and Jurisdiction

Initial Version

'(a) This Agreement is governed by and shall be construed in accordance with English law.

(b)   The Borrower agrees that any legal action or proceedings arising out of or in connection with this Agreement against the Borrower or its assets may be brought in the English courts, in the State courts of or the Federal courts in the State of New York or elsewhere as any Bank or the Agent may elect, irrevocably and unconditionally submits to and accepts the jurisdiction of each such court, irrevocably designates, appoints and empowers (i) .... at present of .... to receive for it and on its behalf service of process issued out of the English courts and (ii) .... at present of .... to receive for it and on its behalf service of process issued out of the State courts of or the Federal courts in the State of New York in any such legal action or proceedings and agrees that failure by such process agent to give notice of such service of process to the Borrower shall not impair or affect the validity of such service or of any judgment based thereon.

(c)   The submission to such jurisdictions shall not (and shall not be construed so as to) limit the right of the Agent or the Banks to take proceedings against the Borrower or its assets in whatsoever jurisdictions shall to it or them seem fit nor shall the taking of proceedings in any one or more jurisdictions preclude the taking of proceedings in any other jurisdiction, whether concurrently or not. The Borrower irrevocably waives any objection it may now or hereafter have to the laying of venue of any action or proceeding in any court and any claim it may now or hereafter have that any action or proceeding has been brought in an inconvenient forum.

(d)   The Borrower agrees that in any legal action or proceedings arising out of or in connection with this Agreement against the Borrower or its assets no immunity from such legal action or proceedings (which shall include, without limitation, suit, attachment prior to judgment, other attachment, the obtaining of judgment, execution or other enforcement) shall be claimed by or on behalf of the Borrower or with respect to its assets, irrevocably waives any such right of immunity which it or its assets now have or may hereafter acquire or which may be attributed to it or its assets and consents generally in respect of any such legal action or proceedings to the giving of any relief or the issue of any process in connection with such action or proceedings including, without limitation, the making, enforcement or execution against any property whatsoever (irrespective of its use or intended use) of any order or judgment which may be made or given in such action or proceedings.

(e)   For the purpose of the foregoing waiver and without prejudice to its generality, the Borrower hereby expressly acknowledges that its consent and submission are intended to be irrevocable under New York and United States law and in particular, but without limitation, under the Foreign Sovereign Immunities Act of 1976 of the United States.'

Modified Version

'(a)   This Agreement is governed by and shall be construed in accordance with English law.

(b)   The Borrower agrees that any legal action or proceedings arising out of or in connection with this Agreement against the Borrower or its assets may be brought in the English courts *or the courts of [country of Borrower]*, irrevocably and unconditionally submits to and accepts the jurisdiction of each such court *and* irrevocably designates, appoints and empowers** .... at present of .... to receive for it and on its behalf service of process issued out of the English courts **in any such legal action or proceedings**. *Additionally, if neither the English courts nor the courts of [country of Borrower] accept jurisdiction in the legal action or proceedings in question or if only the English courts accept jurisdiction but it would be impracticable to obtain an order of the courts of [country of Borrower] enforcing any judgment of the English courts on the legal action or proceedings in question, then the Borrower hereby consents to such legal action or proceedings being brought in New York and hereby irrevocably and unconditionally submits to the jurisdiction of the State courts of and the Federal courts in the State of New York and (without prejudice to the foregoing and for the purposes of such submission only) hereby irrevocably designates, appoints and empowers .... at present of .... to receive for it and on its behalf service of process issued out of such courts.*

(c)   **The Borrower irrevocably waives any objection it may now or hereafter have to the *institution of proceedings in New York on the ground of forum non conveniens.*

(d)   The Borrower agrees that in any legal action or proceedings arising out of or in connection with this Agreement against the Borrower or its assets *in the courts and in the circumstances specified in (b) above (but subject as provided below)* no immunity from such legal action or proceedings (which shall include, without limitation, suit, attachment prior to judgment, other attachment, the obtaining of judgment, execution or other enforcement) shall be claimed by or on behalf of the Borrower or with respect to its assets, irrevocably waives any such right of immunity which it or its assets now have or may hereafter acquire or which may be attributed to it or its assets and consents generally in respect of any such legal action or proceedings to the giving of any relief or the issue of any process in connection with such action or proceedings including, without limitation, the making, enforcement or execution against any property whatsoever (irrespective of its use or intended use) of any order or judgment which may be made or given in such action or proceedings *Provided that the foregoing agreements, waivers and consents by the Borrower do not apply to .... or, for the avoidance of doubt, to the Borrower's title to or possession of property for any diplomatic mission or the property of the Central Bank.*

(e)   For the purpose of the foregoing waiver and without prejudice to its generality, the Borrower hereby expressly acknowledges that its consent and submission are intended to be irrevocable under New York and United States law and in particular, but without limitation, under the Foreign Sovereign Immunities Act of 1976 of the United States.'

Comment

The general intention behind the amendments to this clause is to attempt to cut down the number of potential jurisdictions in which actions might be brought against the Borrower, while trying to stop short of a position which probably would not be acceptable to the lenders for the reasons given elsewhere in these Guidelines. Where New York law is not the governing law of the loan agreement, the Borrower should not have to submit expressly to the jurisdiction of the New York courts, at least in circumstances where the transaction has no substantial connection with New York other than payments in US Dollars having to be made in New York City. The position illustrated in the Modified Version of this clause provides a useful compromise between a refusal by the Borrower to submit to New York jurisdiction in a transaction where the lenders would find such a position commercially unacceptable and a submission to such jurisdiction as a first resort. It should, however, be borne in mind that the deletion of references to jurisdictions other than England, the country of the Borrower and New York does not necessarily mean that the lenders are excluded from bringing actions elsewhere, in jurisdictions where the local courts will accept jurisdiction, but at least the Borrower avoids voluntary submission to those courts where jurisdiction would not exist apart from such voluntary submission and is not seen to be expressly agreeing to actions being capable of being brought in all parts of the world whether at the same time or otherwise.

The space in the proviso added at the end of paragraph (d) is for the insertion of a reference to those assets in respect of which it would be illegal or politically unacceptable to waive immunity.

The Raising of a Syndicated Euroloan Facility: A Case Study of Legal Aspects

BY LARS ANDRÉN AND BENGT KÄRDE

Introduction

This chapter will briefly deal with the raising of a major syndicated Eurodollar loan facility. The perspective is that of the borrower. It should be noted from the outset that this contribution does not purport to be an authoritative guide as to how such a transaction should be negotiated on the part of the borrower. The chapter has been written in the form of a case study for illustrative purposes only.

In 1977, Sweden started a new phase of borrowing abroad. When the loan described here was negotiated, Sweden had been active as an international borrower for a few years. It was, however, considered to be an appropriate stage to propose certain changes in the documentation previously accepted in Sweden.

The borrower

Responsibility for state borrowing in Sweden, including the administration of state debt, rests with Riksgäldskontoret (the Swedish National Debt Office), which is an agency of the Riksdag (the Swedish Parliament). In accordance with a standing authorisation by the Riksdag, Riksgäldskontoret is authorised to raise loans on behalf of the state for a variety of statutory purposes, such as the financing of capital expenditures in the public sector and other expenditures authorised by the Riksdag, and the payment and funding of the national debt.

Ancillary documents

The following documents will usually be provided by Riksgäldskontoret in a foreign borrowing transaction and are referred to below:

1. Resolution(s) by the Board of Directors of Riksgäldskontoret to raise the loan (Appendix A).
2. Legal Opinion of the Chancellor of Justice of Sweden, essentially to the effect that Riksgäldskontoret has the power and authority to raise the loan on behalf of Sweden (Appendix B).
3. A transfer guarantee from the Riksbank (the Swedish Central Bank) stating primarily the Riksbank's undertaking, at the request of Riksgäldskontoret, to sell foreign currency to Riksgäldskontoret for the purpose of enabling Riksgäldskontoret to meet its payment obligations in the currency required by the loan agreement. (The Riksbank controls, according to Swedish law, the Swedish currency reserve.) (Appendix C.)
4. Various certificates and notices as to factual matters including specimen signatures.

Initial approach by lender

After having informally advised several major international banks active in the Eurodollar market that Sweden was interested in discussing the raising of a loan of a substantial amount in that market, Riksgäldskontoret, on January 22, 19.., received a telex which outlined the main features regarding a US dollar floating rate loan facility for the amount of US $500–800 million. The telex was despatched by an international bank (the 'bank') active in the Eurodollar market. It was stressed in the telex that it was meant only as 'a basis for discussions', as the bank would have to know Riksgäldskontoret's precise requirements in order to be committed to put together an entire financial package. The telex contained details as to maturity, disbursement period, repayment, margin, commitment fee and management fee. The bank suggested that the whole amount should be fully underwritten by a small group of not more than three or four international banks. In the opinion of the bank this approach would make it possible to complete the first stage of the transaction 'in a quick and more silent fashion'. The telex closed as follows: 'We are in principle prepared to commit ourselves for an amount of $ ... million'.

Borrower's internal evaluation of preliminary offer

The contents of the telex were discussed internally. It was decided that the proposal was worth further investigation. At this stage considerations were mainly related to the financial terms in the telex rather than the legal issues. Nevertheless it should be noted that a lawyer should already be taking part in this stage of the discussions. This enables the lawyer to advise against unnecessary 'restrictions' with respect to formal and legal matters to be dealt with later. It is also essential that the lawyer is completely familiar with the underlying business considerations relevant to the transaction.

Appointment of managers

The bank was asked to provide suggestions as to banks to be approached initially as managers.

Within the next few days the bank submitted to Riksgäldskontoret a list tentatively setting out a number of names of international banks to be approached at an initial stage. The banks were located not only in Europe but also in the USA, Canada and Japan.

Telexes were exchanged regarding the wording of the initial invitation telex to the prospective managers.

The managers were chosen by Riksgäldskontoret in consultation with the bank, which agreed to act as agent in the contemplated financing. The prospective managers were approached and accepted their appointments in principle.

Acceptance of firm offer

On February 6, 19.. the agent, jointly with the managers, presented a firm offer regarding the proposed financing. The offer was based on 'but not not limited to' terms and conditions with respect to: amount, lenders, purpose of the loan, availability period, final maturity, repayment, prepayment, cancellation, interest rate, fees, taxes, costs and expenses, governing law and jurisdiction. The offer was valid for two days. The offer was subject to the conclusion of mutually acceptable loan documentation and was not intended to restrict the scope of the ensuing discussions among the lawyers regarding the specific wording of the final documentation.

The offer was submitted to the Board of Directors of Riksgäldskontoret. The board resolved in principle to raise the loan on the terms and conditions indicated in the offering telex. The board's resolution was, however, subject to its approval of the wording of the loan documentation.

On February 15, 19.. Riksgäldskontoret received the first draft of the loan agreement which had been prepared by the agent.

The draft was reviewed within the Legal Department of Riksgäldskontoret. The draft was compared with agreements relating to previous transactions of the same kind in which Riksgäldskontoret had been involved, and also with agreements entered into by other sovereign borrowers of equal credit standing.

After the first review the lawyers on the Swedish side found that the large number of changes and modifications which needed to be made in the draft prompted a personal meeting between the negotiators in order to try to reach an agreement as quickly and as smoothly as possible. (In our experience it is often feasible to conduct the negotiations by telex and by telephone. But in cases where the loan documents have to be substantially revised, the most efficient approach normally is to arrange a personal meeting between the borrower and the lender. In this case, the respective parties should preferably be represented by persons with the authority to make agreements with each other without having to refer back constantly to third parties for approval, although it may be necessary to reserve some fundamental points for decision at a higher level. The idea is for the parties to negotiate for one or more days in order to reach as final an agreement as possible, on this sole occasion.) On February 18, 19.. the chief negotiator representing the agent was invitied to Stockholm to discuss the documentation. It is very important for any newcomer to the international capital markets to retain a local lawyer from the country whose law governs the loan agreement. Riksgäldskontoret normally retains such local lawyers when it intends to tap a market for the first time. When dealing with complicated loans, it is also sometimes useful to have the benefit of local lawyers from the outset, even though it is not the borrower's first venture into the relevant market. In the transaction being described (which was governed by English law) we contacted and cooperated closely with a London law firm. It can also materially assist the conclusion of the transaction if the borrower is advised by lawyers who are experienced in the relevant market as this can save the managers having to satisfy the borrower as to the normal practices of the market.

Syndication continued

At the same time as the lawyers were reviewing the loan documentation, the syndication was proceeding on the basis of an 'Information Memorandum' prepared in consultation between the agent and Riksgäldskontoret.

Negotiations with respect to loan documentation

On February 21, 19.. a meeting was held in Stockholm between representatives of the agent and of the Legal Department of Riksgäldskontoret. The meeting lasted for almost two days (about 22 hours) and was broken off at the agent's request in order to give its representatives the opportunity to discuss with colleagues in London some points in the documentation. After the first day's discussions 18 points were declared 'open'. After the second day's discussions, six of them remained open. It was agreed that the discussions concerning these points should continue by telephone and telex, after the agent had had the opportunity to consult with the managers.

Second draft prepared

On February 28, 19.. a second draft of the loan agreement was received by the Legal Department. This draft incorporated all the changes upon which the participants in the meeting in Stockholm had been able to agree. The six 'open' points were in square brackets in the draft.

Continued negotiations

The issues upon which it had not been possible to agree were, for the next couple of days, the subject of lengthy telephone discussions between the parties involved. Telexes were exchanged containing alternative wordings of provisions on which the parties had different views. (Before analysing these points one by one, it should be explained that one of Riksgäldskontoret's main objectives in this context is to try to achieve conformity or 'standard' language throughout its loan documentation with respect to certain key clauses, regardless of the type of borrowing and the market concerned. This applies in particular to the negative pledge clause, the default clause and the clauses dealing with jurisdiction and immunity.)

The points noted as open are set out below:

1. The definition of 'External Indebtedness' for the purposes of both the negative pledge clause and the default clause: Sweden wished, in order to achieve conformity with other dollar borrowings, to define External Indebtedness only as Indebtedness (as defined) in any currency other than Swedish Kronor, and not also as Indebtedness in Swedish Kronor owed to a person resident outside Sweden.

2. The question of penalty interest in case of late payment.

3. Events of Default: Sweden suggested a grace period not only for payments of interest and costs but also for payments of principal. The reason was to avoid any risk of 'default by mistake' in the technical transfer of funds.

4. Events of Default: Sweden suggested that the cross-default clause should be limited to defaults in External Indebtedness (to be defined in accordance with Sweden's proposals referred to in 1 above) of Sweden, in order to give Sweden full freedom of action with regard to its internal borrowings.

5. Events of Default: Sweden suggested that a clause concerning a general moratorium on its debts should be limited to a general moratorium concerning only External Indebtedness (defined as above) of Sweden. The reason was the same as that noted under 4 above.

6. Certain reimbursements to the agent.

Ancillary documents

Simultaneous with the negotiations with respect to the loan agreement were discussions about the wording of the ancillary documents mentioned above. The documents which gave rise to some dispute were primarily the transfer guarantee and the legal opinion to be rendered by the Chancellor of Justice. It should be mentioned that the Chancellor's opinion originally contained some language describing the legal effect of the transfer guarantee which was not acceptable. The description of the transfer guarantee in the legal opinion was found to be phrased too broadly compared with the language contained in the instrument itself. On the Swedish side, the discussions were for practical reasons carried on by Riksgäldskontoret because, clearly, Riksgäldskontoret was familiar with both the Riksbank's and the Chancellor's requirements in this respect. When the negotiating parties had reached agreement among themselves on the wording, Riksgäldskontoret presented drafts of the relevant instruments, together with relevant supporting documents, to the Riksbank and the Chancellor, asking them to execute the respective documents which were to be held in escrow by Riksgäldskontoret and to be released by Riksgäldskontoret at the appropriate time.

Continued negotiations

By March 1, 19.. the managers had been able to consider among themselves the open points. The position taken by the parties could be summed up as follows:

1. The request by Riksgäldskontoret for a change in the drafted definition of 'External Indebtedness' had been considered by the managers in the light of what was deemed to be the 'norm' for agreements with sovereign borrowers. Allegedly, in very few such agreements was the definition of 'External Indebtedness' limited to debt denominated in non-domestic currency, and the managers concluded that it would be inappropriate to exclude from the definition Swedish Kronor debt owed to non-residents.

In a few agreements Sweden had accepted the definition of External Indebtedness worded as the agent suggested, namely, referring to both indebtedness in external currencies and indebtedness in any currency to a person resident abroad. On the other hand, in most of Sweden's agreements the definition of External Indebtedness referred only to external currencies. We stressed that Sweden as a sovereign has absolute control of its own domestic currency—at least with respect to the accessibility thereof (as a last resort by printing banknotes). Consequently, we saw no point in putting in the same category as borrowing foreign currencies the borrowing of Swedish currency, no matter where in the world it was borrowed.

2. Subject to agreement on other points, the banks were inclined to concede to Riksgäldskontoret's suggestion that the penalty interest should be restricted to the margin plus cost of funds and that no additional penalty interest would be added.

Sweden's main objection in this context had been that a penalty interest stipulation would be more appropriate for a corporate borrower and should thus be rejected by a sovereign borrower as a matter of 'national prestige'.

3. Events of Default. One of the managers was inclined to agree that the

same period of grace, i.e. five days, should be allowed both for principal and interest. However, the other managers were absolutely and unequivocally against permitting grace for payment of principal, as this was considered to be contrary to a firm 'norm' in the Eurodollar market. Furthermore, the managers argued that no bank would invoke the event of default provision if for some reason a mistake occurred regarding payments from the borrower to the agent's account.

Clearly, Sweden had no reason to believe that the loan would actually be accelerated in case of a 'default by mistake'. But Sweden didn't find it reasonable for the lenders to oppose a request by the borrower for provisions intended only to avoid any risk of a default situation where the default is not the result of inability on the part of the borrower to pay the loan when it falls due.

4. A majority of the managers was sympathetic to the view that the cross-default clause should be limited to External Indebtedness, leaving open at this stage exactly how that term was to be defined.

5. The managers held that the effect of the suggested change as to the general moratorium stipulation would be to allow the borrower to declare a moratorium on its domestic debt—which, where the borrower is a sovereign, could be re-arranged to favour lenders of domestic currency and leave lenders of foreign currency without remedies to accelerate their loans. The managers were unanimous in their view that Riksgäldskontoret's proposals would not be acceptable in the market.

Sweden's position in this respect was based on considerations of principle. When making preparations for a domestic borrowing Sweden should be in a position to determine, together with the Swedish lenders, the terms and conditions of such borrowing operation. No third party (such as a foreign bank) should be able to exercise an influence upon such a transaction. Again, due to Sweden's control of the accessibility of its domestic currency, no such third party should have any reasonable need to have an influence on the terms of internal borrowings.

6. The agent agreed to Riksgäldskontoret's suggested wording as to reimbursement of certain items.

At this stage, agreement had been reached on all the open points in the loan agreement bar three:

1. The definition of 'External Indebtedness'.
2. The question of grace period for late payment of principal.

3. The provision regarding a declaration of a general moratorium also on internal debt as an Event of Default.

Riksgäldskontoret agreed to the original wording with regard to the grace period. Obviously, days of grace may be allowed for the payment of any sum, but it is more usual for these to be allowed only for interest payments. The concept of a 'norm' in this respect could therefore to some extent be justified.

As to the two remaining points, Riksgäldskontoret had strong views on both of these questions. The definition of External Indebtedness was regarded by Riksgäldskontoret as a 'key clause', the wording of which should be in substance the same in every agreement to which Riksgäldskontoret was party, regardless of the market for borrowing. The argument concerning 'norms' in this respect was rejected by Riksgäldskontoret as being made irrelevant by the mere fact that Sweden already had the definition as desired in several other international loan agreements, even though these agreements related to loans in markets other than this one. The second remaining open point was the question of general moratorium.

After some further discussions by telephone it became evident to Riksgäldskontoret that the managers were not inclined to accept Riksgäldskontoret's view on the two remaining points. Thus a decision had to be made on how to proceed: in other words, whether, temporarily, to withdraw the loan or alternatively to accept the managers' position. The very day a decision on a postponement would have had finally to be made, the chief legal negotiators agreed, by telephone, to give up one open point each, which led to an agreement where the borrower was granted its suggested wording of the definition of External Indebtedness and the managers their wording of the general moratorium clause.

Two important lessons can be learned from the final stage of the negotiations on this loan agreement. These are, first, the importance of careful timing in relation to negotiations and, secondly, the need for flexibility, even at the expense of abandoning an argument (however well supported by logic) where pursuit of that argument is leading to an impasse at a time when a speedy solution is required.

Where in a particular transaction a borrower wishes to achieve specific objectives in relation to loan documentation, it is important from the borrower's point of view that the timetable for concluding the transaction should not be too tight. If it is, the position may well be reached where the borrower is simply faced with a choice of either meeting the timetable or abandoning its objectives. The borrower should, therefore, avoid making any arrangements which require that documentation be concluded by a specific date, even if that date is set at a sufficient distance apparently to allow full time for agreement on documentation. The lenders will have made some form of an 'offer' of loan terms which usually has to be taken up by a given date but, having taken up the initial 'offer', there is normally no firm deadline imposed by the lenders for conclusion of documentation although, as a practical matter, the point will no doubt be reached when lenders will wish either to conclude or to abandon negotiations. It is sensible for a borrower on its entry into the market for the first time to try to settle documentation with which it is comfortable and then to insist on using that documentation as the basis for negotiations on future loan transactions. This is less disruptive from the borrower's point of view than negotiating each loan on the basis of completely fresh documentation. Although the transaction reviewed in this case study was not Sweden's first entry into the market, it was the first occasion on which certain aspects had been negotiated and the timetable had allowed time for that approach.

The second important lesson is the need for flexibility. In the transaction under review, there was considerable logic in favour of the proposal which was put forward by Riksgäldskontoret to limit the general moratorium clause to External Indebtedness, given that the lenders had accepted that the cross-default clause should be limited to External Indebtedness, that the negative pledge clause did not restrict Sweden from granting security to domestic debt and that there was no general restriction against individual renegotiation of arrangements for domestic loans which would result in more favourable terms for domestic lenders. Against this, the argument of the managers that to have the general moratorium language limited to External Indebtedness would leave the borrower in a position to rearrange its domestic debt on favourable terms to the domestic lenders, was not convincing. Moreover, there were certain other transactions then current in the market where the limitation of a general moratorium to External Indebtedness had been accepted. The final decision not to press for acceptance of Riksgäldskontoret's view was conditioned by the belief that the managers had committed themselves to their point of view as a matter of principle. The point, therefore, had become one where, if the view of the managers was not accepted, the managers had no alternative but to withdraw from the transaction. Since Riksgäldskontoret felt that the negotiations had been satisfactory overall, the representatives of Riksgäldskontoret were prepared, on this occasion, not to press their view further, while of course reserving their right to argue the point again in a future transaction.

Final board resolution

On March 13, 19 .. the Board of Directors of Riksgäldskontoret resolved to enter into the loan facility and approve the loan agreement.

Signing of loan agreement and execution of Chancellor's legal opinion and transfer guarantee

On March 19, 19 .. the loan agreement was signed and the Chancellor of Justice's legal opinion and the Riksbank's transfer guarantee together with the board resolution and certain certificates were delivered by Riksgäldskontoret to the agent.

APPENDIX A

Resolution by the Board of Directors of Riksgäldskontoret

2 § Re US $ ... ... Loan Facility
The Board of Directors of Riksgäldskontoret has decided to inform those who may be concerned of the following:

The Board of Directors has earlier this day decided, for purposes mentioned in 23 § of the Law containing Regulations for Riksgäldskontoret, on behalf of the Kingdom of Sweden to enter into a Loan Facility of up to US $ ... ... and to approve of the draft loan agreement (draft March.., 19..).

The Board of Directors has authorised the Director General, Mr Lars Kalderén, or the Deputy Director General, Mr Ingmar Jansson, or the Assistant Director General (Finance), Mr Olof Norell, with countersigning by the Head of the Guarantee and Legal Department, Mr Lars Andrén, or the Deputy Head of the Guarantee and Legal Department, Mr Tord Arnerup, to sign and deliver the loan agreement on behalf of Riksgäldskontoret, at such time and place as the signatories shall agree, in the form of the above mentioned draft with such modifications therein (if any) as may be approved by the individuals signing the loan agreement.

Furthermore the Board of Directors has decided to authorise Sveriges Riksbank, by its published authorised signatories for the time being, to deliver notices of drawing and notices selecting the duration of an interest period under Clause ... of the loan agreement.

Finally, the Board of Directors has decided to authorise the Director General or the Deputy Director General, or the Assistant Director General (Finance) together with the Head or Deputy Head of the Guarantee and Legal Department on behalf of Riksgäldskontoret to sign and deliver all notices (including those described in Clause ...) certificates and other documents required pursuant to the loan agreement.

This clause was declared immediately adopted.

APPENDIX B

Legal opinion of Chancellor of Justice of Sweden

To:

as agent for the Banks hereinafter referred to

Dear Sirs,

I refer to the Agreement ('the Agreement') dated March .., 19 .. and made between the Kingdom of Sweden represented by Riksgäldskontoret, certain banks named as Managers and Co-Managers, the Banks listed on the execution pages of the Agreement ('the Banks') and yourselves as Agent.

I Ingvar Gullnäs being the Chancellor of Justice of Sweden have inspected the following:
(i)   a signed copy of the Agreement;
(ii)   a copy of the resolution of the Board of Directors of Riksgäldskontoret referred to in Clause ... of the Agreement;
(iii)   a copy of the Transfer Guarantee referred to in Clause ... of the Agreement.

I have made such other enquiries as I have considered appropriate for the purpose of giving the opinion set out below.

For the purpose of this opinion, I have assumed:

(A) that the Agreement has been duly authorised, executed and delivered by or on behalf of each of the parties thereto other than the Borrower;

(B) the genuineness of all signatures on all documents and the completeness, and the conformity to original documents, of all copies submitted to me.

All expressions defined in the Agreement have the same meanings in this opinion.

I am of the following opinion:

(a) all acts, conditions and things required to be done and performed and to have happened prior to the execution and delivery of the Agreement in order to constitute all of the obligations of the Borrower under the Agreement valid and binding in accordance with their respective terms have been done and performed and have happened;

(b) the execution and delivery of the Agreement and the performance by the Borrower of its obligations under the Agreement and compliance with the terms thereof have been duly authorised by all necessary action of Riksgäldskontoret and do not and will not (i) violate any provision of any law, rule or regulation presently in effect having applicability to the Borrower or (ii) result in a breach of, or constitute a default under, any agreement or other instrument to which the Borrower is a party or by which it or any of its assets may be bound or affected;

(c) the Agreement is a legal, valid and binding obligation of the Borrower enforceable against the Borrower and the obligations of the Borrower thereunder are direct, unconditional and general obligations of the Borrower and (subject to the operation of Clause ... of the Agreement) rank *pari passu* with all other External Indebtedness of the Borrower;

(d) there is no income or other tax of the Borrower, imposed by withholding or otherwise on any payment to be made by the Borrower pursuant to the Agreement to any person who is not otherwise subject to taxation in Sweden or is imposed on or by virtue of the execution or delivery of the Agreement by the Borrower or any document or instrument to be executed and delivered thereunder by the Borrower, and the arrangements contemplated by the Agreement give rise to no charge for Swedish stamp or documentary taxes of any kind;

(e) Riksgäldskontoret is duly established under Swedish law and has full and unconditional authority to enter into the Agreement on behalf of the Borrower and to pledge the full credit of the Borrower for the due performance by the Borrower of its obligations thereunder;

(f) to the best of my knowledge and belief no such violation as is referred to in paragraph (b) (i) of this opinion and no such breach or default as is referred to in paragraph (b) (ii) of this opinion has occurred and is continuing which might materially and adversely affect the Borrower's ability to perform its obligations under the Agreement;

(g)   the legal consequences of the execution, delivery and performance of the Agreement by the Borrower are governed by private law.

In respect of the obligations of the Borrower under the Agreement:

(i)   in the courts of the Kingdom of Sweden the Borrower does not enjoy any right of immunity from suit; in the event of a judgment being obtained in such courts, the assets of the Borrower do not enjoy any right of immunity from attachment or execution; and

(ii)   the assets of the Borrower do not enjoy any freedom from set-off.

The waiver by the Borrower contained in Clause ... of the Agreement is irrevocably binding on the Borrower and the consent by the Borrower to the jurisdiction of the courts specified in Clause ... with respect to matters arising from the Agreement and the provisions thereof that the laws of England shall govern the Agreement as contained in Clause ... of the Agreement are also irrevocably binding on the Borrower;

(h)   all authorisations, statutes, public decrees, laws, approvals, consents and licences from all legislative bodies of government, ministries, agencies, exchange control authorities or other authorities required by the Constitution or the laws of the Kingdom of Sweden in order for the Borrower to execute and deliver the Agreement and to execute and deliver all other documents and instruments to be delivered by the Borrower thereunder and to perform and observe the terms and provisions thereof and to make all payments in dollars thereunder, have been duly obtained and are in full force and effect;

(i)   the Transfer Guarantee referred to in Clause ... of the Agreement is irrevocably binding on Sveriges Riksbank;

(j)   no litigation or administrative proceeding before or of any court or governmental authority is at the date of this opinion pending or, to my knowledge, threatened against the Borrower or any Government Entity or any of their respective assets which might materially and adversely affect the Borrower's ability to perform its obligations under the Agreement.

My opinion herein expressed is limited to matters of law of the Kingdom of Sweden. I express no opinion with respect to the law of any other jurisdiction.

Yours faithfully

APPENDIX C

Transfer guarantee from the Riksbank

Stockholm, March.., 19..

To: Riksgäldskontoret

As foreseen in Clause ... of the Loan Agreement of March .. ,19 .. between you on the one hand, representing the Kingdom of Sweden, and a group of banks on the other hand concerning a loan facility of US $ ... ... we hereby undertake to sell to you in all circumstances the US dollars or such other currencies as are (in order that any obligations which arise under Clause ... may be fulfilled) necessary for the payment of interest and principal of the said loan and all other sums payable to the banks in accordance with the Loan Agreement, and to ensure that sufficient foreign exchange in US dollars or such other currencies as aforesaid is available to us enabling us to carry out such sale in order that you can make all payments in full under the Loan Agreement as they become due in accordance with its terms.

This undertaking is irrevocable.

SVERIGES RIKSBANK

Governor

Chief Legal Adviser

Contributors

Lars Andrén has a law degree from the University of Lund. After court practice he was employed by the Swedish National Debt Office as a lawyer in 1971. Since 1979 he has held the post of Director and Head of the Legal and Guarantee Department. He is also the Vice-Chairman of the Board of Ship Credit Guarantees in Sweden.

J. Speed Carroll graduated from Harvard Law School in 1962. An associate of the New York firm of Cleary, Gottlieb, Steen & Hamilton for some years, three of which he spent in their Paris Office, and a member of the firm since 1971, his career has been centred on international business and financial law. He spent one year as consultant on foreign law to Messrs. Nagashima & Ohno of Tokyo, Japan, and five years as resident partner in Cleary, Gottlieb's London office. Since late in 1981 he has again been resident in their New York office.

Francis Chronnell joined Norton, Rose, Botterell & Roche in London in 1963, shortly after qualification as a solicitor. He became a partner in 1968 and since then has been extensively involved in advising in respect of all types of Euromarket transactions, initially mainly for lenders but in recent years frequently also acting for borrowers. He read law at Manchester University and obtained an LL M at the London School of Economics. He is an occasional lecturer on various topics related to international financial transactions.

Paul I. Harris graduated in law from the University of Birmingham, England, in 1966 with the degrees of LL B and LL M. He joined the London firm of Linklaters & Paines in 1967 and became a partner in 1976. He has concentrated on international financial matters both as to banking and investment work, has spoken at various seminars and conferences on legal issues concerning borrowers and lenders, and, together with a colleague, has published a book on 'Unit Trusts'.

Lars Kalderén is an economist who has served in Sweden's Ministries of Finance and Foreign Affairs as well as with the Swedish International Development Authority, the World Bank and Harvard's Institute for International Development. In 1977 he became Director General of the Swedish National Debt Office. He has written and lectured extensively on problems of international development and finance.

Bengt Kärde is a lawyer and has been an Assistant Director at the Swedish National Debt Office since 1978. Previously he was a junior judge and an associate of the Swedish law firm Wetter and Wetter.

Göran Ohlin has been Professor of Economics at Uppsala University since 1969. He was a staff member of the Pearson Commission, in 1968−69, a Fellow of the Development Centre of the OECD in Paris, in 1962−66, and Executive Secretary of the Independent Commission on International Development Issues (the Brandt Commission), in 1978−79.

Shridath S. Ramphal is the Secretary-General of the Commonwealth. He was Minister of Foreign Affairs and Justice in Guyana from 1972 to 1975 and served as Attorney-General and Minister of State for External Affairs in 1966−72. He is a member of the Independent Commission on International Development Issues (the Brandt Commission).

Qamar S. Siddiqi is Assistant Director of the Economic Affairs Division of the Commonwealth Secretariat. He studied economics and international law at Karachi and Geneva.

William Tudor John graduated from Cambridge University in 1966. He has practised law since 1967 and became a partner in Allen and Overy in 1972. Between 1970 and 1972, he worked as a banker with Orion Bank Limited.

K. Venkatachari is a consultant (law and industrial relations) to the Central Office of the State Bank of India in Bombay. He holds a Master of Laws degree from Madras University and has served both in the legal department of the Reserve Bank of India and in the Law Department of the State Bank of India, whose chief he was for more than two decades. He has handled all matters of the State Bank of India in respect of its international finance and borrowings and has taken part in the negotiation and documentation of many Eurocurrency loans.

Patricia Watson read law at Durham University and joined Norton, Rose, Botterell & Roche in London in 1978, where she is now a member of a department which handles international financings of all kinds. Within the work of that department she has principally specialised in syndicated loan transactions, fixed and floating rate securities issues, and export finance. During the last two years she has increasingly represented the interests of borrowers in major non-domestic borrowing operations.

Nicholas Wilson studied law at Sheffield University, Harvard and the University of California. He has been a partner in Slaughter and May, London, since 1968 and is a member of the Bank of England's City Capital Markets Committee.

Philip Wood was born in Livingstone, Zambia. He read English at the University of Oxford and subsequently joined Allen and Overy, where he is a partner. He is the author of *Law and Practice of International Finance* and part-author of the *Encyclopaedia of Banking Law.*

Richard G.A. Youard read law at the University of Oxford after which he joined Slaughter and May, London. His work in the last few years has been concerned to a considerable extent with international finance and in particular, loans to sovereign borrowers. He is the author of articles in banking journals on topics concerning international finance.

Literature

The literature on the constitutional and legal issues of sovereign borrowing is very limited. A few references are given by some of the authors in this volume. The short list which follows contains books and periodicals which may be consulted by those who wish to follow the subject closely.

Books
Mendelsohn, M.S., *Money on the Move. The Modern International Capital Market,* New York, McGraw-Hill, 1980.
Rendell, Robert S., (ed), *International Financial Law, Lending, Capital Transfers and Institutions,* London, Euromoney Publications Ltd., 1980.
Wood, Philip R., *Law and Practice of International Finance,* London, Sweet & Maxwell Ltd., 1980.

Periodicals
The Banker, London, Financial Times Business Publishing Limited.
Euromoney, London, Euromoney Publications Ltd.
Euromoney Trade Finance Report, London, Euromoney Publications Ltd.
International Financial Law Review, London, Euromoney Publications Ltd.